Nursing and Health Care for the Homeless

Nursing and Health Care for the Homeless

Edited by Juanita K. Hunter

STATE UNIVERSITY OF NEW YORK PRESS

This book was supported in part by the Special Project Grants Program in the Nursing Education Practice Resources Branch, Division of Nursing, U.S. Department of Health and Human Services, Public Health Service, Health Resources and Services Administration, Bureau of Health Professions Administration. Grant #5D1060003-05.

Published by
State University of New York Press, Albany

For information, address State University of New York
Press, State University Plaza, Albany, N.Y., 12246

Production by Cathleen Collins
Marketing by Dana Yanulavich

Library of Congress Cataloging in Publication Data

Nursing and health care for the homeless / edited by Juanita K.
  Hunter.
       p.   cm.
    Includes bibliography references and index.
    ISBN 0-7914-1349-7 — ISBN 0-7914-1350-0 (pbk.)
    1. Homeless persons—Medical care. 2. Community health nursing.
  I. Hunter, Juanita K., 1930–
    (DNLM: 1. Community Health Nursing—United States. 2. Community
Health Services—United States. 3. Homeless Persons—United States.
WA 300 N974]
RT98.N8517   1992
362.1'0425—dc20
DNLM/DLC   92-2172
for Library of Congress   CIP
10   9   8   7   6   5   4   3   2   1

Contents

Acknowledgments

I wish to express my sincere appreciation to Dr. Marietta Stanton, Ph.D., R.N., Director of Continuing Nurse Education in the School of Nursing at the State University of New York at Buffalo, for encouraging me to investigate the possibility of having the "Homelessness: An Issue for the Nineties" conference papers published. I would also like to thank Ms. Alice Stein, editor, for her able assistance in shaping the format of the book through conscientious review of the manuscripts. Finally, I am most grateful for the efforts put forth by Ms. Barbara Herman, secretary, who diligently worked throughout this process typing the papers and related correspondence and who provided much encouragement for the task at hand.

SECTION 1

Overview

CHAPTER 1

Introduction

Juanita K. Hunter

Homelessness is a complex and emotionally provoking contemporary problem. To date organizational responses to this phenomenon have often been conflicting, contradictory, and ineffective. Current statistics and predictions substantiate that the homeless problem will increase in the next decade, with estimates on the number of homeless varying from six hundred thousand to three million. This increasing proportion of homeless citizens in the U.S. population poses many challenges for both health-care professions and the entire society. Health-care providers are becoming more and more concerned about the health needs of this vulnerable population for whom homelessness itself prevents access to health services and health maintenance. The number of homeless women with children is a particular concern, as they are now the fastest growing subgroup within the homeless population.

The lack of a permanent address and health insurance are two obvious barriers to health-care services for the homeless; other health-related problems such as substance abuse, alcoholism, and emotional disorders may further complicate the process of providing a coordinated plan of care. The environment in overcrowded shelters promotes the rapid spread of communicable diseases, upper respiratory infections, infestations of head lice, scabies, hepatitis, and tuberculosis. Of great concern are the homeless children who have often been subjected to physical, sexual, or emotional abuse and/or neglect, and who are more susceptible to disease because of malnutrition and lack of immunizations. Homeless women are also a vulnerable group, and one-third of them report they have been raped or are victims of domestic violence. Many of the homeless are caught in a cycle where health problems become a precipitating cause of their homelessness, and, in turn, the homeless condition causes a further decline in their health.

Before 1990 health-care professionals concerned with the homeless had to focus much of their effort on gathering a base of demographic data needed to plan relevant and cost-effective health services for this group. Health care for the homeless has become a special concern for many nurses, and several models for providing nursing care to the homeless are being implemented throughout the country.

Specifically, in 1989, the Special Project Grants Program in the Nursing Education Practices Resources Branch, Division of Nursing, U.S. Department of Health and Human Services, Public Health Service, Health Resources and Services Administration, Bureau of Health Professions Administration had funded five special project grants to schools of nursing to demonstrate models that increase access to health care for this disadvantaged population. The Nursing Center for the Homeless, sponsored by the State University of New York at Buffalo School of Nursing, is one of those funded projects and it sponsored a national conference, entitled "Homelessness: An Issue for the Nineties," on May 3–4, 1990, in Buffalo, New York. The conference was co-sponsored by four of the other university programs funded by the Special Grants Program in the Nursing Education Practice Resources Branch, Division of Nursing, U.S. Department of Health and Human Services, Health Resources, Public Health Service and Services Administration, Bureau of Health Professions Administration. They include Pace University Lienhard School of Nursing, Pleasantville, New York; University of California at Los Angeles School of Nursing; Medical University of South Carolina School of Nursing, Charleston, South Carolina; and University of Kentucky College of Nursing, Lexington, Kentucky.

The purpose of the conference was to provide a forum for those health-care professionals actively involved in the administration and implementation of homeless projects. Papers were presented that addressed main topical areas. Through this publication, that information will now be shared with the growing number of nurses and other health-care professionals committed to active involvement in establishing and maintaining homeless health-care services. This book will be a resource for health professionals and others who seek information and reports of firsthand experiences about the current status of the homeless, their health-care needs, and various programs.

The keynote addresses and papers presented at the conference are included in this manuscript. Dr. Porter-O'Grady gives an excellent overview of the scope of the problem. Dr. Bob Prentice discusses the issues related to solutions of the problem and the critical importance of housing regulations and policies in effecting viable, preventive strategies. The current demographic profile and health needs of the homeless and the nurses' role in providing health care to this group are described. The other papers provide a rich source of firsthand information about the impact of homelessness on individuals, families, communities and the nation.

Topical areas include: demographics and characteristics of various homeless populations; issues related to homeless children; cost effectiveness of nurse managed clinics; considerations in the design, implementation and evaluation of a homeless nursing project; mental health and homelessness; selected contributions of various nursing roles in care of the homeless; and innovative approaches for nursing service, practice, and education.

Creative student learning activities are another focus of the presentations, and reports of ongoing research will inform the reader about significant questions being addressed by nurses. Several nursing models also include collaborative practice designs. Nurses have assumed a leadership role in identifying and meeting the health and related needs of the diverse homeless population. This book demonstrates that nursing is on the cutting edge of meeting the challenges of the contemporary homeless issue.

CHAPTER 2

Nursing Care for the Underserved: Crisis and Opportunity

Tim Porter-O'Grady

Abstract

Regardless of the rhetoric, economic and social commitment to the needs of the homeless and other underserved persons continues to decline at all levels of the health-care system. As the mainstream health-care system continues to constrain and tighten its economic resources, the impact on those at the periphery of the system accelerates radically. Therefore, it is unlikely that the homeless and other underserved will have available to them increasing resources to address the growing needs of this increasing population.

This chapter specifically addresses some of the issues affecting service to the underserved from an economic and social perspective. Also included is identification of the role of health professionals, specifically nurses, and how that role can be applied to addressing and even resolving some of the problems affecting the underserved. Using the role of the nurse as a framework, recommendations and suggestions related to alternative approaches to providing services to unique populations are discussed, some suggested existing models are highlighted, and some specific recommendations for organized nursing with regard to responding to the expanding need of the population are given.

Introduction

In spite of increased interest in problems of the underserved, commitment in terms of dollars and services continues to decline at all levels of the health-care system. In all spectra of services, financial support for addressing the needs of the underserved continues to shrink, and the problems continue to grow. As a proportion of our society, it appears that the middle class is shrinking, and both the monied class and the poor are increasing. About 10% are without assets necessary to pay for health-care services. More Americans lack access to health care than the total population of Canada, all of whom are covered. In a country that touts the best of health-care technology, it is clear that that technology is available only to those who can afford it.

As the United States continues to fight its consumption behavior and the resultant deficit spending, the administration must cut programs that address some of the nation's major health concerns. Because of continuous cuts in Medicare allocations, mainstream health care is in danger of losing the funds necessary to maintain the level of service to 90% of the American population. An average of $2 billion a year for the past five years has been cut from the Medicare Medicaid budget, the prime source of funding for underserved and indigent populations. The 1990 budget is now $2.8 billion. Because of this, hospitals, which were the largest providers of care services to this group, have pulled back from serving them.

In addition, pre-election commitments of money promised by the Bush administration have been reduced in two budgets that have emerged since President Bush took office. Specifically, full funding of the McKinney Homeless Assistance Act was promised prior to elections, yet the act has been reduced successively by substantial percentages, affecting health care and social services to the homeless.

Because of payment and service problems in the mainstream health system, it is unlikely that hospitals and physicians will be able to increase their own commitment and efforts to incorporate the underserved into their already constrained service framework. This puts those on the fringe of the social system at jeopardy for adequate services which address their unique needs; therefore the homeless and impoverished must wait until they are seriously ill with no choice but to crowd the emergency rooms of hospitals that can't afford to serve them but cannot legally turn them away. These "Catch-22" situations further complicate and erode the efficacy of the health-care delivery system.

The failure of the American political process to provide a policy framework and a plan for the delivery of health-care services creates a patchwork of efforts directed at addressing the diverse health care needs of the public. Each administration or Congress has its own, separate, noncontiguous agenda for what will be provided and paid for during the next Congressional budget period.

In a disseminating process, the health-care system tries to piece together the services required by society in a way that can assure some level of survival and that some services are provided. The result is an ever-increasing cost base for care, reduced continuity, and thus lowered quality and an increasingly fragmented approach to the delivery of services. All this occurs at a time when the insurance industry is more carefully and critically assessing what it pays for and intervening when the service promised is either inappropriate or inadequate. Increasing problems with higher physician costs, increasing intervention services, and the use of high-tech options in providing medical service continue to create a burden on both the insurance industry and the consumer. This further tightens the grip of the payers, and concerted efforts at intersecting with the provider system by insurers increases scrutiny, reduces covered illnesses or procedures, and pushes more of the payment for health care back on the consumer.

The Role of Nurses

Nursing has a strong history of responding to public need for health-care services. Even when taking the lead to provide services for underserved people puts nurses at legal and personal risk, they have persevered. When assessing services for the underserved, it is clear that many of the service structures and systems which address the needs of the underserved are planned and operated by nurses. From before birth to after death, a whole spectrum of services frequently has been provided by nurses to people who can't pay for them.

In many states a large portion of rural health-care services is provided by nurses in the public health agencies and the community health services which provide outreach to people who have no access to physicians or other health-care providers. In some states nurses provide nearly 60% of both the hospital and nonhospital services available to the rural population. In many counties nurses may be the only primary providers of services.

Out of this reality emerges a number of creative and innovative programs that address the broad spectrum of health-care services offered for underserved or disadvantaged populations. From urban, nurse-managed birthing centers to migrant worker health centers, to health clinics for the homeless, to community-based elder-care programs, nurses provide places where those who could not otherwise receive services have an opportunity to access them without a compromise in quality. And in spite of the shrinking dollars allocated to such services.

There are three key reasons for the growth and success of nurse-managed service structures for the underserved:

1. The resourcefulness of nurses in a time of increasing need and decreasing dollars
2. The increase in the number of non-institutional needy representing a broader spectrum of the population
3. Lack of a concerted or clear public policy plan or consolidated initiative to address health-care problems.

Nurses have been very successful in providing a broad range of health-care services to a number of segments of society in their history in America. Frequently, such services have been provided to those for whom no one else cared. In times of pestilence and other socially threatening outbreaks, nurses were available to address the issues and bring relief. It can be said unequivocally that this commitment remains unchanged.

However, to be successful in today's world, no service provider can function alone. It is increasingly difficult for any single discipline to respond to the whole spectrum of needs in the underserved community. Because of the desire of service providers to break the cycle of indigence or disadvantage, it becomes essential to join with others in addressing a broad base of responsive strategies which aim at intervention from a number of directions on behalf of those being served.

In addition, the reality of attempting to serve the disadvantaged with currently available resources is challenging at best. The effort is made impossible if the attempt is undertaken unilaterally. There is no single public or private service agency or provider that can access sufficient funding to provide the broad range of services that may be required in order to adequately address the basic needs of the underserved community. In addition, if the service provider is also committed to breaking the cycle of illness, personal pain, or social condition, it is essential that the effort include those who can join in the effort to effectively access the full range of supports necessary to make that endeavor successful.

What is even more paramount is the need to provide care other than medical model approaches, which serve merely to address the critical condition without reference to either its root causes or the conditions that created it. Short-term interventions deal with the immediate issues but do nothing to impact on the living situation that accompanies the illness. Further, it is essential that the client's health or social problems be dealt with where the client lives, rather than expecting him to come to the health-care provider. Mobility, combined with a high level of noncompliance, make the underserved, especially the unhoused, difficult to serve and almost impossible to follow if the health service of choice is fixed and demands that the client seek it out for follow-up on a health problem requiring continued intervention. The medical model that often expects the client to come to the physician does nothing to meet the needs of this unique population.

Perhaps the greatest concern to the underserved is the lack of health resources devoted specifically to their needs. The number of physicians either available or willing to serve this population is appallingly inadequate. Because physicians have an overriding influence on the use of the fiscal resources of the health-care system, they control compensation paid to nurses for their services. Thus, even though they are often the primary health-care providers, they are dependent on physicians for payment. Also, resources allocated to serving the underserved are never adequate to provide even basic services. Complicated mechanisms must therefore be created in the service sector to make creative and sometimes artificial connections to physicians in order to get services to the people who need them. In cases where unique arrangements can be worked for nurses and others to provide direct services, frequent constraints emerge either from the professional disciplines, the payers or the politicians, creating battles that have to be fought in order to continue to provide services. Subsequently, there are many individuals in service professions like nursing who burn out from the struggle to offer appropriate services to this group.

It must be said that the primary contribution that nursing makes to the issues of health care to the underserved is to assist in forcing key policy initiatives to emerge at both the national and state levels. There will be no substantive changes in the delivery of services or payment for such services until the nursing profession and other providers have an agenda for change that enumerates both the characteristics of this change and the processes necessary to achieve them. In the current health-care environment, no single discipline or unilateral strategy for change is going to be acceptable or adequate. However, each party to the enterprise will have to be familiar with the current situation and its constraints and be willing to participate in a process that will seek solutions that represent the best national interest and commit themselves to its achievement.

Nurses must also be willing to take risks to enter into service arenas and enterprises where the underserved are a major constituency and enlarge the system to attend to their needs. That includes challenging legal and practice restrictions for nurses providing services that other disciplines seek to have regulated but do not otherwise address themselves. Nurses must continue to challenge the delivery system and current assumptions about the ascendancy of medical models and practices when the evidence does not support those arguments and when needed services are not provided. Where that has occurred in a number of settings and circumstances around the country, evidence abounds that nurses provide as full a range of health-care services as physicians, in many instances with better outcomes and lower cost. This has been especially true in the care of the elderly and the homeless, birthing, and continuity of care.

Examples of Successful Programs

Perhaps one of the most successful examples of community-based, interdisciplinary elder-care services can been seen at the On Loc Senior Health Services program in San Francisco. Here, nurses and others provide residential-based health-care support services to a predominantly Asian elderly population in a manner that respects their culture and independence. Along with other health-care providers, nurses coordinate, plan, and intervene in case managing the care that these elderly people receive. All data indicate that the kinds of services offered in this program are well received and result in improved quality of life and higher levels of satisfaction. Nurses act both independently and interdependently to provide a range of elder-care services which are effective, cost-efficient, and indicative of a high level of quality. The process is eminently replicable and could serve as a model of community-based elder-care services for the underserved older consumer anywhere in America.

In Boston at the Pine Street Inn, in New York at the Pace University Homeless Clinics, and in Atlanta at the Atlanta Community Health Program for the Homeless, nurses not only provide a full range of health-care services for homeless individuals and families but direct and control their operation and service payment process. While data related to the efficacy of such services are just now emerging, costs are lower than those for the same kinds of services offered in the mainstream by physicians and hospitals. Cost savings to the health system also are beginning to indicate that a significant contribution to the care of the homeless is emerging at a tremendous cost reduction. The coalitions entered into by the nurse leaders in these clinics and programs are indicative of the coordinative and integrative skills of nurse-managed centers and services. Clear also is the ability of nurses in accessing an extensive range of existing services which provide support for the homeless in a context beyond their need for health care. Here again, by background and education, the nurse often is the most able to provide and access what is necessary to take care of the underserved beyond their medical needs.

An emerging body of data and overwhelming evidence indicates that what is happening with the elderly and the homeless also is true for pregnant women. The growth of nurse-run birthing centers such as the Maternity Center Association of New York is indicative of the quality and effectiveness of nurse-midwifery in the birthing process. These freestanding centers serving a broad socioeconomic range of women are testimony to the ability of nurses to meet a need in a manner consistent with good health care and the sensitivities of the women who come to them for prenatal, birthing, and postnatal care. Not only are there excellent data on the safety and efficacy of these nurse-run birthing centers, they are very cost effective as well. The average cost of a normal nurse-midwife managed delivery is $994, while the same normal delivery done by a physician costs about $1492. Here again, the value and contribution of nursing to both service and cost is well documented.

At Beth Israel Hospital and St. Mary's Hospital in Tucson, continuity and integration of patient care has moved to new heights. The nurse case manager coordinates and integrates care for patients during the entire course of their health and/or illness experience in moving from home to institution and back to the home again. The nurse pulls together all the essential resources, is a provider of both institutional and home care, and stays connected with the patient and other providers through the entire health-care experience. In some settings and circumstances, the nurse determines the kind and level of care the patient should receive, arranges for it, and follows the patient through service provision and beyond. Integrating the patient's support and relational systems into the process strengthens the patient's response and involves the patient's loved ones in the healing process. Creative cultural and social interactions are established, such as including the Indian medicine man in the healing team as is done at St. Mary's. Here again, nurse-driven care models connect the consumer with the system and assure that the full range of health needs is incorporated into the process with the resultant increase in satisfaction, continuity, quality, and cost reduction.

Examples of nursing effectiveness in the health-care system abound. The above simply represent a small sample of the kinds of creative and innovative steps nursing has already taken within an adversarial health system to meet the requirements of those in need. It has not been an easy process and continues to be fraught with questions, compromises, and outright opposition. As the health-care system struggles out of a dominantly medical paradigm, trauma and transformation will emerge. The system is not effective as currently configured, and all associated with it are aware of this reality. Script writing for a new reality becomes increasingly important. Nurses and others who are able to present viable responses to a constraining payment structure with the assurances of sound outcomes and high quality will succeed.

Concern has been voiced by some that nursing is always burdened with providing services for the poor and undeserved where the chances of mainstream economic and personal gain for the nurse and the profession are minimal. However, as our health-care system strives to better serve all segments of the population, alternatives such as the rapidly growing birthing centers become more important. Also, differentiation between the poor and the middle class in the United States becomes blurred when neither can afford to pay for health care in the future. What will inevitably emerge will be a broader mix of managed health services. The principle of primacy of provider will be played out in a system that will expect the nurse to assess, triage, treat, and/or refer, based on the nursing diagnosis which indicates the kind and cost of service the consumer will receive at any given time. Such models exist now in a number of successful health maintenance organizations in this country.

New Strategies Needed

There are five major strategies that organized nursing will need to undertake to effectively address the role of the nurse in health care to the community, including those inadequately served by the current health system.

1. *Nursing must participate in the formation of a strong social health policy.* There will be little of substance accomplished in terms of affecting the current health quagmire without a major policy shift in the United States. Medical-model–driven strategies have proven to be of little value in improving or altering the social health condition of the nation. The biological response to the environment, which is the focus of medical practices, is simply not sufficient to address the variables of the human experience which affect health and illness. In this model, cost will always incline while the nation's general health continues to decline. Interdisciplinary dialogue and a plan design for the future system will have to emerge if health care is to rise above its current crippled state in the United States.

2. *Nurses must be prepared to assert their role in health-care decisions and delivery in order to have a place in defining the future of health care.* Nursing has often appeared to be a responsive-active rather than prescriptive-proactive profession. For a myriad of reasons, nurses have not sat at the policy or political tables where the future is defined and played out. If the role of the nurse is to prescribe the future and nurses' response to it, nursing leadership must participate. This means that nurses must not wait for an invitation, but, instead, expect to be there when

policy makers meet and, if at all possible, should call for the meeting. If nurses are to be adequately involved and compensated for the services they provide, they must have some role in defining the legislative, legal, policy, and regulative processes that govern such action. Without these changes and influence, all desire is simply reduced to rhetoric.

3. *The power of coalitions should never be underestimated.* It is often surprising that nurses who are gifted at putting together coalitions for patient care do not do as well in advancing their cause or the social circumstances of health care. Coalitions are life-giving and enhance power and opportunity. The future will not well tolerate unilateral action and precipitous behavior. The interaction and investment of the partnerships necessary to meet the health-care needs of the future must be identified and accessed by health-care providers if any of us are going to survive. Coalition forming and relational strategies will be essential to nurses if the political or social reforms desired are ever going to emerge.

4. *The framework for health care must change as the social conditions of the time shift and demand newer models.* Society is changing. The demographics indicate a major aging shift. Along with this shift will come the need for preventive, chronic, and long-term care strategies that more directly address the needs of the society. While most of the underserved are currently younger, demographic shifts will demand a change in the kind of and approach to health-care services in the United States. Nursing education and service must be retooled to accommodate these realities and prepared to meet new ones as they emerge.

5. *Nursing practice must shift from the institution to the community.* Institutional nursing practice is, by default, a captive of the medical system. The hierarchy and clinical arrangements necessitate the role of the nurse operating within narrowly defined, medically driven parameters. When nurses do manage to create structures that represent the nursing value context, it is often at the risk of confrontation and anxiety with the organized medical staff or the operation of the institution. The full range of the benefits of nursing practice can only be achieved when the walls of the hospital are scaled and the continuity of health services is established and coordinated. Both hospital and community nursing care takes on a whole new dimension, and the power and effectiveness of the nursing role are fully played out. This transition is central to nursing's future and the future of health care in America.

Services to the underserved will continue to be a major issue in the United States for some time. It can be expected that the need for them may even increase in the short term. Practice and policy changes will be essential if the community needs are to be adequately addressed. It is not only unfortunate but a national disgrace that people don't have access to basic health care. Further, when nurses try to address the needs of those who don't have health care, it is a major effort to change policy or law influencing practice. The degree of difficulty that nurses confront from many in the public sector in the localities and communities where they seek to provide services is ample testimony to the effort that must go into nurses' providing health-care services to those who need them.

It is said that challenge never diminishes, it simply changes its appearance. There is no end of challenge in health care today. Nurses, however, are wiser, stronger, and better prepared to address the challenges before them. There are no brighter, more creative, or better prepared people in America today than nurses. Concerted and definitive action taken by nursing leadership today, knowing what needs to be done, will make all the difference. If one doubts the truth of this commitment, one only needs ask the underserved of America whose only experience of health care most likely was provided by a nurse.

References

The American Nurses' Association. (1977). *One Strong Voice*.

Beatty, J. (February 1990). "A Post Cold War Budget." *The Atlantic Monthly*; 75.

Burda, D. (February 19, 1990). "Major Healthcare Reform Not Likely." *Modern Healthcare*; 8.

Ethridge, P. (January 1987). "As I See It: Nursing Centers Make Nursing Care Accessible," *American Journal of Nursing*; 5, 6.

Georgia Nurses Association. (1989). "Proposal for the Payment of Nursing Services for the Underserved." (Now part of the Georgia Nurse Practice Act, passed 1990).

Georgia State Department of Human Resources Annual Report. (1989).

Goldsmith, J. (May/June 1989) "A Radical Prescription for Hospitals," Harvard Business Review, 104–113.

Gunn, I. (Winter 1990) "Carpe Diem: Dead Poets of Nursing Movement." *Specialty Nursing Forum*, 2, no. 1; 2.

Haddon, R. (January 1990). "An Economic Agenda for Healthcare." *Nursing and Healthcare*; 21–25.

Inlander, C. (1988). *Medicine on Trial*. Englewood Cliffs, N.J., Prentice Hall.

Jahiel, R. (1989). *Homelessness and Its Prevention*. Baltimore, Md., Johns Hopkins Press.

Kaiser Permanente of California. Group Health Cooperative. Seattle, Wash. 1990.

Kessler, D. M. (March 1988). "Viewing Healthcare As a War Theatre." *Healthcare Strategic Management*; 5–9.

The Land Corporation. (1990). "The Land Corporation's Study of Physician Extenders, Nurse Practitioners, and Physician Assistants." Santa Monica, Calif., University of Minnesota School of Public Health, Minneapolis; Boston University School of Public Health.

Levitt, T. (March/April 1988). "The Pluralization of Consumption." *Harvard Business Review*; 7–8.

Maraldo, P. (January 1990). "The 90's: A Decade In Search of Meaning." *Nursing and Healthcare*; 11–14.

McKinney Homeless Assistance Act. (1990). *Budget of the United States of America*.

Minor, A.F. (December 1989). "The Cost of Maternity Care and Child Birth in the United States 1989." *Research Bulletin*. Health Insurance Association of America.

Proceedings of the 2nd Annual Conference of the The National Commission on Nursing. (1988). Futures for High Quality, Cost Effective Nursing Care Delivery Systems of the Future. San Diego.

National Commission on Nursing Implementation Project. (1988). *Models for the Future of Nursing*.

The National Commission on Nursing Implementation Project, Models for the Future of Nursing. (1989). "Community Care for the Frail Elderly: Innovative Nursing Roles: The On Loc Senior Health Services Program."

Nornhold, P. (January 1990). "Prediction for the 90s." *Nursing 90*; 35–41.

Olivae, G., et al. (November 1989). "Case Management A Bottom Line Care Delivery Model." *The Journal of Nursing Administration* 19, no. 11; 16–20.

Payne, S. (December 1987). "Identifying and Managing an Appropriate Hospital Utilization." *Health Services Research*; 407–418.

Peterson, P. (October 1988). "The Morning After." *The Atlantic Monthy*; 43–69.

Porter-O'Grady, T. (1990). *Reorganization of Nursing Practice*. Rockville, Md., Aspen Publishers.

Rooks, J. P., et al. (December 28, 1989). "The Outcomes of Care in Birth Centers." *New England Journal of Medicine*. 321, no. 26; 1804–1811.

Wagner, L. (February 19, 1990). "Hospitals Reject AMA's Overture to Join Forces Over Medicare." *Modern Healthcare*; 2.

Zander, K. (1988). "Nursing Case Management Strategic Management of Cost and Quality Outcomes." *The Journal of Nursing Administration* 18, no. 5; 23–30.

CHAPTER 3

Homelessness and Public Policy

Bob Prentice

Abstract

This chapter argues that the dramatic increase in homelessness over the past decade is the direct outgrowth of changes in public policy. Contemporary homelessness is associated in particular with policy changes affecting housing, employment, public assistance, and health care. The transformation of public policy is traced from the New Deal, which for decades served as the political framework for public policy debate in the United States, to the market-oriented reforms and general assault on the public sector ushered in by the Reagan presidency. The chapter concludes with an argument that a homeless movement will achieve limited victories at best in the current hostile climate and that homeless activists must forge coalitions with other groups to develop a larger social agenda that includes restoring the legitimacy of the public sector.

This chapter departs from the assumption that the homelessness we see around us is simply the historical legacy of people who have always lived on the margins. It is based instead on the premise that contemporary homelessness exists on a scale unprecedented in this country since the 1930s and that it is the direct outgrowth of changes in public policy. Moreover, it argues that those changes have occurred under the ideological banner of the private market, which has been used to whittle, and in some cases chop, away at the already limited public sector support system for the poor. Perhaps just as ominously, the assault on the legitimacy of the public sector is seen as dampening the prospect of forging a public policy that will effectively reverse the growth in homelessness.

The chapter begins with an analysis of some of the major structural factors that have increasingly converted poverty into homelessness before turning to a review of the political realignments that have ushered in what one commentator has called a neo-Dickensian social policy (Kuttner 1987).

A Profile of Contemporary Homelessness

Homelessness is an exacerbation of poverty. In the longer view, urbanization and industrialization transformed the primary locus of support for the poor from family and community to a wider, collective responsibility manifest through the public sector, first by towns and cities, then increasingly by state and national governments. However, in the general ideological assault on government that began in the 1970s but flourished in the 1980s, much of the public sector support system for the poor was also undermined. In some instances it resulted from a direct attack on government programs; in others, it was a conscious refusal to take an active governmental role in reducing the destructive consequences of developments that occurred in the private economy. The combined effects of those policies in housing, employment, public assistance, and health care became the force that pushed more people than we have seen in decades over the edge of poverty into homelessness.*

Housing

If there is one dominant factor underlying the explosive growth of homelessness during the 1980s, it is the crisis in low-cost housing. People can be poor for many reasons, but they are homeless because they do not have a place to live.

The roots of the low-cost housing in the cities can be traced back at least as far as the 1950s, which were characterized by suburbanization as primarily a residential phenomenon, with people still commuting to the cities for jobs, shopping, and cultural activities. During the 1960s and 1970s, however, industry and commerce joined the exodus. As disinvestment hollowed out their economic base, cities struggled to revitalize their economies in part by promoting tourism, office high rises, and retail trade. Under the rubric of urban renewal, local redevelopment agencies leveled large chunks of the low-cost housing stock to clear the way for convention centers, office buildings, hotels, and sports stadiums. San Francisco, for example, lost 40% of its residential hotel rooms (from 32,000 to 18,000) in a fifteen-year period due to demolition and conversion to uses better suited to the expanding downtown, a familiar theme in cities throughout the country.

In addition to the loss of low-cost housing stock, the price of housing that remained skyrocketed over the past decade. During the 1980s housing prices increased at twice the rate of median income. Housing prices for poor people, on the other hand, outstripped income by a factor of three to one during the same period. While many people adapted by adjusting their expectations about home ownership or the type of house in which they would live, poor people had few options for downward adjustment. Families doubled and tripled up, or families of four lived in one-bed-

*Much of this analysis was previously published in Agnos, 1989.

TABLE 3.1
**Reductions in Federal Housing Aid Budget Authority for the U.S. Department
of Housing and Urban Development,
1981–1989 (selected years)**

Year	Budget Authority ($ Billions)	Percentage Decrease Since 1981 (%)
1981	32.2	------
1986	10.3	68
1987	8.4	74
1988	8.4	74
1989	6.9	79

SOURCE: Low Income Housing Information Service 1988

room or studio apartments, but it became increasingly difficult to maintain housing on public assistance or a minimum-wage job without some form of subsidy.

And what has been the public policy response to the housing crisis? New budget authority for the Department of Housing and Urban Development (HUD) declined from $32 billion in 1981 to $7 billion in 1989, which amounts to more than a 75% reduction in federal housing subsidies (see Table 3.1). It is hard to imagine a more thorough decimation of a federal department short of its outright elimination. Hidden in those general figures is an even more dramatic 90% reduction in federally assisted new housing starts as what was left of federal housing subsidies shifted away from new construction to vouchers, which in effect increases competition for existing housing stock. As reported by the Center on Budget and Policy Priorities and the Low Income Housing Information Service, data from HUD and the U.S. Census Bureau indicate that there was a surplus of 2.4 million low-rent units over low-income households in 1970, but by 1985 there were 3.7 million *fewer* low-rent units than low- income households. Nearly half (45%) of the poor pay 70% or more of their income for housing, yet only 25% of eligible poor households live in federally subsidized housing (Leonard et al. 1989).

Income

A crucial link in the equation between housing and homelessness is the declining capacity of some people to generate income sufficient to secure market-rate housing.

The restructuring of the U.S. economy in the latter part of the twentieth century has resulted in four out of five new jobs being created in retail trade and services, which pay roughly half the wages of manufacturing jobs and generally have fewer benefits and less job security. In California three out of ten workers earn less than the official poverty wage for a family of four. Nationally, one-quarter of the work force is in "contingent" classifications, which includes casual labor, on-call work and involuntary part-time or self-employed occupations. Temporary work has outpaced the growth of the labor force as a whole by a factor of nine, resulting in a four-fold increase in the number of temporary workers between 1973 and 1988 (Hatfield 1989). In short, there is a growing pool of the working poor, who comprise 15% of the homeless population according to the most recent survey by the U.S. Conference of Mayors (1989).

Life has also become more difficult for those who are out of work. Even at a relatively low unemployment rate of 5%, more than 6 million people are out of work in a total work force of 123 million. In 1988 only 32% were receiving unemployment benefits, in contrast to 81% in 1975, reflecting the failure of unemployment insurance to keep pace with the duration or frequency of unemployment episodes. None of this, of course, even takes into account what the Bureau of Labor Statistics conservatively estimates to be the roughly 855,000 people who have given up looking for work (Hatfield 1989).

For those who rely on public assistance, the outlook was no better. According to the Center on Budget and Policy Priorities, the official poverty rate increased from 11.7% (26.1 million people) to 14% (33.1 million people) between 1979 and 1985, with 30% of that increase being accounted for by reductions in federal assistance programs (Greenstein 1987). A change in the 1981 regulations for the Aid to Families with Dependent Children (AFDC) program, for example, eliminated benefits for about a quarter of a million poor working families and reduced benefits for almost an equal number (Hopper and Hamberg 1984). In 1979, unemployment insurance, AFDC, Social Security, and other social programs lifted one in five families out of poverty, but by 1985 this figure had dropped to only one in nine families (Greenstein 1987).

Health Care

The lack of a universal and comprehensive national health-care program has kept open one of the avenues to impoverishment on one hand, and on the other denied access to health care for many who are already poor. The passage of the 1965 amendments to the Social Security Act that established Medicare and Medicaid was accompanied by rhetoric about providing access to the "mainstream" health-care system for the elderly, disabled, and poor. It also unleashed a series of proposals that would extend the scope of federal health-care legislation moving in the direction of a more universal national health-care program. By the end of the 1970s, however, the rhetoric had changed, and cost containment became the overarching framework for health-policy reform. The emphasis on competition in the health-care marketplace, new reimbursement formulas from both public and private insurers, and a diminished government role in the health-care system were the hallmarks of health policy in the 1980s. Meanwhile, roughly 37 million people have no health insurance coverage, and the United States continues to be in a league it shares only with South Africa as industrialized countries with no national health-care program. As the AIDS epidemic has reminded us dramatically, homelessness can be one result of a serious illness when people lose their health insurance along with their employment.

Two health issues in particular—mental health and substance abuse—have often been used to explain the growth of homelessness during the 1980s. While mental illness and substance abuse are often significant problems among the homeless population, they do not by themselves explain why homelessness has increased so significantly over the past decade.

The most common distorting mythology surrounding homelessness is that it was caused by the deinstitutionalization of the mentally ill, which dumped thousands of mentally disabled people into the streets. Between 1960 and 1985 there was a 75% reduction in state mental hospital beds nationwide, from roughly 554,000 to about 134,000. However, more than half of that reduction occurred prior to 1970 and more than 95% occurred prior to 1980. It is a tenuous argument at best to attribute the growth of homelessness during the 1980s to deinstitutionalization. Moreover, the psychiatric inpatient census has actually increased during the same period, although it is now in veterans' hospitals and local general hospitals rather than state mental hospitals (Goldman et al. 1983). Psychiatric hospitalization is today more likely to be a series of episodes than a constant way of life (Goldman et al. 1983).

It is more likely that the number of mentally disabled people on the streets is a combination of the crisis in low-cost housing and the lack of adequate community-based support services. Many people who are chronically mentally ill, for example, are also poor and rely on Supplemental Security Income (SSI) benefits as their primary source of income. During the infamous purges of the SSI rolls during the early days of the Reagan Administration, nearly half a million mentally disabled people lost their benefits (Hopper and Hamberg 1984). Those who retained their benefits still faced the escalating price of low-cost housing. At the same time, the community-based system of care, ranging from residential treatment facilities to board-and-care to outpatient services, was greatly underfunded. Accordingly, the important goal of deinstitutionalization to enable people to live with the greatest degree of independence possible was difficult to realize when increasing numbers of mentally disabled people had neither the minimal stability of a place to live nor access to community-based care.

Substance abuse also has been pointed to as a primary cause of homelessness. Studies of homelessness throughout the twentieth century have indicated that 25–35% of the homeless population has suffered from alcohol problems (Stark 1987; Wilhite 1989). The use of illicit drugs has varied more, depending upon region, time, and availability. There is no doubt that addiction to alcohol or other drugs can destroy family, job, and home and lead to homelessness. However, there is no evidence of a precipitous increase in alcohol or drug addiction that can by itself explain the growth of homelessness over the past decade. It is more likely that the destruction of skid rows through urban renewal has made street alcoholics (now called "public inebriates") more visible because they are no longer confined to a single, isolated section of a city, that the marginal existence of chronic alcoholics and drug users living in residential hotels has also been affected by the jump in housing prices, and that lack of adequate treatment programs has contributed to both the reality and perception that associates substance abuse and homelessness.

The Transformation of Public Policy

Contemporary homelessness is the consequence of several related factors, including the crisis in low-cost housing, a restructuring of the labor market, an assault on public assistance programs, and a retreat from a commitment to comprehensive health care. As even *Time* magazine recently acknowledged, we know the causes of homelessness, and they are not insoluble (Gibbs 1990). If we are to dramatically reduce homelessness, however, we must make a commitment to an aggressive federal housing policy, a full-employment economy, and comprehensive health and social services. Unfortunately, political realignments over the past two decades have not only ushered in the policies that have helped create homelessness as a common feature of contemporary American life, but continue to frustrate efforts to reverse those trends.

In its simplest characterization, that realignment was built upon an antigovernment sentiment that has made a near-fetish of the virtues of the private market as the prescription for every ill—if the government stops subsidizing low-cost housing, private investment will spur housing production and the market will maintain affordability; eschew public employment programs in favor of incentives to business to hire and train the poor; ease the tax burden on the wealthy to stimulate investment and contain the costs of government in part by reducing public assistance programs; and introduce competition into health care to force efficiencies and lower costs.

If progress is to be made in carrying out the policy reforms necessary to successfully confront homelessness, on the other hand, it must emerge from a broader political culture that reestablishes the social legitimacy of the public sector. Whatever the virtues of the market economy, it does not by itself provide decent housing that poor people can afford; it does not provide secure jobs with living wages to anyone who seeks them; it does not protect those who are unable to provide for themselves; and it does not provide universal access to health care. If we are to build a movement that can revive the possibility of a public policy that is capable of addressing the roots of contemporary homelessness, it is useful to first review the political transformations that got us to where we are today to better understand what we are up against.

How Did We Get Here?

This chapter began with the observation that homelessness now exists on a scale unprecedented since the 1930s. The association of developments separated by five decades is more than a rhetorical device. The political response to the crisis of the 1930s, and the coalition that brought it into being, have, until recently, been the backbone of the American political culture, providing not only a framework for social policy but the more fundamental images of the appropriate relationship between civil society and the state. Much of what we have come to take for granted— Social Security, unemployment insurance, welfare, public housing, the right to organize and join labor unions, regulation of banking, etc.—had its origins in the New Deal of the 1930s. In the midst of a widespread economic crisis, government was established as the regulator of the private economy and as the guarantor of basic life necessities for those who, for temporary or enduring reasons, were unable to provide for themselves. Moreover, the political coalition of labor, immigrants, minorities, poor people, liberal professionals, and business men and women who understood that the conditions for private gain require a measure of social harmony formed the foundation not only for the New Deal but for political discourse in the United States for decades to come.

While the decade of the 1930s was a fractious period, the ambitious program of the New Deal was able to be carried out in part because the economic collapse affected a broad spectrum of people, from immigrants and industrial laborers to stockbrokers and bankers. As the economy began to recover, with new safeguards and regulations, World War II provided a boost to production and helped forge a new national consensus. When the United States emerged from the war as both an economic and military power, it was the beginning of what was being called the American Century, in which all sectors of society would benefit.

In the postwar period, economic growth was seen as the solution to all social problems. Organized labor agreed to link wages and benefits to increases in productivity, abandoning much of its previous militance. Similarly, poverty would be solved as people's individual slices grew along with the expanding economic pie. The new American dream of home ownership, underwritten in part by the Federal Housing Authority (FHA), became attainable for more people with the growth of the suburbs, and public housing remained for those (such as returning veterans) who needed a temporary period to get back on their feet. Health-care insurance became more widely available as a benefit tied to wage negotiations between employers and labor unions, which deflated the efforts to create a national health insurance program. We had achieved, in the infamous phrase of the sociologist Daniel Bell, the "end of ideology." The promise of social harmony inherent in economic expansion and abundance brought musings over the survival of the individual in an era of conformity to the center of cultural debate. Against the deadening obsession with conformity manifest in McCarthyism, commentators such as

Galbraith (*The Poverty of Affluence*), Reisman (*The Lonely Crowd*), Packard (*The Status Seekers*), and Whyte (*The Organization Man*) questioned whether individual autonomy and initiative were being destroyed (Ehrenreich 1989).

The cracks in the foundation of the apparent postwar consensus began to surface, however, first with the civil rights movement and then with the rediscovery of poverty commonly associated with the publication of Michael Harrington's *The Other America*. The problems of racism and poverty proved to be more intractable than the apostles of economic expansion had anticipated. The public policy response to the civil rights movement and the rediscovery of poverty was at once the pinnacle of the New Deal legacy and the beginnings of its demise. On the one hand, when, as part of his Great Society programs, Lyndon Johnson signed the Civil Rights Act and declared the war on poverty, he reaffirmed the legitimate role of the federal government as the guarantor of social justice and ultimate source of support for the poor and disenfranchised. On the other hand, the War on Poverty coincided with a war in Vietnam that helped spawn a student movement that split apart what remained of the New Deal coalition and ushered in an era of limits that challenged, among other things, the very role of government.

The War on Poverty had important potential constituencies insofar as it overlapped with the concerns of the civil rights movement and appealed to the sensibilities of a burgeoning student culture that sympathized with the poor and disenfranchised as an outgrowth of their rejection of the vapid consumerism and conformity of the suburban milieux from which many of them came. The Vietnam War, however, contributed to the further alienation of many who were active in the civil rights and student movements, which led to a broadly based counterculture that clashed with the national pride and traditional values of other potential allies in the New Deal coalition. The various movements that emerged from this counterculture—black nationalism, new student left, hippies, feminism, ecology, antinuclear, gay liberation, etc.—seemed a far cry from, and, for some, antithetical to, the issues of wages, benefits, and Parent Teacher Associations (PTAs). The political coalition that for three decades had sustained the legacy of the New Deal was divided.

Perhaps more significantly, however, the near-universal faith in economic expansion that had dominated American political culture since the end of World War II was being shaken to its foundations from other sources. The geopolitical limits on U.S. economic expansion became more significant as third world countries demanded a fair share of the world's resources, and as new centers of economic power surfaced in Germany and Japan. The ecology movement called attention to the questionable ability of the environment to sustain even current levels of economic development. For many Americans the most dramatic indication that we had entered a new era of limits came in 1973 when the oil boycott forced people to wait in long lines for gasoline and pay significantly higher prices for petroleum products. The United States was no longer dominant or even in control of its own destiny.

Richard Nixon was elected to office in 1968 with the aid of a badly divided political base in the Democratic party and a growing antigovernment sentiment that was articulated more forcefully during the campaign by George Wallace ("We'll throw the bureaucrats' briefcases into the Potomac") than by Nixon himself. However, Nixon was able to establish certain themes that were amplified later during the Reagan presidency. He set about the business of dismantling the Office of Economic Opportunity, a cornerstone of the War on Poverty. He began the process of shifting responsibility for programs from the federal to state and local governments under the rubric of revenue sharing. He also promoted public policy goals by using government subsidies of the private sector as opposed to government-administered programs, such as all but abandoning public housing in favor of federal subsidies to private developers as the linchpin of federal housing policy during his administration.

If there was any chance for a resurgence of the Democratic party as the dominant national party (it could still win local elections to send members to Congress), it disappeared with the crushing defeat of McGovern in 1972. Even when the Republicans were discredited in the aftermath of Watergate, it was an outsider, Jimmy Carter, not the Democratic party itself, who surfaced to preside over the interregnum. Ronald Reagan's great accomplishment was to capitalize on the political realignments that had taken place over the previous decade, aided by a well-organized new right and an incipient tax revolt movement that achieved an important victory when, in 1978, California voters approved the infamous Proposition 13. Although Reagan had previously sought the presidency, the Republican Party was wary because of the fate of other recent ideological candidates (Goldwater in 1964 and McGovern in 1972). By 1980, however, Reagan was in a unique position to consolidate trends that had been developing during the 1970s.

The Reagan presidency represented a political watershed potentially on a par with Roosevelt's New Deal coalition. Reagan was able to maintain the traditional base of the Republican party, integrate new forms of professional and technical labor, capture new regions of economic power in the Sunbelt, and break off sectors traditionally loyal to the Democratic party by mobilizing their resentment toward the villainous forces that were accused of eroding family and community. The backlash against the social movements and sensibilities of the 1960s, combined with an antigovernment sentiment that glorified the virtues of competitive individualism, gave an ideological coherence to an otherwise tenuous coalition.

Reagan was able to parlay his new political base into some very significant changes in public policy. If Nixon set out to dismantle the Great Society, Reagan attempted to reverse the legacy of the New Deal. Supply-side economists assaulted Keynesian policies. Deregulation of industries, from banking to airlines, and the removal of obstacles such as environmental protections, were designed to unleash the forces of the market. Tax reform resulted in an income shift from poor and middle-income people to the wealthy (Phillips 1990).

The overarching theme, however, was to reduce the role of government—with the notable exception of the military—which had direct consequences for the major structural factors associated with homelessness. Sam Pierce, Reagan's new secretary of Housing and Urban Development (HUD), declared that the federal government was going to get out of the housing business, a commitment he kept very well, as the dramatic reduction in HUD's budget would indicate. (Of course, he meant the federal government was going to get out of the low-income housing business, since middle- and upper-income homeowners receive an estimated $65 billion per year in housing subsidies through the mortgage interest deduction, and the savings and loan industry is in line for an estimated $500 billion bailout.) The response to structural shifts in the economy and changes in the types of employment available did not include economic planning to minimize dislocation, sanctions against plant closures, a major commitment to retrain laid-off workers, or public sector employment in the tradition of the Works Project Administration (WPA) or even Comprehensive Employment Training Act (CETA), but rather incentives to business and private industry councils to hire and train the unemployed. Health policy reforms fostered the development of large, for-profit hospital chains and mergers of community-based hospitals as they fought for market shares in the new competitive environment, but federal funding for community health centers was substantially reduced and access for the poor and uninsured worsened. Public assistance programs were targeted for reductions while Reagan dismissed claims about a growing homeless population as the artifice of a small band of malcontents.

Where Do We Go From Here?

While there have been some successes—the Stewart B. McKinney Homeless Assistance Act is a limited one—the outlook still is bleak for the kind of public policy changes that will be required to significantly reduce homelessness. Rather than wring our hands over the enormous task of reversing a decade of political momentum or take refuge in the small victories we are able to achieve, however, homeless activists must engage in a broad discussion of a strategy that can frame our immediate goals within a larger agenda of social change.

Perhaps one of the most formidable challenges is to change the terms within which public debate over homelessness occurs. The appeal to the primacy of the individual, family, and community as a means of discrediting a broader collective responsibility embodied in the public sector has produced a political culture that does not readily grasp the structural aspects of poverty. We do not easily associate homelessness with housing policy, economic policy, or our health and social service system. Instead, we individualize poverty. Social work, for example, has tended to move away from community organizing as a means of confronting the conditions of poverty toward individual therapy and—the panacea for the 1990s— case management. The path out of homelessness is individual rehabilitation.

Even the backlash against homeless people is fueled in part by the individualization of poverty. Most people's perceptions of homelessness are shaped by personal experience, whether in the form of being asked for money by a panhandler or seeing people sleeping in doorways or parks. Without a political vocabulary that makes a clear connection between public policy and the fact that people are living in the streets, however, there is a tendency to focus only on the moral character of the homeless person rather than the moral character of a society that produces so many people who beg money for food or life-numbing chemicals.

The transformation of the public debate over homelessness requires more than the public relations campaigns that have preoccupied some advocates for the homeless. To counter the hostile images of homeless people as drunks and crazies, we offer sympathetic images of families. The goal, though, must be to make poverty the issue and to acknowledge that poverty ravages people's lives, whether able-bodied adults, runaway youth, mentally disabled people, or children of homeless families. The point is not to soft sell homelessness, but rather to help people see the connections among public policy, poverty, and homelessness.

Health-care workers are in a unique position to contribute to this revitalized public debate. Who knows better both the damage that homelesness does to individuals and the limits of seeking solutions exclusively in individual rehabilitation? Clinics used by homeless people see disease profiles more characteristic of third world countries, conditions that could have been prevented or easily treated, and complex problems that go beyond the capacity of any one clinician or clinical discipline to solve (Brickner et al. 1990; Wlodarczyk and Prentice 1988). Even the best effort with individual patients reaches its limits, however, if there are inadequate treatments programs, no housing that they can afford, or no jobs that pay a living wage. For those who provide health care to homeless people, the relationship between homelesness and housing policy, economic policy and the health and social service system is not so abstract.

Coinciding with the attempts to change the terms of public debate is the need to broaden the goals of a homeless movement. Even a strong homeless movement will be limited in what it can achieve. The Stewart B. McKinney Homeless Assistance Act is a good example. While it has funded programs that have provided important assistance to homeless people, its annual appropriation of well under $1 billion must be considered in relation to the $25 billion annual reduction in federal housing subsidies over the last decade. Legislative victories in an unsympathetic climate will of necessity be limited. It is therefore essential to build alliances with other groups who share a broad social vision while continuing the efforts to effect legislation targeted specifically to homeless people. This alliance must, at a minimum, include groups that have a common commitment to the legitimate role of the public sector, whether it is in the monitoring of civil rights and equal opportunity, protection of the environment, regulation of the vagaries of the market economy or guaranteeing human rights to decent and affordable housing, gainful employment, and health care. In short, the forging of such a coalition would require the mobilization of groups traditionally loyal to the Democratic party as part of the New Deal legacy (labor, ethnic minorities, immigrants, the poor, liberal professionals, etc.) with those who identify with more recent social movements (feminists, environmentalists, gay activists, etc.).

Is the appeal to a coalition of groups that are struggling for survival and in a general state of disarray an exercise in futility? There could be some signs of hope. Republican political strategist Kevin Phillips has written an important book, *The Politics of Rich and Poor: Wealth and the American Electorate in the Reagan Aftermath* (Phillips 1990), in which he not only chronicles the concentration of wealth and power during the Reagan years but speculates that it might have set the stage for a populist upsurge. After more than a decade of confrontation with the legacy of the Great Society and New Deal, we might have gone too far in the other direction. Are the redistribution of income toward the wealthy, the decline of basic industry, 37 million people with no health insurance, and homelessness in virtually every city and town our monuments to the domestic policy of the Reagan era? The prospects for organizing in such a climate are not entirely dim.

The social vision of a revitalized public sector could also emanate from an unlikely source. The people of the Soviet Union and Eastern Europe have captured our attention because they have cast aside the restrictive political and economic institutions that for so long stifled the freedoms we value as the essence of democracy. The self-congratulatory interpretation of those events is that they are finally looking more like us — political democracy, market economy, and diminished public sector. While the people of the Soviet Union and Eastern Europe have reason to exult in their new freedoms, there is a more sobering side to the dramatic reforms they have introduced. As unemployment and even homelessness begin to surface in the newly liberated economies of Eastern Europe, people might very well conclude that there are aspects of the public sector that they are unwilling to surrender, particularly those that guarantee housing, employment, and health care. It will be interesting to see how those events unfold over the course of the next decade and how they might help to shape events in the United States. If the central dynamic in political debates in this country over the last several decades has been the issue of the proper relationship between civil society and the state, we might have something to learn from people who are struggling with the same questions, albeit from a different direction.

References

Agnos, Mayor Art (August November 1990). *Beyond Shelter: A Homeless Plan for San Francisco, Office of the Mayor.* City and County of San Francisco, Calif.

Brickner, P. W., L. K. Scharer, B. A. Conanan, M. Savarese, and B.C. Scanlon, eds. (1990). *Under the Safety Net: The Health and Social Welfare of the Homeless in the United States,* New York: W. W. Norton and Co.

Ehrenreich, B. (1989). *Fear of Falling: The Inner Life of the Middle Class.* New York: Harper Collins Publishers.

Gibbs, N. (December 17, 1990). "Answers at Last." *Time*.

Goldmann, H. H., N. Adams, and C.A. Taube (February 1983). "Deinstitutionalization: The Data Demythologized." *Hospital and Community Psychiatry 34*, no. 2. 129–134.

Greenstein, R. (1987). Washington, D.C. Center on Budget and Policy Priorities.

Hatfield, L. D. (April 23, 1989). "Experts Divided: Is Jobless Picture Rosy or Really Grim?" *San Francisco Examiner*.

Hopper, K., and J. Hamburg (December 1984). *The Making of America's Homeless: From Skid Row to New Poor, Housing and Development Policy Unit and Institute for Social Welfare Research*. New York: Community Service Society of New York.

Kuttner, R. (August 31, 1987). "A Blueprint for Affordable Housing." *Business Week*.

Leonard, P. A., C. Dolbeare and E. B. Lazere (April 1989). *A Place to Call Home: The Crisis in Housing for the Poor*, Washington, D.C.; *Center on Budget and Policy Priorities and Low Income Housing Information Service*.

Phillips, K. (1990). *The Politics of Rich and Poor: Wealth and the American Electorate in the Reagan Aftermath*, New York: Random House.

Stark, L. (Spring 1987). "A Century of Alcohol and Homelessness." *Alcohol Health and Research World*.

U.S. Conference of Mayors (January 1989). *A Status Report on Hunger and Homelessness in America's Cities: 1988*. Washington, D.C.: U.S. Conference of Mayors.

Wilhite, J. (September 1989). *The Disappearance of the Skid Row Alcoholic as a Public Problem*. Alcohol Research Group: University of California, Berkeley.

Wlodarczyk, D., and R. Prentice, (June 1988). "Health Issues of Homeless Persons." *Western Journal of Medicine* 148:717–19.

Demographics and Characteristics of Various Homeless Populations

CHAPTER 4

Evolution and Population Characteristics of a Nurse-Managed Health Center for the Homeless and High-Risk, Low-Income Families

Mary Margaret Gottesman
Mary Ann Lewis
Ada M. Lindsey
Mary-Lynn Brecht

Abstract

The School of Nursing, University of California Los Angeles (UCLA) operates two full-time nurse-managed clinics for the homeless in downtown Los Angeles. This chapter describes the evolution of the initial center that opened in 1983 in the Union Rescue Mission on Skid Row. This center, developed by the School of Nursing's faculty members, opened offering services two afternoons per week, and progressed to providing services on a full-time basis.

Data from the Union Rescue Mission Center describe the personal and social characteristics, health-care needs, and functional status of children and adult clients according to age and gender. The majority of clients are minority adult males between nineteen and forty-nine years of age. There is a prevalence of alcohol and drug abuse, as well as smoking, among adult clients. During 1989, the number of women and children seeking services at the clinic increased.

Nursing has the expertise and the social responsibility to take the lead in providing services to this disadvantaged population. Future nurses must be prepared to assume leadership roles in development of health and social welfare policies related to provision of health-care services for the homeless.

Introduction

Health care for the homeless is both a challenge and necessity (Reuber 1989). The University of California, Los Angeles, School of Nursing provides primary health-care services for the homeless population in Los Angeles' inner city. This nurse-managed health center has received funding from the Robert Wood Johnson Foundation; Pew Charitable Trust; Special Project Grants Program in the Nursing Education Practice Resources Branch, Division of Nursing, U.S. Department of Health and Human Services, Public Health Service, Health Resources and Services Administration, Bureau of Health Professions Administration; and funds allotted by the Stewart B. McKinney Homeless Assistance Act of 1987. Additionally, in-kind contributions were received from Los Angeles County, the mission, and the UCLA School of Nursing.

Location

Dubbed the "Homeless Capital of the Country," with 34,000 to 50,000 homeless persons, Los Angeles has one of the largest homeless populations in the United States. The homeless of the 1980s are "younger, better educated, and dispropor-tionately non-white, compared with previous generations" (Ropers and Boyer 1987, 38). Nationally, the number of homeless individuals continues to increase, with families comprising the most rapidly growing segment of the homeless popu-lation (Freeman and Hall 1986; Institute of Medicine 1988)).

In Los Angeles the majority of the homeless population is concentrated in the Skid Row area located in the heart of downtown metropolitan Los Angeles. The Skid Row area has varied little since the turn of the century, but its boundaries are more psychological than physical. Skid Row contains a concentration of business-es in rundown buildings, light manufacturing industries, railroad tracks, bridges, and a multitude of shabby, deteriorating structures. Numerous bars and small gro-cery/liquor stores stocked with cheap wine and liquor occupy the center of the row. There also are dilapidated, cockroach- and rodent-infested hotels that house the poor. Religious missions and private shelters serve the homeless population. These missions offer thousands of free meals each day as well as approximately 1,200 beds each night. The less fortunate (estimated at between 1,500 and 3,000 on any given night) are forced to sleep in the alleyways, abandoned buildings, garbage bins, or under bridges and bushes. Rape, assault, robbery, and murder are com-monplace.

In the past, the police tended to leave the residents of the Skid Row area alone, and the residents tended to avoid the police. However, recently police have been di-rected to "sweep" the streets and sidewalks in the Skid Row area. The intent is to re-move temporary housing structures (Jones 1987). The homeless mentally ill of Skid Row have learned that if they wander outside the Skid Row area, their chances of being picked up by the police and taken to public institutions for care are significantly greater.

In a probability sample of sheltered and nonsheltered homeless individuals in the Los Angeles Skid Row area, more than half of the sample was less than fifty years of age. Koegel and Burnam (1987) report that 49.5% of the sample had children. Ninety percent of the individuals with children had problems with alcohol or other substance-abuse disorders (Koegel and Burnam 1987). Almost half of those with histories of alcohol abuse problems had experienced their first episode of homelessness at least six years earlier.

Nearly 80% of homeless persons in Los Angeles lack access to medical coverage (Ropers and Boyer 1987). Only 2% of these individuals receive veterans' benefits, although more than 45% of the males are veterans. In the Los Angeles study Ropers and Boyer (1987) conclude that many homeless persons are unaware of their rights to health-care services and fail to recognize the seriousness of their need for health-care services. For example, only one-half of the homeless persons suffering from either acute or chronic health problems contacted health professionals for treatment of symptoms that were obvious to the data collectors as needing professional services. Access to health-care services is extremely limited for the Skid Row adult population (Jones 1987). Services for adolescents and children are almost nonexistent (Social and Human Services Committee 1987).

Service Area and Potential Population

The service area for the Health Center covers twenty inner-city census tracts. According to 1980 census data provided by the State of California Census Data Center, the racial/ethnic breakdown of this population is: white not Hispanic 21%, black not Hispanic 18%, Hispanic 45%, and other 16%. Nearly 71% of this population lives at or below 200% of the federal poverty level. These numbers fail to reflect the constantly increasing numbers of undocumented immigrants flooding the inner city. Finally, 1980 census data do not reflect the minimum population increase of 464,982 projected for the city of Los Angeles based on the E–5 Report released January 1, 1990, by the California Department of Finance Demographic Research Unit.

Development of the Health Center

The administrators of the Union Rescue Mission, located in Skid Row, requested the assistance of the UCLA School of Nursing in providing consistent health-care services to the mission's adult clients. In March 1983 the School of Nursing faculty initiated a nurse-managed clinic to provide primary health-care services. During the initial operation of the nurse-managed clinic, nurse practitioner faculty members volunteered their services two afternoons per week. Within a short time, the demand for the services of a full-time nurse practitioner was so great that in 1984 the mission obtained funds from the federal Comprehensive Employment Training Act (CETA) for this position. Under the direction of the UCLA School of Nursing faculty, a full-time nurse-practitioner began providing care forty hours per week.

With the rapidly increasing homeless population in Los Angeles, it became clear that the nurse-managed clinic required more extensive and comprehensive funding. In 1985 the UCLA School of Nursing received a Robert Wood Johnson Foundation–Pew Charitable Trust grant which funded the Los Angeles Health Care for the Homeless Program (also known as the Los Angeles Homeless Health Care Program). A portion of this money was used to fund the UCLA School of Nursing Health Center to support the existing free clinic and to add social services and out-reach efforts.

The major objective of the UCLA School of Nursing Health Center at the Union Rescue Mission is to offer primary health care to the homeless, including episodic, acute-care services and the management of stable chronic conditions. The primary emphasis is on the provision of services for adult males and adult women with non-pregnancy-related problems. Pediatric care and services for childbearing women are provided only in urgent care situations. An additional goal is to increase the number of referrals to formal social and public welfare agencies through the clinic's social services. In order to insure appropriate follow-through, services include provision of transportation to these agencies. Two vans have been donated by the city of Los Angeles for this purpose.

In November 1986 the UCLA School of Nursing Health Center Development Committee met to formulate plans for opening a pediatric clinic. A grant was submitted to the Division of Nursing, PHS, DHHS, which was approved in July 1987 and funded in October 1987. The funds were used during April 1988 to open a second health center site for children, located outside the Union Rescue Mission. This report is restricted to data about the original site, however, since its clients are most representative of the homeless population in other urban centers.

Organization of Nursing Practice

The School of Nursing's Health Center occupies 750 square feet on the second floor of the Union Rescue Mission. It operates five days a week, providing thirty-six hours of clinical services, reserving four hours for administrative functions. These functions include ordering supplies, implementing quality-assurance activities, and staff development meetings.

The UCLA School of Nursing Health Center is a nurse-managed practice staffed by nurse practitioners who use physicians as consultants. The nurse administrator manages the Health Center and supervises all professional and nonprofessional staff and volunteers.

Ancillary services, such as urine and blood tests, X-rays, pulmonary function tests, and electrocardiograms are provided mostly through a special arrangement with the Knights of Malta and St. Vincent's Hospital. Patients with illnesses unresponsive to treatment or requiring services the clinic does not offer are referred to the Los Angeles County Hudson Comprehensive Care Center. Unstable acute and chronic conditions and emergencies are referred to the Los Angeles County/University of Southern California (LAC/USC) Medical Center four miles away. Psychiatric emergencies are referred to the Skid Row Mental Health Center four blocks from the Health Center or to the LAC/USC Medical Center.

The small core of professional paid staff at the Health Center in 1990 consisted of one full-time nurse practitioner and two part-time nurse practitioners, a full-time nurse administrator, a part-time physician, and a full-time licensed vocational nurse (LVN) and social worker. The nurse practitioner provides services for an average of fifteen to twenty patients per day. Each nurse practitioner performs a thorough assessment, makes diagnoses, and develops treatment plans as well as furnishes medications as permitted by California law. The nurse practitioners also administer treatments, provide tuberculin testing, and perform simple laboratory tests such as urinalysis (dipstick), blood glucose determination (BG chemstrip), and stool guaiac tests. In addition, they also teach, refer patients, and prepare examining areas in between providing patient-care services. The LVN triages incoming patients, interprets tuberculin tests, and provides self-care supplies to patients.

Participants in the Union Rescue Mission's alcohol and drug rehabilitation program are assigned as clinic aides. These men take measurements of blood pressure, heights, weights, and temperatures. However, these volunteer aides lack previous health-care training and frequently are handicapped either educationally, physically, or emotionally. Therefore, the nurse administrator must continuously monitor and evaluate their performance. A general internal medicine physician is on site 20% of the time. He is also available by telephone. The physician consults on questionable cases, reads X-rays, and orders medications that cannot be furnished by the nurse practitioners.

A full-time social worker provides psychosocial assessments and counseling. The social worker screens patients for Medi-Cal coverage and other social welfare programs, deals with suspected child abuse cases, and works with local mental health agencies to provide services. Case management activities include: locating new housing; facilitating entrance into rehabilitation programs for alcohol or drug abuse treatment; assisting individuals to obtain food, clothing, and medications; and acting as an advocate for individuals in their dealings with social institutions.

Client Characteristics

From 1985 to 1989 the UCLA School of Nursing Health Center has provided 39,879 primary care visits to 11,605 individuals. This does not include the clients who receive only transportation, self-care supplies, and social services. These primary-care visits include all visits provided where there was a medical diagnosis, a service provided, or both, regardless of the provider's professional background.

For 1990 data presented in this report, a somewhat different definition was used for primary-care visits, which excluded services provided by LVNs and nonprofessional personnel but included visits where there was a nursing diagnosis only and the service was health education. Prior to 1990, health education visits provided by the nurse practitioner were not included in the primary-care count because they were not recorded as such on the encounter form until 1989, and their consistent use was not established until 1990.

The sample described in this report includes 3,112 clients seen from January 1–December 31, 1990, at the Health Center's Union Rescue Mission Clinic. Data are abstracted from the encounter forms completed by the nurse practitioners for each of the 9,172 primary-care visits and entered into a computerized database.

Demographic Characteristics

Table 4.1 describes the demographic characteristics of the clients. Sixty percent of the clients were thirty to forty-nine years of age, whereas only 5.6% were eighteen years of age or less. Thirteen percent of clients were female. The majority of clients were black and Latino. Nearly 90% of the clients had no public or private health insurance coverage. The most often reported place of residence was the shelter and the street/car/camper categories. Only 17% of the individuals reported living in rooms, apartments, or houses. Children zero to eighteen years of age were more likely to live in rooms, apartments, or houses than were adults.

Health Status of the Sample

Five dimensions of functional status are widely accepted as essential to a proper evaluation of client needs: social resources, economic resources, mental health, activities of daily living, and physical health (Duke University, Center for the Study of Aging and Human Development 1978). Although Health Center clients were not surveyed with a functional status instrument, the encounter forms captured data relevant to each of these dimensions.

Child Clients

For children, social resources were represented by the housing variable. Of the ninety-eight children from birth to five years of age, 32% lived in shelters, cars,

TABLE 4.1
*Frequency of Demographic Characteristics by Age of Health Center
Clients Receiving Primary Care in 1990*

	Years of Age				
	0–5 (N = 98) 3.1%	6–18 (N = 78) 2.5%	19–29 (N = 735) 23.6%	30–49 (N = 1860) 59.9%	50–older (N = 340) 10.9%
Gender					
Male	58	54	633	1,639	318
Female	40	24	102	221	22
Race					
White	6	7	81	190	77
Black	65	19	377	1,321	174
Latino	25	50	260	320	76
Asian	2	2	6	9	5
Other	0	0	11	20	8
Insurance					
Medi-Cal	30	7	11	62	32
Medicare	0	0	0	3	4
VA	0	0	2	22	3
Other	5	5	26	84	30
None	63	66	696	1,689	271
Residence					
Street/Car/Camper	4	12	139	288	44
Shelter	27	21	493	1,311	239
Room/Apt/House	67	45	103	261	57
Average # of clinic visits	2.08	1.94	2.84	3.09	2.87

campers, or the street, compared to 42% of six to eighteen year olds (N = 78). The remainder lived in rooms, apartments, or houses.

In terms of economic resources, 31% of children zero to five years of age were identified as Medi-Cal recipients, and 64% were listed as having no health insurance. Only 9% of six to eighteen year-olds reported having Medi-Cal coverage, and 85% had no health coverage.

The mental health of children is closely tied to the quality of parenting they receive (McCall 1981; National Center for Children in Poverty 1990). There were no cases of abuse or neglect identified among the 176 children seen during 1990. However, there were nine diagnoses of poor growth, with anthropometric measures of height and weight below the fifth percentile for age, and four cases of developmental delay, all among children five years of age or less.

Children seen at the Health Center had the usual childhood illnesses (these data are presented later). Their impact on functional status is limited by their episodic nature. However, chronic illnesses often have greater impact on functional status by limiting physical activity and altering body image and self-esteem (Rose and

TABLE 4.2
Frequencies of Diagnoses Reflecting Deficits in ADLs
for Children 0–18 Years of Age in 1990[a]

Diagnosis	Frequency
Injuries	24
Pediculosis	22
Tinea	14
Malnutrition	9
Scabies	7

[a] $N = 174$

Thomas 1987). There was little evidence of chronic illness in this sample of children. Four children were diagnosed with asthma and one with seizures.

Activities of daily living (ADLs) include the abilities to feed and bathe oneself and to provide a clean environment for oneself to live in (Moinpour, McCorkle, and Saunders 1988). Children are dependent upon their parents for the quality and quantity of the food they eat, their personal and environmental cleanliness, and safety. Accordingly, the following diagnoses were chosen to measure the adequacy of ADLs for children: malnutrition; contagious skin diseases associated with poor hygiene, a dirty environment, or both; and preventable injuries. Their frequencies in childhood clients are presented in Table 4.2. Preventable injuries and contagious skin conditions were the most frequent diagnoses reflecting deficits in safety and cleanliness.

Tables 4.3 and 4.4 present data describing the five most frequent health problems by age and sex. Diagnoses varied little by sex and age group. Respiratory infections and otitis media were common diagnoses in this population as in other child groups, regardless of socioeconomic status.

Adult Clients

It is more difficult to describe social resources for the adult population served by the Health Center. Homelessness necessarily means limited social resources (McGeary and Lynn 1988). Health Center data do not reflect the social networks homeless, needy individuals may have developed and rely upon daily (Burt and Cohen 1989). However, data are available which describe the incidence of risk factors in the Health Center's adult population which are associated in the literature with loss of social support resources and increased health risks. These are presented in Table 4.5. Sixty-six percent or more of Health Center clients identified smoking as a health risk factor. More than 50% of all adult clients reported alcohol abuse. In addition, more than 50% of clients nineteen to forty-nine years old reported drug abuse. Less than 10% of adults reported histories of mental illness.

Although mental illness was self-reported in the health histories from 212

TABLE 4.3
Five Most Frequent Diagnoses by Gender for 0–5 Years of Age in 1990

Males (N = 56)[a]		Females (N = 40)[b]	
Diagnosis	Frequency	Diagnosis	Frequency
Respiratory infections	67	Upper respiratory infections	43
Otitis media	19	Dermotologic problems	24
Dermatologic problems	13	Otitis media	10
Health maintenance	7	Health maintenance	7
Urinary tract infection	4	Tonsillo-pharyngitis	5

[a] 154 diagnoses
[b] 121 diagnoses

TABLE 4.4
Five Most Frequent Diagnoses by Gender for 6–18 Years of Age in 1990

Males (N = 54)[a]		Females (N = 24)[b]	
Diagnosis	Frequency	Diagnosis	Frequency
Respiratory infection	26	Dermatologic problems	16
Health maintenance	12	Respiratory infection	9
Pharyngitis	11	Health maintenance	6
Otitis media	9	Reproductive	4
Open wounds	7	Otitis media	2

[a] 137 diagnoses
[b] 46 diagnoses

TABLE 4.5
Social and Health Risk Factors for Adult Clients Based on Primary-Care Visits in 1990

Risk factor	19–29 Years of age (N = 735)	30–49 Years of age (N = 1862)	50 & over (N = 340)
Alcohol abuse			
Frequency	434	1,305	231
Percent	59	70	68
Drug abuse			
Frequency	366	1,040	89
Percent	50	56	26
Smoking			
Frequency	483	1,372	223
Percent	66	74	66
Mental illness			
Frequency	33	152	27
Percent	5	8	8

TABLE 4.6
Frequency of Mental Disorders Among Adult Health Center Clients
19 Years of Age or Older in 1990

Disorder	Frequency
Psychosis	119
Depression	75
Anxiety neuroses	22
Thought disorders	13
Other[a]	98

[a] Includes unspecified mental illness conditions.

TABLE 4.7
Frequency of Chronic Conditions in Health Center Adult Clients
19 Years of Age and Older in 1990

Condition	Frequency
Hypertension	326
Asthma	176
Arthropathies	77
Heart disease	74
Stasis ulcers	70
Diabetes	64
AIDS/ARC	56
Seizures	42
Arthritis	32

encounters, mental health disorders that appeared as diagnoses were more numerous (see Table 4.6). Psychoses and nonspecific mental illness were the most frequent diagnoses.

Adults had few economic resources. Ninety-one percent of adult clients reported having no public or private health insurance coverage. In housing, 87% reported living on the streets or in cars, campers, or shelters.

For adults, as for children, most episodic visits were for acute illnesses with time-limited impact on functional status. Table 4.7 presents the types of chronic conditions identified for adults that were likely to impact on functional status. Hypertension was by far the most prevalent chronic condition. This is consistent with the high rates of alcohol abuse and smoking in this homeless population, as well as the increased prevalence of hypertension in the black population, who represent 63% of Health Center clients (Institute of Medicine 1988).

Finally, for adults as for children, diagnoses were selected as proxies for ADLs which reflected the individual's ability to meet basic needs for food, personal cleanliness, sleep, and exercise. These diagnoses and their frequencies are listed in Table 4.8. Contagious skin diseases and dental disease were the most frequent

TABLE 4.8
Frequency of Diagnoses Reflecting Problems in ADLs for Adult Clients 19 Years of Age and Older in 1990

Diagnosis	Frequency
Contagious skin disease	1,188
Dental disease	594
Wound infections	300
Reportable communicable disease[a]	121
Malnutrition	48
Obesity	16
Sleep deprivation	10

[a] Does not include suspected but unconfirmed reportable communicable disease.

diagnoses. They clearly reflected the lack of access to bathing and laundry facilities in the urban homeless population.

Tables 4.9–4.11 present data describing the five most frequently encountered health problems by adult age and gender categories. Several interesting patterns are worth noting. At all ages, respiratory infections were the most frequent illnesses treated at the Health Center. Also, among female clients nineteen to twenty-nine years and thirty to forty-nine years of age, reproductive problems including pregnancy were the second most frequent diagnoses.

Table 4.12 summarizes the number and percent of visits provided at each level of prevention. Children more often came for wellness visits than did adults. Adults had more chronic illnesses than did children. For all clients, episodic services were sought most often.

Discussion

The UCLA School of Nursing Health Center served 3,112 individual clients during the 1990 calendar year, providing 9,172 primary-care visits. Health Center clients were most often adult black and Latino males thirty to forty-nine years of age. Many clients reported histories of alcohol and drug abuse. The majority of clients did not have public or private health-care coverage, and over 80% reported living on the streets or in shelters. Management of chronic conditions was the principal reason for 8% of adult visits and 2% of child visits. Health maintenance/wellness was the principal purpose of 8% of child visits and 1% of adult visits. Thus, episodic care for acute conditions was the most frequent type of care provided by the Health Center for clients of all ages.

The demographic profile of Health Center clients reflects the characteristics of homeless populations reported from all parts of the country: adult males; minority group members; and a high incidence of substance abuse (Institute of Medicine 1988; Wright 1989). The data also reflect the growing number of homeless families

TABLE 4.9
Five Most Frequent Diagnoses by Gender for 19–29 Years of Age in 1990

Males (N = 633)[a]		Females (N = 102)[b]	
Diagnosis	Frequency	Diagnosis	Frequency
Respiratory infection	450	Respiratory infection	100
Open wounds	285	Reproductive	58
Dental disease	213	Open wounds	33
Tinea	211	Dental disease	22
Tonsillitis	55	Otitis media	10

[a] 2,151 diagnoses
[b] 378 diagnoses

TABLE 4.10
Five Most Frequent Diagnoses by Gender for 30–49 Years of Age in 1990

Males (N = 1,641)[a]		Females (N = 221)[b]	
Diagnosis	Frequency	Diagnosis	Frequency
Respiratory infection	1,478	Upper respiratory infection	255
Open wounds	973	Reproductive	76
Contagious skin diseases	718	Open wounds	55
Dental disease	290	Contagious skin diseases	39
Alcohol/drug abuse	208	Dental disease	38

[a] 7,031 diagnoses
[b] 860 diagnoses

TABLE 4.11
*Five Most Frequent Diagnoses by Gender for Clients
50 Years of Age and Older in 1990*

Males (N = 318)[a]		Females (N = 22)[b]	
Diagnosis	Frequency	Diagnosis	Frequency
Respiratory infection	211	Upper respiratory infection	13
Open wounds	174	Contagious skin diseases	12
Contagious skin diseases	143	Dental disease	11
Hypertension	80	Reproductive health	6
Cellulitis	56	Chronic obstructive pulmonary disease	5

[a] 1,316 diagnoses
[b] 74 diagnoses

TABLE 4.12
Frequency of Diagnoses at Each Level of Prevention for Children[a] and Adults[b]

Level	Frequency	
Health maintenance/wellness		
Children	33	(8%)
Adults	152	(1%)
Acute illness		
Children	418	(90%)
Adults	9,694	(91%)
Chronic illness		
Children	7	(2%)
Adults	961	(8%)

[a] Clients 0–18 years of age
[b] Clients 19 years of age or older

(Schorr 1988; U.S. Congress 1985). Although women were only 12% of the adult sample, and children eighteen years of age or less were only 6% of the whole sample, this is an increase over the figures for 1988, when women were 8% and children 4% of the clinic's clients.

The increase in the number of women and children reflects the increased demand for food at the Union Rescue Mission by women with children. The Mission's staff has set aside a special area of their dining facility for these families. Subsequently, the clinic has experienced an increase in the number of women and children seeking care.

The data for women and children also are consistent with reports identifying the harsh impact that reductions in the social safety net have had on the most vulnerable citizens of the country (McGeary and Lynn 1988; Schorr 1988). They also reflect the difficulty such individuals have in accessing public welfare programs (Gelberg and Linn 1988). Only 31% of zero to five year-old and 9% of six to eighteen year-old children were enrolled in Medi-Cal coverage. This was true despite California's relatively generous Aid to Families with Dependent Children and Medi-Cal funding parameters. This fact was also reflected in a report by Policy Analysis for California Education (PACE) published in 1989 and a report by Health Access in 1988.

Single, adult males form the largest portion of the homeless population nationwide. Unlike other reports of homeless males naming up to 45% as veterans, less than 1% of the Health Center's clients identified themselves as having veterans' benefits (Robertson and Greenblatt 1989; Schutt and Garrett 1986). There is a scarcity of public benefits to help this group, since most do not qualify for state and federal public assistance programs (Maurin, Russell, and Memmott 1989). They must rely largely on the services of philanthropic organizations who face an increasingly difficult battle for resources as public sympathy for the homeless wanes. The full impact of the tragedy for the nation as a whole in terms of lost productive workers has not been fully appreciated. Among the Health Center's clients, 83% are nineteen to forty-nine years of age, the years of greatest work productivity for most adult citizens. It is impossible to calculate the personal cost to individuals of the inability to have a job and a stable living environment. Homelessness and poverty are also sources of great embarrassment, loss of self esteem, and depression among children (Bassuk and Rubin 1986; National Center for Children in Poverty 1990).

Implications for Practice

The very poor and homeless of all ages require primary-care services that address their physical, psychological, and social needs. The nursing profession is uniquely prepared to meet this multiplicity of needs, given its focus on the interaction between the whole person within the person's unique environment (Fawcett 1984).

Nursing care of the homeless challenges the provider to adapt caregiving to the conditions of homelessness (Sutherland 1988). For example, lack of a watch makes complicated medication schedules impractical. Exposure to the sun prohibits the use of medications which sensitize the skin to sunlight. The homeless diet in soup kitchens emphasizes dairy products and therefore limits the choice of medications to those not inactivated by dairy products.

The emphasis on episodic health-care visits for both child and adult clients highlights the need to incorporate health maintenance care into all health visits (Miller and Lin 1988). The very poor may of necessity focus on meeting survival needs. Thus, they may require assistance to recognize the value of incorporating health-preserving and disease-preventive strategies into their lives. Tooth brushes, dental floss, soap, combs, and socks are important preventive resources for providers to offer, given the prevalence of skin diseases, dental caries, and foot problems among the homeless.

The prevalence of alcohol and drug abuse among homeless adults highlights the need for provider awareness of rehabilitation programs and requirements. Smoking is another frequent risk behavior among the homeless (Institute of Medicine 1988). Providers should assess smoking habits and offer a variety of cessation techniques.

Homeless women often require reproductive health services. They need food, vitamin supplements, shelter, and social services to assure the birth of a healthy infant. Careful risk assessment and counseling regarding smoking habits and substance abuse are also important. Screening for sexually transmitted diseases, AIDS counseling, and family planning services are other critical dimensions of care that providers should offer to women of childbearing age.

Conclusion

It is obvious that the primary and most critical needs of the homeless relate to their basic requirements for safe housing and the opportunity for employment and, hence, to become more self-reliant (Wright 1989). The pathogenesis of their homelessness is complex and beyond the interventions that can be provided by nurses and other health-care practitioners alone. Nevertheless, the health problems of this population must be met and dealt with by health-care professionals (Institute of Medicine 1988). Although the services may not represent health promotion and disease prevention in the most traditional sense, they are a fundamental service that must be offered to this population in a creative manner. Health promotion and disease prevention measures require a high level of commitment for homeless individuals.

Providing services for episodic illness and reducing subsequent illness and co-morbidities will likely reduce the overall costs of care for this population.

Nurses must also be advocates for this disenfranchised population. Significant contributions to the health-care delivery system can be made by participating in social and political actions that address the more fundamental social issues that lead to homelessness (Abdellah, Chamberlain, and Levine 1986).

The UCLA School of Nursing has demonstrated that it is possible to take the lead and provide the opportunity to engage both students and members of the faculty in redesigning the delivery of services for this population. The Health Center has also provided a "social laboratory" for nurse researchers to study a variety of key issues and contribute further to nursing practice and the formation of health policy for the homeless population.

The homeless have always been with us. However, they are more visible now and more numerous. Unfortunately, given the current economic and political tenure, they are likely to continue to represent a population who will desperately require health-care services for years to come (National Center for Children in Poverty 1991). Nursing has not only the expertise and opportunity but a social responsibility to take the lead in providing services for this disadvantaged population. Indeed this type of effort is part of our heritage. To meet this challenge, we must prepare future nurses to assume leadership roles in the provision of care and the development of health and social policies related to the homeless.

References

Abdellah, F. G., G. Chamberlain, and E. Levine, (1986). "Role of Nurses in Meeting the Needs of the Homeless: Summary of a Workshop for Providers, Researchers, and Educators." *Public Health Report* 101 (5); 494–498.

Bassuk, E. L., and L. Rubin. (1986). "Homeless Children: A Neglected Population." *American Journal of Orthopsychiatry* 57(2); 279–286.

Burt, M. R., and B. E. Cohen. (1989). "Differences Among Homeless Single Women, Women with Children, and Single Men." *Social Problems* 36(5); 508–24.

Conditions of Children in California. (1989). Berkeley, Calif.: Policy Analysis for California Education (PACE).

Duke University, Center for the Study of Aging and Human Development (1978). *Multidimensional Functional Assessment: The OARS methodology* (2nd ed.).

Fawcett, J. (1984). *Analysis and Evaluation of Conceptual Models of Nursing.* Philadelphia: F. A. Davis Company.

Freeman, R. B., and B. Hall. (1986). *Permanent Homelessness in America?* (Working paper No. 2013). Cambridge, Mass.: National Bureau of Economic Research.

Gelberg, L., and L. Linn. (1988). "Social and Physical Health of Homeless Adults Previously Treated for Mental Health Problems." *Hospital and Community Psychiatry* 39(5); 510–516.

Health Access. (1985). *The California Dream, the California Nightmare.* San Francisco: Health Access.

Institute of Medicine. (1988). *Homelessness, Health, and Human Needs.* Washington, D.C.: National Academy Press.

Jones, J. C. (March 7, 1987). "City May Sue for More Homeless Services." *Los Angeles Times*; 1, 6.

Koegel, P., and Burnam, M. A., (1987). "Traditional and Nontraditional Homeless Alcoholics." *Alcohol World: Health and Research* 11 (3); 28–34.

Maurin, J. T., Russell, L., and Memmott, R. J. (1989). "An Exploration of Gender Differences Among the Homeless." *Research in Nursing and Health* 12; 315–321.

McCall, R. B. (1981). "Nature-nurture and the Two Realms of Development: A Proposed Integration with Respect to Mental Development." *Child Development* 52; 1–12.

McGeary, M. G. H., and L. E. Lynn, eds. (1988). *Urban Change and Poverty.* Washington, D.C.: National Academy Press.

Miller, D. S., and E. H. B. Lin, (1988). "Children in Sheltered Homeless Families: Reported Health Status and Use of Health Services." *Pediatrics* 81(5); 668–73.

Moinpour, C. M., R. McCorkle, and J. Saunders, (1988). "Measuring Functional Status." In *Instruments for Clinical Nursing Research*, edited by M. Frank-Stromberg. Norwalk, Conn.: Appleton and Lange.

National Center for Children in Poverty. (1991). *Alive & Well? A Research and Policy Review for Health Programs for Poor Young Children.* New York: Columbia University Press.

National Center for Children in Poverty. (1990). *Five Million Children: A Statistical Profile of Our Poorest Young Citizens.* New York: Columbia University Press.

Reuber, J. B. (1989). "Health Care for the Homeless in a National Health Program." *AJPH* 79(8); 1033–1035.

Robertson, M., and M. Greenblatt, (1989). *Homelessness: The National Perspective.* New York: Plenum Press.

Ropers, R. H., and R. Boyer. (1987). Homelessness as a Health Risk. *Alcohol World: Health and Research* 11 (3); 38–41, 89–90.

Rose, M. H., and R. B. Thomas, eds. (1987). *Children with Chronic Conditions.* New York: Grune and Stratton.

Schorr, L. B. (1988). *Within Our Reach: Breaking the Cycle of Disadvantage.* New York: Doubleday.

Schutt, R. K., and G. R. Garrett. (1986). *Homelessness in Boston in 1985: The View from Long Island.* Boston: University of Massachusetts at Boston Press.

Social and Human Services Committee. (January 1987). *Medical Services in the Los Angeles Skid Row Area.* Los Angeles County Grand Jury.

Sutherland, A. R. (Fall 1988). "Health Care for the Homeless." *Issues in Science and Technology.* 79–86.

U.S. Congress, House of Representatives, Committee on Ways and Means. (1985). *Children in Poverty.* Washington, D.C.: U.S. Government Printing Office.

Wright, J. D. (1989). *Address Unknown: The Homeless in America.* New York: Aldine De Gruyter.

CHAPTER 5

Health Perceptions of the Homeless: A Survey of Buffalo's City Mission

Anne H. Skelly
Cathleen Getty
Martha J. Kemsley
Juanita K. Hunter
Jeanne Shipman

Abstract

Several faculty members at the State University of New York at Buffalo School of Nursing were interested in developing a nursing center in Western New York to serve the homeless population. The City Mission in Buffalo was selected as a site to conduct a survey to identify the demographic characteristics of one group of homeless subjects and their perceived needs. One hundred and twenty-four questionnaires were completed and analyzed statistically. The profile of the typical respondent was that of a young, single, Protestant, white male from the Buffalo area with a history of local residence. A large proportion of the subjects perceived themselves as experiencing health problems. Both disease prevention and health promotion needs were recognized.

The findings of this study were consistent with those of earlier studies including those completed in Boston Massachusetts (1984). These data have served as a base for the provision of primary nursing interventions for this population within a nursing center model.

Reprinted with permission from *The Journal of the New York State Nurses Association* 21, no. 2, June 1990.

Introduction

Although there is no consensus on the extent of homelessness in the United States, a 1985 report of the Erie County Legislative Task Force on the Homeless estimated that there were 5,000–6,000 persons in Erie County were homeless.

While homelessness of individuals has long been recognized, it is estimated that families now comprise more than 30% of the homeless population (Bassuk, Rubin, and Lauriat 1986). *The Buffalo News* (Hill 1986) reported that increasing numbers of families with young children were being cared for in local shelters and halfway houses. In addition, a study indicated that about one-third of all persons occupying emergency shelters in Western New York needed assistance as a consequence of the state's policy of deinstitutionalization of the mentally and developmentally disabled (Hill 1986).

One of the agencies that has served the needs of the homeless in the Western New York area is the City Mission of Buffalo, New York. In 1981, the Mission provided food and shelter to twenty to thirty persons daily and had an annual budget of $50,000. By 1986, the mission served up to 150 individuals daily and had increased its budget to $500,000. Estimates made by Mission staff at the time of the survey suggested that 50% of the people who sought services at their facility suffered from alcoholism, 30% were mentally ill, and 20% were the "new poor," or victims of the depressed economy seen in the Western New York area. These estimates of the percentage of homeless persons having psychiatric problems is in keeping with figures reported by Hill (1986).

Health Care of the Homeless

The health problems of the homeless are often more serious than those of other populations. They lack insurance coverage, eligibility for social services, and access to health care. This is often compounded by unwillingness on the part of health-care providers to serve the homeless, impaired social supports, and feelings of passivity, helplessness, and despair within the homeless themselves. Provision of appropriate health care for the homeless remains a critical issue (Brickner Scharer, Conanan, Elvy and Savarese 1985; Lenshan, McInnis, O'Donnell, and Hennessey 1985). Although specific statistics that document the medical problems of the homeless population are not readily available, the major reported health problems include diabetes, hypertension, seizure disorders, skin irritations, and leg ulcers. These conditions, when untreated, often have resulted in chronic complications that could have been prevented through prompt identification and treatment. The lack of continuous adequate nutrition also places homeless individuals further at risk for the development of disease (Brickner et al. 1985).

Several faculty members at the State University at Buffalo School of Nursing in were interested in developing a nursing center in Western New York and explored possible populations to be served by such a center. They found that homeless persons were in need of health assessment, health-care planning, implementation, and evaluation. During the summer of 1985, State University of New York nursing faculty reviewed the services provided at several sites serving the homeless in Buffalo. After interviews with the directors of the various programs, it became apparent that minimal data had been collected on the specific demographic characteristics of the homeless clients or their perceptions of their individual health needs. The City Mission at that time served the largest population of homeless individuals and expressed an interest in on-site health services. It was selected, therefore, as a site to survey the health needs of homeless persons. The data gathered were viewed as essential to the development of a comprehensive nursing approach to address the health needs of the homeless at this shelter.

Methodology

The goals of this survey were: (a) to develop a demographic profile of the homeless persons currently using the services of the City Mission; (b) to document the perceived health problems of this population; and (c) to identify their perceived health needs. The survey used an interview format. A computer-based questionnaire developed and previously utilized by the University of Massachusetts at Boston (Schutt 1984) was modified for use in this study. This questionnaire elicited information about demographics, social support, work experience, residential history, general and mental health, substance abuse, social service agencies utilized, and services needed.

Data were collected two evenings per week by two undergraduate nursing student research assistants who had both an interest and previous experience in working with this population. Prior to data collection, the interviewers spent time at the City Mission to familiarize themselves with the surroundings and daily routine of the residents. In addition, two training sessions using role playing were conducted by project faculty to orient the interviewers to the questionnaire. Each interview was conducted in an area of the mission where privacy could be assured and lasted anywhere from twenty minutes to one hour. The sample consisted of those individuals who were receiving services at the City Mission during a four-month period (February–May 1986) and were willing to participate in the study. The staff of the City Mission assisted in eliciting the cooperation of the participants by explaining the purpose of the study. The issue of informed consent in a population often considered unprotected was recognized. Therefore, an explanation of the project was given verbally. Then a written consent was signed by the respondent and the project interviewer and witnessed by a staff member. One hundred and thirty-four individuals consented to participate; approximately thirty residents refused.

Results

Characteristics of the Sample

The sociodemographic profile of the sample was that of a young, single, Protestant, white male from the Buffalo area who is a citizen of the United States (Table 5.1). These findings were generally consistent with the research conducted in Boston which demonstrated a shift in the composition of the homeless from the primarily older, white male with alcoholism problems of the 1950s and 1960s to a younger, more racially diverse group seen today (Schutt 1984; Bahr and Garrett 1976). The majority of the subjects had received a high school education or vocational training, contradicting the prevalent view that the homeless lack education and that this deficit subsequently accounts for their unemployability. One hundred and twenty-one individuals responded to a question regarding their employment history. Twenty-three percent (23%) of those responding to this question were employed in 1990, 65% had worked in the past, and 12% stated that they had never been employed. Seventy-two individuals responded to a question regarding their last work date. Of these, 47% had been employed within the last year. This suggests that many are potentially employable. However, psychiatric and legal problems, and alcohol and drug use may limit employment prospects. Overall, most of the respondents had been homeless for less than six months, and their homelessness was primarily due to economic reasons, perhaps reflective of the depressed economy of Western New York.

Social Support

Out of the 124 respondents who answered questions related to social support, 71 (57%) were single, 39 (32%) were separated or divorced, and only 9 (7%) were married (Table 5.1). Fifty-five (84%) of 124 respondents reported that their parents were living (Table 5.2). A majority of the respondents reported having caring parents with whom they had contact ranging from once a week to a few times a year. Of these, 27 (49%) reported having contact with their parents on a weekly or monthly basis, while nineteen (35%) had contact with them only a few times a year and nine (16%) had no contact. Forty-nine (40%) of the 122 respondents reported having children. Residents were asked whether they had a special person with whom they felt close. Fifty (42%) of the 120 respondents reported having such a special person. Of these, 37 (79%) identified a friend while only 6 (13%) identified a relative, one of these being a spouse. The residents were also asked whether they could count on anyone for financial help. Ninety-three (77%) of the 121 responding said no. Of the 28 who reported having someone to count on for financial aid, 11 (41%) identified this individual as a friend and 16 (59%) identified a relative.

TABLE 5.1
Characteristics of the Subjects of the City Mission

	Number*	Percent (%)
Age		
1–29	44	38
30–49	47	39
50–65	24	19
65	5	4
Sex		
Male	97	78
Female	27	22
Race		
Caucasian	68	55
Black	44	35
Hispanic	5	4
Native American	6	5
Other	1	0.8
Marital status		
Single	71	57
Married	9	7
Separated	15	13
Divorced	24	19
Widowed	5	4
Education (completed grades)		
1–8	21	18
9–11	38	32
12	55	43
13 +	6	5
Work		
In 1990 looking for employment	51	30
Presently employed	28	16
Worked in the past	79	46
Never been employed	14	8
Length of homelessness		
Less than 6 months	89	72
Six to twelve months	16	13
One to five years	13	10
Greater than five years	6	5
Reasons for homelessness		
Financial	55	47
Family Problems	34	29
Unemployment	27	24

*Totals will vary according to the number of respondents to the item.

TABLE 5.2
Perceptions of Social Support by the Homeless

	Number	Percent (%)
Parents living	55	84
weekly of monthly contact with parents	27	49.1
One of more siblings	98	73
weekly contact with sister	22	16.4
weekly or monthly contact with brother	30	22.4
Children	49	36.6
weekly or monthly contact with sons	10	7.4
weekly or monthly contact with daughters	10	7.4
Spouse living	2	1.5
Identified a special person the respondent felt close to	50	41.3
friend	37	78.7
relative	6	12.7
Identified a person on whom the respondent		
could count on for financial help	28	40.7
friend	11	40.7
relative	16	59.3

Perceptions of Health

Data related to the subjects' perceptions of their health indicated that a large proportion, 90 (73%) of the 124 responding, perceived themselves as experiencing
health problems (Table 5.3). The most frequently identified health problem was
dental, 45 (36%); gastrointestinal, 36 (29%) was second.

Of those who reported health problems, 43 (48%) indicated a need for help with
their health problem at the time of the interview. The most frequently identified need
was for dental care. Other identified health needs were for regular checkups, help
with medications, improved nutrition, fitness activities, and vision exams or treatment. Thirty-six of the 105 respondents (34%) said they were currently taking medications for a physical problem, with non-narcotic medications being most frequently
cited (18%). Anticonvulsants, antihypertensives, antianginal agents, and antibiotics
each represented 4% or less of the current medications used. Finally, 26 of 81 respondents (32%) reported being hospitalized during the past year.

Although there were few statistically significant relationships between specific
health problems and demographics, several patterns emerged. A large percentage of
younger respondents, (34%) reported no health problems. However, subjects fifty to
sixty-five years of age reported a higher percentage of health problems than those
who were over sixty-five. The incidence of dental, cardiovascular, and gastrointestinal problems increased with age whereas injuries and psychiatric problems were prevalent in the thirty to forty-nine year age group.

There were few variations in reported health problems based on sex. Although a

TABLE 5.3
Subject-Reported Health Problems*

	Number	Percent (%)
Dental	45	36
Gastrointestinal	36	29
None	34	27
Injury	32	25.8
Cardiovascular	30	24
Allergies	29	23
Respiratory	24	19.3
Neurological	20	16
Psychiatric	15	12
Musculo-skeletal	15	10
Genito-Urinary	13	11
Visual	10	8
Skin	6	5
Pregnancy	5	4

*Figures shown are based on 124 respondents.

greater percentage of females than males denied any health problems, the total number of female respondents was signficantly smaller than that of males. Greater numbers of males reported injuries, stomach, lung, and psychiatric problems; whereas greater numbers of females reported head injuries, dental, and cardiac problems. Forty-six percent of the total sample was composed of persons of color, and 35% of them denied any health problems, as did a comparable 34% of the white respondents. White respondents reported higher frequencies of dental, gastrointestinal, circulatory, and lung problems and injuries.

Greater numbers of married respondents denied any health problems than did those who were single. However, married respondents reported greater frequencies of injuries and dental, gastrointestinal, and psychiatric problems. Explanations for the distribution and frequencies of these disorders are not readily apparent. They may be specific to this particular sample.

Perceptions of Mental Health

In the psychiatric profile of the respondents, 42 (36%) reported a history of treatment for mental and nervous problems with 29 (25%) of the 119 respondents reporting a history of hospitalization for mental or nervous problems. However, only 15 (12%) identified themselves as currently experiencing psychiatric difficulties. "Nervous problems" was the most frequently reported condition. Nine subjects (7%) reported that they were taking psychotropic medications (Table 5.4).

TABLE 5.4
Psychiatric Profile as Reported by Subjects

	Number	Percent (%)
Currently reporting psychiatric problems:	15	12.1
History of psychiatric diagnoses:	31	23
Psychosis	1	0.7
Depression	5	3.7
Anxiety	1	0.7
Personality disorder	2	1.5
Nervous problem	14	10.4
Substance abuse	1	0.7
Other mental conditions	7	5.2
History of treatment for mental or nervous problems:	42	35.3
History of hospitalization for mental or nervous problems:	29	24.3
Number of individuals in 1990 taking psychotropic medications:	9	7

Alcohol and Drug Use

When asked a series of questions related to their use of alcohol and drugs, 84 (69%) stated that they consumed alcoholic beverages. Of these, 18 (21%) reported drinking alcohol daily, 26 (31%) drank alcohol a few times a week, 13 (16%) once a week, and 27 (32%) drank less often.

Twenty-five respondents or approximately 27% of 94 responding subjects reported past treatment for alcohol abuse (Table 5.5). Of these, 10 were treated at a public alcohol treatment center, six at a VA alcohol program, and two at a private alcohol treatment center.

Responses to the questions on drug usage revealed that 46 (38%) said they used street drugs. The types used were: Barbiturates, 4 (3%); cocaine, 10 (8%); opiates, 7 (6%); psychedelics, 10 (8%); volatile substances, 3 (2%); and, tranquilizers, 12 (10%). Twelve of 77 respondents (10%) reported prior treatment for drug use (Table 5.5). Brickner et al. (1985) have estimated that between 35 and 40% of homeless persons have a primary alcohol, drug abuse, or mental disorder.

Utilization of Community Services

Social services and shelters were reported as the most frequently utilized services. Although 61% of the respondents indicated that they had contact with social services, only 30% reported that they had received services requested or needed. The services most frequently requested were for financial assistance, (70%); housing, (65%); medical referral, (60%); and employment referrals or work experience programs, (58%).

TABLE 5.5
Reported Tobacco Use; Reported Alcohol and Drug Use and Treatment

	Number	Percent (%)
Reported Tobacco Use	85	63.4
Reported Alcohol Use	84	69
daily	18	21
few times a week	26	31
once a week	13	16
less than once a week	27	32
Treatment for Alcoholism	25	27
Reported Drug Use	46	38
marijuana	41	30.6
amphetamines	14	10.4
barbiturates	4	3
cocaine	10	7.5
opiates	7	5.2
psychedelic	10	7.5
volatile substances	3	2.2
tranquilizers	12	10
Treatment for Drug Use	12	10

Approximately 77% of the subjects had no contact with the Social Security Administration Vocational Rehabilitation or Municipal Housing Authority. Lack of knowledge about or prior negative experiences with these services may account for this minimal use. In addition, more than 80% of the respondents stated they did not request or need referrals for alcoholism treatment. These data raised the question of whether the respondents were able to recognize the need for these services.

Although the respondents were receiving few benefits, they were quite clear in identifying the specific services they believed they needed. Questions related to the benefits respondents received may have been too vague to elicit the anticipated responses. For example, the wording may have confused the client, and the response may have been given in relation to knowledge about the benefit rather than whether the respondent received the benefit. As anticipated, the results suggest that more attention should be given to servicing the needs of this population, particularly in relation to employment and housing. A listing of needed services may be found in Table 5.6.

Discussion

The findings from this study demonstrate that the homeless population has significant health problems and is in need of assistance in obtaining health-care services. Not only treatment but disease prevention and health promotion needs were recognized by the respondents through their identification of dental and vision exams,

TABLE 5.6
Services Requested by the Homeless Population

	Number	Percent (%)
Financial assistance	83	70
Housing referral	77	65
Medical referral	71	60
Work experience program	69	58
Employment referral	69	58
Legal advice	47	40
Veterans service referral	26	22
Alcoholism evaluation or referral	22	19
Department of Mental Health	18	15
No services needed at this time	13	11
Other	10	8

improved nutrition, and exercise. The fact that a younger population acknowledged these needs provides an opportunity for early intervention by nurses to change health behaviors, and, ultimately, to prevent chronic illnesses.

The data related to psychiatric/mental health problems are consistent with national reports which indicate that 30–40% of homeless persons "suffer from serious and persistent mental illness" (Morrissey and Levine 1987). The mentally ill are twenty times more likely to be homeless than others according to Freeman (1987). A reciprocal connection has been posited also, suggesting that homelessness tends to increase the severity of psychiatric symptoms (Rousseau 1981) and contributes to mental health problems (Baxter and Hopper 1982). It has been recognized in the literature that medical problems in homeless persons with psychiatric conditions often are not identified or treated (McCarrick et al. 1986; Roca 1987). This problem is thought to be related to both client and caregiver factors.

It appears that the large numbers of unmarried individuals may be best accounted for by the young age of the subjects or their economic situation rather than interpreted as an indication of problematic adult interpersonal relations. On the other hand, it is interesting to note that while the parents of half the sample were living, and almost half of that number had weekly contact with them, few of the subjects identified relatives as persons with whom they felt "close." These findings may point to a disturbed family relationship or, again, to the limited financial resources of the relatives.

The gap in community services was demonstrated by the fact that needed services far exceeded in 1990 those utilized by the respondents. These data indicate important deficits in services provided to the homeless. Deficits in services included: Difficulties with the referral process itself, lack of follow up, and demeaning bureaucratic procedures. Housing problems are especially important, as this group includes not only transient individuals, but families who have been evicted from substandard housing.

Limitations of the Study

A major limitation of this study was that the sample was voluntary. Approximately thirty individuals refused to be interviewed. Those who refused appeared to be the older residents. Further, review of the instrument revealed that the questions were male-oriented and did not address the special needs of women and children. Although women were included in the sample, children were not interviewed nor were questions asked about their health status when they accompanied a caretaker. Finally, subjects were drawn from only one shelter site, and persons who chose not to use a shelter or who were turned away from this specific shelter (e.g. for prior disruptive behavior) were not included. Their exclusion might have skewed the results.

Alcohol and substance abuse have been perceived to be a long-standing problem with the homeless population. Questions were not asked regarding past alcohol and substance abuse. The data in this study related only to present consumption. Therefore, no overall estimates of the degree of present alcoholism in the population could be determined. The number of younger respondents in this study may account for the few reports of chronic manifestations of alcohol and drug abuse which usually are found in an older population.

It is difficult to elicit accurate information regarding alcohol and drug use; therefore, the reported consumption of alcohol and substance abuse was generally considered to be well under the estimates given. This could be related to the reluctance of the respondents to give accurate information and to their concerns about possible legal ramifications from admitted usage. In addition, the homeless population is often fearful and alienated from society and generally does not seek alcohol and substance abuse services. Therefore, participation in a data-gathering process would, by its very nature, be intimidating to most within this group.

Implications for Nursing

The results of this study have several important implications for nursing practice. Few nursing school curricula include content or clinical experiences related to the care of homeless individuals. Therefore, nurses lack information about the special health and psychosocial needs of the homeless and the skills to meet those needs. However, as the numbers of homeless increase and particularly the numbers of young adults, nursing will be faced with the challenge of providing care for these individuals.

Nurses working in emergency rooms and ambulatory care settings should be alert to clients who present social histories indicative of problems related to actual or potential homelessness and should initiate appropriate referrals. Schools of nursing and individual nurses need to seek creative approaches in planning and implementing service-delivery programs for this population. Nurses should actively assist in the prevention of homelessness through counseling of and advocacy for vulnerable populations. These data indicate a need for a more systematic, comprehensive assessment of this population and its needs. Nurses need to implement research projects that will increase understanding of the special health needs of the homeless. Future studies should target the diverse groups present in the homeless population such as women and children, the elderly, and street persons who typically do not use established shelter services.

Attempts to meet the health needs of the homeless population have often been ineffective. Homeless individuals are frequently isolated from the mainstream of society and do not engage readily in health-care seeking behaviors, as the process of seeking health care is often threatening. A primary role of nursing in securing health care for the homeless should include assisting clients to overcome these fears and helping them surmount the institutional barriers to receiving care. Alternative models of care are needed that will address the special needs and concerns of this group. Such models should promote the clients' active role in their health care.

Many factors such as rising health-care costs, changing population needs, consumerism, and health promotion have prompted examination of alternative methods and settings for health-care delivery. The establishment of a nursing center within a homeless shelter is one approach to providing health care for homeless persons. Such a nursing center is an organization of health services managed and staffed by nurses. The primary goal of a nursing center is to provide an alternative health-care modality that is cost effective and compatible with client needs. Education and research components are built into its activities.

Nursing centers emerged about a decade ago and were designed not only to provide health services to a particular community but also to serve as teaching and research centers. They provided a setting in which nursing practice could be demonstrated and simultaneously evaluated through nursing research. Although the community served, the nursing services provided, and the sources of funding may vary, nursing control is inherent in the organization of these services. It is thought that nurses within such organizations are able to provide comprehensive, less fragmented, and more cost-effective care to their specific client/patient populations. A nurse-managed clinic in a homeless shelter provides an opportunity for nursing to demonstrate how its unique services can meet the specific health needs of this equally unique and growing population.

Authors' Note: This survey provided the data for a grant proposal for "A Nursing Center for Homeless Persons in Buffalo, New York." This project was funded by the Special Projects Grants Program in the Nursing Education Practices Resources Branch, Division of Nursing, United States Department of Health and Human Services–Public Health Service, Health Resources and Services Administration, Bureau of Health Professions Administration, Grant 5D1060003-01. A nursing center was established and has been in operation at the City Mission of Buffalo since January 1, 1988.

References

Bahr, H. M., and Garrett, G. A. 1976). *Women Alone*. Lexington, Mass.: Lexington Books.

Bassuk, E. L., Rubin, L. and Lauriat, A. (Sept. 1986). "The Characteristics of Sheltered Homeless Families." *AJPH* 76(9); 1097–1101.

Baxter, E., and Hopper, R. (1982). "The New Mendicancy: Homelessness in New York City." *Am. J. Orthopsychiatry* 52; 393–408.

Brickner, P. W., Scharer, L. K., Conanan, B., Elvy, A., and Savarese, M. (1985). *Health Care of Homeless People* (Chapters 1 and 2). New York: Springer Publishing Co.

Freeman, R. B. (1987). *Permanent Homelessness in America?* Stanford, Calif.: National Bureau of Economic Research.

Hill, R. (Sept. 24, 1986). "Y Cottage Offers Home to Homeless." *Buffalo News*.

Lenehan, G. P., McInnis, B. N., O'Donnell, D., and Hennessey, M. (Nov. 1985). "A Nurses' Clinic for the Homeless." *American Journal of Nursing* 85 (11); 1236–40.

McCarrick, A. K., Manderscheid, R. W., Bertolucci, D. E., Goldman, H., and Tessler, R. C. (1986). "Chronic Medical Problems in the Chronic Mentally Ill." *Hospital and Community Psychiatry* 37; 298–91.

Morrissey, J. P. and Levine, I. S. (1987). "Researchers Discuss Latest Findings, Examine Needs of Homeless Mentally Ill Persons," *Hospital and Community Psychiatry* 38 (8); 811–12.

Roca, R. P., Breakey, W. R. and Fisher, P. J., (1987). "Medicare of Chronic Psychiatric Outpatients," *Hospital and Community Psychiatry* 38 (7); 741–45.

Rousseau, A. M. *Shopping Bag Ladies*. New York: Pilgrim Press, 1981.

Schutt, R. K. (1984). *Boston's Homeless: Their Backgrounds, Problems, and Needs*. University of Massachusetts at Boston.

Skelly, A. H., Getty, C., Kemsley, M. J., Hunter, J. K., and Shipman, J. "Health Perceptions of the Homeless," *Journal of the New York State Nurses Association*. 21,2; June 1990, 20–24.

Task Force on the Homeless, Erie County. (1985). Report of Erie County Legislator's Task Force on the Homeless. Buffalo, N.Y.

CHAPTER 6

Analysis of the Differences and Similarities Between Homeless People Seen at On-site Health Clinics in Soup Kitchens and Shelters

Virginia E. Taylor

Abstract

Are the homeless who frequent health-care facilities in soup kitchens and shelters the same population or different? To answer the question, a year was randomly selected from the five-year Statistical Package Social Services computer data of the Erie County Health Department Medically Indigent Project funded by the New York State Health Department. Two thousand six hundred forty-nine visits were analyzed using chi-square and z distribution. Factors analyzed included race, age, sex, health-care provider, medical on-site visits (referral and compliance at community agencies), and substance abuse on-site visits (referral and compliance at community agencies), social service on-site visits (referral and compliance at community agencies). A significant profile was deduced for soup-kitchen users of on-site health clinics and shelter users of on-site health clinics.

Many studies of the homeless done in the past treat the homeless living in shelters and those eating in soup kitchens as the same population. As these studies are reviewed, there is a divergence of data from one to the next. Therefore we are hypothesizing that shelter users and soup-kitchen users are not the same population and need to be viewed as different populations with different health needs.

A 1987–1988 random sample from five years of computerized data of client visits in the Medically Indigent Project (MIP) funded by the Health Department of New York State and Erie County was sorted to distinguish two populations. Six on-site clinics were studied, four in soup kitchens and two in shelters. During that year, there were totals of 1,133 visits to soup-kitchen clinics and 1,516 to shelter clinics.

Results:

TABLE 6.1
Soup Kitchen (SK) and Shelter (SH) Users of On-site Health Clinics
Significant z Distributions of Race, Age, and Sex.

	RACE			AGE			SEX	
RACE	SK	SH	AGE	SK	SH	SEX	SK	SH
Black	0.48%*	0.37%	0–14	0.01%	0.02%**	Female	0.36%*	0.19%
Caucas.	0.49%	0.52%	15–19	0.02%	0.03%**	Male	0.64%	0.82%*
Hispan.	0.01%	0.09%*	20–44	0.47%	0.60%*			
Indian	0.14%	0.07%	45–64	0.34%*	0.25%			
Other	0.01%	0.01%	65 +	0.16%*	0.10%			

*Sig. at $p < 0.001$
**Sig. at $p < 0.05$

Various factors were reviewed to identify similarities and differences between users of the two types of clinics. The factors include: race, age, sex, health-care provider, medical/mental health, substance abuse, social service health problems, and on-site visits (referrals and compliance to community agencies).

The SPSS computer system was used, and a chi-square statistical analysis was done on each factor. Significant chi-squares at .05 or less were: race, sex, age, health-care provider, medical on-site visit, community agency visit and compliance, substance abuse on-site visit, community agency visit and compliance, social service on-site visit, community agency visit and compliance, and health problems.

The nonsignificant similar factors were: urine; blood pressure; tuberculosis assessment; number of referrals to medical, substance abuse, mental illness, and social services and public assistance at onset and closure.

The significant chi-square factors were further analyzed using a z distribution, a two-tail distribution using percentages to test the hypothesis and alternate hypothesis. The first factors analyzed were age, sex, and race.

Table 6.1 documents that use of the soup kitchen clinic was equally divided between blacks and Caucasians whereas Caucasians used the shelter the most. This was interesting in spite of the fact that the two soup kitchens were in predominantly black communities. Significantly more Hispanic clients were seen in the shelters than in the soup kitchens. This could be accounted for by the fact that many Hispanics were in transit to Canada because of their working paper status. Families and younger adults used shelters more, and older adults, especially women, used soup kitchens more than men who tended to use the shelters more.

Another factor analyzed was the utilization pattern by soup-kitchen users and shelter users of community health-care facilities.

Table 6.2 provides information on shelter and soup-kitchen users of on-site health clinics and other health-care providers. More soup-kitchen users had private medical doctors or used Erie County health clinics for care. Shelter users of on-site clinics had no health-care provider and used emergency rooms in hospitals and

TABLE 6.2
***Utilization of Health Care Providers by Soup Kitchen (SK) and Shelter (SH)
Users of On-site Health Clinics***

Health Provider	(SK)	(SH)
None	0.06%	0.09%***
Emergency Room	0.08%	0.21%*
Walk-in Clinics	0.01%	0.01%**
PMD	0.33%*	0.03%
ECMC Hosp.	0.12%	0.18%*
BG Hosp.	0.21%*	0.15%
ECH Clinic	0.07%*	0.04%*

*Sig. at $p < 0.001$
**Sig. at $p < 0.05$
***Sig. at $p < 0.009$

walk-in clinics for care. The utilization patterns of soup-kitchen users and shelter users of on-site health clinics were then analyzed.

Tables 6.3 and 6.4 indicate that soup-kitchen clinic users continued to return to the on-site health centers and community agencies for medical care from year to year. They also maintained a close contact with the MIP team regarding substance abuse and mental health. Shelter clinic users made more initial contacts with the MIP team regarding substance abuse and mental illness but did not keep follow-up appointments.

Although not shown in the tables, the pattern of referrals to community agencies by the MIP team was not significantly different. However, utilization of those community agencies by clients in the two types of clinic sites differed significantly.

The initial referrals kept at community agencies for medical, substance abuse, and mental health problems were significantly higher among shelter clinic users (Table 6.4); however, kitchen clinic users remained in those services longer. Social service encounters differed; the number of inital community agency visits was significantly higher among soup-kitchen users, but the ongoing continuous participation was greater among shelter clinic users. Interestingly, there were more on-site social visits at shelters, with fewer initial contacts with community agencies, but those who went made repeated visits. However, there was not a significant increase of persons getting public benefits at the opening and closing of the case file. The primary reason for the on-site encounter was analyzed as stated by clients and as diagnosed by health professionals.

The major reasons the clients came to on-site clinics at soup kitchens were substance abuse and mental illness (Table 6.5) whereas the major reasons the clients came to on-site clinics at shelters were skin problems and emergencies. In contrast, the health professional diagnosed the major problem of soup-kitchen clinic users as cardiovascular, that is, hypertension and heart problems. The major problems identified by professionals of shelter clinic users were infections of the ear, nose, and throat; skin problems; muscle problems, that is, arthritis, low back pain, muscle

TABLE 6.3
Users of On-site Health Clinics in Soup Kitchen (SK) and Shelter (SH)

	Medical		Substance Abuse		Mental Health		Social	
	SK(%)	SH(%)	SK(%)	SH(%)	SK(%)	SH(%)	SK(%)	SH(%)
Initial	0.34	0.37	0.51	0.65**	0.37	0.54*	0.47	0.56**
Ongoing	0.58	0.58	0.49**	0.36	0.63*	0.46	0.53*	0.44
Continuous	0.08*	0.05*						

*Sig. at $p<0.001$
**Sig. at $p<0.01$

TABLE 6.4
*Community Agency Visits of Soup Kitchen (SK)
and Shelter (SH) Users of On-site Health Clinic.*

	Medical		Substance Abuse		Mental Health		Social	
	SK(%)	SH(%)	SK(%)	SH(%)	SK(%)	SH(%)	SK(%)	SH(%)
Initial	0.2%	0.42%	0.06	0.12**	0.11	0.29**	0.41*	0.28
Ongoing	0.24*	0.11	0.02	0.07	0.06	0.22**	0.17	0.27**
Cont.	0.08*	0.02	0.25*	0.04	0.4*	0.10	0.01	0.08**

*Sig. at $p<0.001$
**Sig. at $p<0.01$

TABLE 6.5
Primary Reasons for On-site Encounters of Soup Kitchen (SK) and Shelter (SH)

	Client		Professional	
Reasons	SK(%)	SH(%)	SK(%)	SH(%)
Cardiovascular			0.224*	0.07
Dental	0.002	0.01	0.22	0.03
Ear/nose/throat	0.01	0.005	0.11	0.17*
Dermatological	0.05	0.12*	0.04	0.07*
Gastro intestinal/metabolic	0.03	0.01	0.06	0.05
Musculo skeletal	0.02	0.01	0.03	0.07*
Neurological			0.01	0.01
Respiratory	0.19	0.21	0.04	0.05
Emergencies	0.25	0.31**	0.003	0.01**
Substance abuse	0.04*	0.01	0.09	0.09
Mental health	0.098*	0.06	0.1	0.08
Social work	0.27	0.23	0.22	0.26**

*Sig. at $p<0.001$
**Sig. at $p<0.05$

spasms; emergencies such as epilepsy, bruises, lacerations, and burns; and the need for social services.

Interestingly, one soup kitchen was in the vicinity of the state psychiatric center and another near a methadone program. It would seem that the mentally ill and substance abusers congregate at soup kitchens near the center for their care. Many live, go for care, and eat in the same area.

Summary of Similarities and Differences

Similarities between on-site users of a health clinic in soup kitchens and shelters were:

1. Race: Percentage of Caucasians.
   Percentage of Native American.
2. Blood pressure, PPD, Tuberculin Purified Protein Derivative (Mantoux), and urinalysis abnormalities.
3. Veteran hospital usage.
4. The number of referrals made for medical problems, mental health, substance abuse, and social service.
5. Health problems such as dental, gastrointestinal, neurological, respiratory, and social problems.

The significant chi-square factors were further analyzed using a z distribution. Significant differences of z distribution at the .05 level or less were:

Soup-Kitchen Profile

1. Aged 45 to 65 +.
2. Race–black.
3. Continued in ongoing care at on-site health clinic for substance abuse, mental illness, and social service.
4. Continued in care for medical problems from year to year at on-site clinics.
5. Continued in care at community agencies for medical problems, substance abuse, and mental illness.
6. Made more initial contacts with social agencies.
7. Health problems: cardiovascular, substance abuse, mental health.
8. Health providers: private medical doctor, Erie County health clinics.
9. More often elevated blood pressure and abnormal urinalysis.

Shelter Profile

1. Aged infant–44 years.
2. Made more initial contacts with community agencies for medical problems, substance abuse, and mental health.
3. Made more ongoing contacts for mental health and social service at on-site clinics
4. Health problems: infections; eye, ear, nose, throat, and skin; and trauma injuries.
5. Had more active cases of tuberculosis by a ratio of 15–2 than soup-kitchen clients.
6. Decrease in ongoing contacts for mental health and social services from initial contacts.

Summary

In this study, homeless clients of clinics in soup kitchens and shelters were found to differ in several significant ways, both in their health-care needs and their patterns of clinic use. Clients of clinics in soup kitchens visited the clinics more regularly, whereas those who patronized shelter clinics tended to lack primary health-care providers and use emergency facilities more often. This group showed a need for more networking and motivation to maintain health-care contacts and, thus, reduce their use of hospital emergency rooms and walk-in clinics. For both categories, there was a breakdown after initial contact in connecting clients with needed social services. On-site and community agency visits by clients did not appear to result in a change in the status of their public benefits. Individuals who attended mental health care facilities and substance abuse programs tended to live near counseling centers and take their meals in nearby soup kitchens.

At clinics in soup kitchens, the dominant needs of the patients were for chronic care and women's and geriatric health services. At the clinics in shelters, the dominant needs were for acute, pediatric, and adolescent services.

All of these factors must be considered by planners seeking to establish nurse-managed health-care facilities that provide the most cost-effective and beneficial service to the homeless. Targeted care, based on a thorough understanding of group and individual needs, is an essential step toward accelerating the return of homeless persons to more stable and productive lives.

CHAPTER 7

Characteristics of Homeless Families: A Research Report

Joseph L. Halbach
Lillie M. Shortridge

Abstract

The purpose of this study was to obtain descriptive data on the characteristics of emergency-housed homeless families in Yonkers, New York, including basic demographic data and information on resources and physical and mental status. The study is part of a larger research project on homelessness being conducted by the Center for Nursing Research and Clinical Practice, Lienhard School of Nursing, Pace University, with a large research team. Thirty-minute structured interviews were administered anonymously to forty-six adults at a coordinated services site in Southwest Yonkers. Respondents were paid five dollars for participating. The interview survey guide was adopted, with permission, from one developed by the Social and Demographic Institute of the University of Massachusetts to study the homeless in Chicago. The psychometric estimates of the survey are acceptable with the inter-rater reliability of .99.

Homeless families in this study in Yonkers were primarily poor, minority women with young children. Half lost their homes due to eviction. A few problems were identified as more frequent than expected in a comparably housed group: lack of education, a history of abuse, and multiple indications of poor health status in the adults and developmental/emotional problems in the children. These findings agree with those of the few other studies on homeless families. The investigators also suspected that drug abuse was much more frequent than reported.

Introduction

While there have always been homeless people in the United States, the past decade has witnessed increasing attention and concern as the number of them and their visibility have increased. Not only has the number of homeless people increased dramatically over the past few years, but the composition of the homeless population has changed drastically during that period. The former stereotyped concept of the homeless as being limited to the "alcoholic bum" or "bag lady" is no longer valid. There is growing awareness that, in addition to these stereotyped single individuals, entire families, adults and children, are part of the homeless population.

Exact data on the number of homeless people are not available and the range of estimates is wide (Institute of Medicine 1988). At the low end, the U.S. Department of Housing and Urban Development estimates 200,000 to 300,000 homeless people. At the higher end are estimates of greater than 3 million by advocates for the homeless. In the area of this study, data from the Westchester County Department of Social Services in March 1990 showed that they had registered on their caseload 961 families which included 1,909 children; in addition, there were 1,529 homeless singles and childless couples. In fact, per capita, Westchester County has twice the rate of homelessness as New York City (Westchester County Commission on the Homeless 1988; Westchester County Department of Social Services 1990).

In Yonkers, which had a population of about 200,000 in February 1990, there were 364 homeless families with 727 children. Two hundred ninety-five of these children were school age—six and over. In 1989 Westchester County spent approximately $64.5 million for housing, food, travel, and needs for the homeless. Two recent reports confirm that these statistics still remain (Bowie et al. 1990; Bernstein et al. 1990). It is obvious that because of this sky-rocketing cost, as well as the inherent human concern for people lacking the basic necessity of shelter, the problem of homelessness has become a national crisis. While there has been much research and literature on the etiology and problems of the single homeless, there has been a paucity in the literature describing the population of homeless families, most appearing after data collection for this study (Bass et al. 1990; Bassuk and Rosenberg 1990; Berne et al. 1990; Bowdler 1989; Breakey et al. 1989; Brickner et al. 1986; Council on Scientific Affairs 1989; Miller and Lin 1988; Robertson and Cousineau 1986; Weinreb and Bassuk 1990).

In addition to the lack of basic data on homeless families, data also are scarce on the health status, health problems, and resources available to them. The present study, part of which is reported here, was designed to gather basic demographic information as well as information about the health status of homeless families in Yonkers, New York. The pilot study is one small portion of a larger research project on homelessness being done by the Center for Nursing Research and Clinical Practice at Pace University. This study, implemented between March and October 1988, was a structured, thirty-minute interview administered to forty-six people at a coordinated services center for homeless families in southwest Yonkers. This group was a sample of convenience. To enhance motivation, participants were paid five dollars. The original survey instrument was a modification of an instrument that included eighty-five questions and was designed to gather information from homeless individuals as well as families. Questions were asked in four areas: demographics; physical health status; mental health status, including substance abuse and resources available. The survey was administered anonymously by two interviewers together.

A second portion of this study involved administering a two-hour, in-depth, videotaped or audiotaped interview to a selected sample of the initial interviewees and a physical examination of all family members. The purpose of that part of the study was to get more objective measures of health status and to verify some of the information from the initial interview. New families continue to be recruited into the structured interview study.

Results

The results are given in three principal areas: demographics, physical health status, and mental health status, including substance abuse. The purpose of this chapter is to make health professionals aware of the characteristics of the homeless families population and of their social health needs. Again, this is one group in one city in New York and may not be entirely representative of homeless families in other areas.

Demographics

What are the basic characteristics of the people interviewed; who were they? Of the forty-six interviewed, eight were found not to meet the definition established of a homeless family for this study, and they were excluded from the data analyzed. The thirty-eight remaining ranged in age from twenty-one to fifty-five, with a median age of thirty years. There were thirty-six women and two men. Seventy-one percent were black and 16% were Hispanic. On marital status, 55% reported themselves as single, 24% were married or partnered. The others described themselves as divorced, separated, widowed, or other. In terms of education, more than half of the respondents had not completed high school; 15.8% had some college education; the remainder were high school graduates.

Next, a description of the family composition was presented. The respondents had parented an average of 3.2 children, of which an average of 2.4 children currently lived with the respondent. The average age of the children living in the family was 8.2 years. When asked about other people in the current family, six women reported boyfriends, and two reported spouses living with them. There were five other people, including, among others, a brother-in-law, a nephew, a grandmother, and a friend's child. In terms of their current housing, almost all were living in motels, hotels, or emergency temporary apartments. Fifty percent had been home-less for one year or less when we interviewed them. According to the Department of Social Services in Westchester County, the average duration of homelessness is about eighteen to twenty months.

When the interviewer tried to elicit the reasons for homelessness in this group, people were permitted to give more than one cause, and responses were coded on the questionnaire into one or more of nine reasons, including unemployment, other financial problems, divorce, death of spouse or caretaker, hospitalization, family problems, and other. Fifty percent of the respondents said eviction was the reason, or one of the reasons, they were homeless. Sixty-eight percent mentioned a reason categorized as other. For example, 13% mentioned fired. Four of the thirty-eight re-ported they lost their apartments because of either a paperwork mistake by the Westchester Department of Social Services or because Department of Social Ser-vices refused to pay the rent when it was increased by the landlord. Five noted they moved out because the apartment was unsafe or in bad condition. Three could not get their leases renewed. Many other reasons were given, some extremely tragic. Nearly one quarter reported that they had been homeless before.

Use of Resources

When asked about their use of available resources, all families stated that they re-ceived welfare or Aid to Families with Dependent Children (AFDC). Eighty-seven percent were receiving food stamps. Twenty-nine percent were on the Women In-fants and Children's Program (WIC); however, the data were not available on how many of the other families were eligible for WIC and not receiving the food coupons.

The principal source of financial support was welfare and other entitlements. The average woman with one child received $417 in money, bus fare, and food stamps per month. A woman with four children averaged about $589 per month. Forty-seven percent of the respondents reported other resources of cash, mostly gifts from family or friends, which averaged about $215 per month.

A total of 36.8% of this group reported having been physically or emotionally abused in their lives. Most were abused by parents and stepparents as children and battered by boyfriends or spouses as adults. Within this sample, 15.8% had been in foster care themselves as children. Interestingly noted are the data that 78.9% re-ported having held a steady job for three months or more, but only 5.3% had worked for pay in the past thirty days.

Health Status

It is extremely challenging to try to measure health status by questionnaire. How-ever, the homeless were asked a number of questions that are traditionally used to measure health status. One of the first measures is the general self-report of overall health, where most people placed themselves in the middle. Comparative data to help interpret these figures are not available. A number of measures were used to see how healthy or sick this population was.

One of the first questions asked was whether the respondent had a history of chronic illness, and 29% did. The most frequently mentioned illness was asthma. Other illnesses included heart disease, disc disease, anemia, epilepsy, migraines, and depression. Forty-two percent stated that a family member living with them had a chronic illness. Asthma and bronchitis were again the most frequently cited, followed by heart murmurs or other cardiac problems. Other problems mentioned included sickle cell disease, epilepsy, lead poisoning, and hepatitis. Almost 45% were taking or supposed to be taking medication. Asthma medications and vitamins were mentioned most frequently. Other medications listed were seizure and thyroid medications, oral contraceptives, methadone, and antibiotics.

Twenty-nine percent reported a hospitalization in the past year. Most were for childbirth; however, a few serious illnesses also were noted. Almost 40% reported an illness in the family in the last thirty days. Most were febrile illnesses in children. Asthma, trauma, poison, and gynecologic problems also were noted. When asked about the presence of any of a list of common illnesses like hypertension, diabetes, or arthritis, only asthma was mentioned by many.

Several questions related to the health of children. Fifty-two percent reported significant behavior problems. A total of 36.8% reported children doing poorly or having been kept behind in school. There were 28.9% reporting serious illnesses other than coughs or colds. There were 23.7% reporting that the children were behind in their shots. Twenty-one percent had dental problems. Thirteen percent of the children had been in foster care. Only four of the thirty-eight families reported children having been taken away for abuse or neglect. These results suggested that the families had a significant amount of health needs.

In the area of mental health, almost 45% reported having spoken with someone about "emotional problems or problems with nerves," but only about 15% had ever been admitted to a hospital for psychiatric reasons. Twenty-one percent admitted having made a suicide attempt at some time in their lives.

One of the most frequently abused substances reported by respondents was cigarettes, and more than 80% smoked. Most of the smokers admitted to smoking less than half a pack a day. Some data on self-report of drug use in the past month were obtained; however, the interviewers came away feeling there had been significant underreporting of drug use, and, therefore, are not reporting these numbers. They were asked about inpatient and outpatient drug treatment, and very few people gave these histories.

One of the final areas to be discussed was their sources of health care. Surprisingly, more than 90% could identify one or more sources of regular health care. Most identified one of the local hospitals or private clinics, but eleven of the thirty-eight also mentioned the on-site health care provided by nurse practitioners as one of their regular sources of health care.

Conclusions and Discussion

This study had four very important limitations. The first was the small sample; although it was intended as an initial pilot survey, the plan was to interview many more families. This couldn't be done because it took a long time to develop the instrument and because of the erratic availability of families for interview.

The second limitation was the use of a convenience sample. All of our families were from a selected population that had obtained some emergency housing and were taking advantage of the coordinated service site where free food, health care, and social services were available. It would be preferable to identify a sample of the whole population of emergency-housed families in the city or the county.

The third limitation was the use of self-report data. In subsequent in-depth interviews, and in discussions with the nurse practitioners, it seems likely that substance abuse and illegal activity were underreported. Self-reporting of the other data also is liable to be biased, but less so than the drug-use data.

The fourth limitation is not unique to this study. Most studies of the homeless do not include a control group or do not use an appropriate control group. The use of a control is essential to answer the questions of how much of what is found is the result of being a poor minority family in the location studied and how much is related to lack of adequate housing.

Given these limitations, the following is a summary of the conclusions drawn from the study: This was a descriptive study designed to generate hypotheses, not to test them. Homeless families in Yonkers are primarily poor, single, minority women with young children, half of which lost their homes due to eviction. A more complete understanding of how this happens is necessary. There appear to be a few factors associated with family homelessnesss that occur more frequently than one would expect in a comparably housed group. These factors are: 1) lack of education, 2) a history of abuse, 3) multiple indicators of poor health status in the parent group and developmental/emotional problems in the children, and 4) probable frequent substance abuse. Access to care did not appear to be a problem in this group.

We must continue to obtain better and more controlled data to test these hypotheses, and if they are true, then family homelessness is a complicated problem that may not be solved with housing alone.

References

Bass, J. L., Brennan, P., Mehta, K. A., and Kodzis, S. (1990). "Pediatric Problems in a Suburban Shelter for Homeless Families." *Pediatrics* 85:33–38.

Bassuk, I. L., and Rosenberg, L. (1990). "Psychosocial Characteristics of Homeless Children and Children with Homes." *Pediatrics* 85:257–261.

Berne, A. S., Dato, C., Mason, D. J., and Rafferty, M. (1990). "A Nursing Model for Addressing the Health Needs of Homeless Families." *Image—Journal of Nursing Scholarship* 22(1):8–13.

Bernstein, A. J., Mitchell, D. H., Banks, R. B., Dhir, A., and Rippy, E. (1990). *Addressing the Problem of Homelessness in Westchester County.* White Plains, N.Y.: Skadden, Arps, Slate, Meagher, and Flom, and McKinsey and Company, Inc.

Bowdler, J. E. (1989). "Health Problems of the Homeless in America." *The Nurse Practitioner* 13:47–51.

Bowie, J. M., Mitchell, D. H., Bernstein, A. J., and Banks, R. B. (1990). *Addressing the Problems of Homelessness in Westchester County: The Legal Analysis.* White Plains, N.Y.: Skadden, Arps, Slate, Meagher, and Flom.

Breakey, W. R., et al. (1989). "Health and Mental Health Problems of Homeless Men and Women in Baltimore." *JAMA* 252:1352–57.

Brickner, P. W., et al. (1986). "Homeless Persons and Health Care." *Annals of Internal Medicine* 104:405–9.

Council on Scientific Affairs. (1989). "Health Care Needs of Homeless and Runaway Youths." *JAMA* 262:1358–61.

Institute of Medicine, Committee on Health Care for Homeless People. (1988). "Homelessness, Health, and Human Needs." Washington, D.C.: National Academy Press.

Miller, D. S., and Lin, E. H. B. (1988). "Children in Sheltered Homeless Families: Reported Health Status and Use of Health Services." *Pediatrics* 81:668–73.

Robertson, M. J., and Cousineau, M. R. (1986). "Health Status and Access to Health Services among the Urban Homeless." *AJPH* 76:561–63.

Weinreb, L. F., and Bassuk, E. L. (1990). "Healthcare of Homeless Families: A Growing Challenge for Family Medicine." *Journal of Family Medicine* 31:74–80.

Westchester County Commission on the Homeless. (1988). *Westchester Homeless Data.* White Plains, N.Y.: Housing Office, Westchester County Department of Social Services.

Westchester County Department of Social Services. (1990). *Number of Homeless Families, Children and Singles*, March 1990. White Plains, N.Y.: Westchester County Department of Social Services.

SECTION 3

Issues Related
to Homeless Families

CHAPTER 8

A Nursing Model for Addressing the Health Needs of Homeless Families

Andrea S. Berne
Candy Dato
Diana J. Mason
Margaret Rafferty

Abstract

Homelessness in the United States continues to be a major social problem directly affecting an estimated 3 million persons, of whom nearly 30% belong to families without permanent shelter. This chapter reviews recent research concerning homeless families and the conditions in which they live and outlines the significant health and mental health problems that these families experience. Effective nursing interventions for homeless families using Peszneckers' Adaptational Model of Poverty are proposed. Nurses must advocate for changes in the social and political conditions that bring about homelessness since the resources to meet the needs of these families are either nonexistent or woefully inadequate.

Introduction

Homelessness in the United States is a major social problem, directly affecting an estimated 3 million persons, of whom 30% are in family units. Of these families, 85% are headed by single women, a disproportionate number of whom are minorities. While families were the last subgroup to join the ranks of the homeless, they are now the fastest growing segment of that population. It is projected that in the near future a majority of the United States' homeless will be single mothers

---

NOTE: Reprinted with permission from *Image*, 22, No. 1, Spring 1990.

with children (City of New York Human Resources Administration 1986a, 1986b; Institute of Medicine 1988; Molnar 1988).

Etiology of Family Homelessness

Homelessness is a relative condition that exists worldwide in both developed and underdeveloped countries, although it expresses itself differently in different parts of the world (Patton 1988). It encompasses Britain's growing poor who are housed in the bread and breakfast rooms in London that have been described as the equivalent of third world shantytowns (Clines 1987). It includes the Ethiopian refugees in the Sudan and other countries where war and politics have uprooted entire communities (Smith 1989). It can be seen in the increasing number of young adults sleeping in hostels and shelters in Denmark, Austria, and Belgium (Hope and Young 1987a; Tennison 1983; Thomas 1985). It is evident in the explosion of slums in the cities of developing nations such as the Philippines, Mexico, and India (Busuttil 1987). And it can be seen in the so-called hidden homeless in Hungary— the growing number of people who are doubled-up in the dwellings of friends or families or who are living in decrepit housing (Hope and Young 1987b). In 1985, the United Nations reported that 100 million people worldwide had no shelter, and it proclaimed 1987 as the International Year of Shelter for Homeless (Ramachandran 1988).

Homelessness used to occur predominantly in third world countries where material resources were underdeveloped or scarce. Its rise in developed countries suggests a maldistribution of existing resources. Nowhere is this more evident than in the United States, where homelessness is primarily caused by the lack of affordable housing and increasing poverty.

The lack of affordable housing in the United States is the result of several factors:

- Gentrification, or a process in which low-income housing is replaced by middle-income and high-income housing;
- A freeze on the welfare shelter allowances in most states, resulting in an allowance that has not kept pace with the rising cost of renting an apartment;
- The Reagan Administration's decision to withdraw the federal government from its prior commitment to build and maintain low-income housing (Report of the Committee on Legal Problems of the Homeless 1989; Institute of Medicine 1988).

Since most of the homeless would not be without permanent housing if they could afford to pay the rents on the housing that is available, homelessness in the Unites States is largely a by-product of the increasing gap between the rich and poor. From 1980 to 1984, family income for the poorest 20% of the population declined by almost 8%, while that of the wealthiest 20% of families increased by almost 9% (United Auto Workers 1985). The poorest three-fifths of all families received only 32.7% of the total national income, while the wealthiest two-fifths received 67.3% of the income; these were, respectively, the lowest and highest percentages recorded since 1947 (Bureau of the Census 1985). The relative nature of poverty that is associated with homelessness is illustrated by data indicating that 35% of homeless mothers and fathers outside of New York City work, but their incomes are insufficient to pay for the rising cost of housing (Schmitt 1988). Indeed, a recent study found that the poor are paying an increasing percentage of their income on housing—now 63%, as opposed to the standard of 30% that is deemed the "affordable" limit by the Department of Housing and Urban Development (Dionne 1989).

Family Homelessness as Poverty: A Model for Nursing

Pesznecker (1984) synthesized the literature on poverty and delineated an interactional, adaptational model of poverty (see Fig. 8.1). It postulates that one develops health-promoting or health-damaging responses to the stress of poverty, which are shaped by interactions between the individual/group and the environment—interactions that are further mediated by factors such as public policy. It presents the poor as individuals and groups who are continually faced with multiple and chronic stressors, including frustration over few employment options, inadequate and unsafe housing conditions, repeated exposure to violence and crime, inadequate child-care assistance, and insensitive attitudes and responses of social service and mental health agencies. The coping abilities of the poor are strained by the unpredictable and unrelenting accumulation of these stressors. Mastery may be diminished so that a sense of helplessness develops with a resulting decrease in motivation as well as a sense of helplessness and hopelessness. The stigmatization of being poor in a society that measures one's worth by income only adds to the stress of poverty and makes it difficult to maintain any semblance of self-esteem or self-efficacy. Anxiety, depression, and feelings of powerlessness are thus predictable concomitants of poverty.

The experience of homeless families can be described within this context. Pesznecker's (1984) model provides a basis for being particularly concerned about the children of these families and the bleak present and future that they face. It incorporates the effect that the stigmas of poverty and homelessness can have on people who are often stigmatized also by their race and gender in a society that continues to contain covert and overt sexism and racism. It also provides a basis for nurses to incorporate social activism in their role as advocates and providers of care for homeless families.

Individual/Group Factors		Environmental Factors
Early childhood experiences		Stress
Unique coping problems		High life change
Multiple-concurrent problems		Enduring life conditions
Limited opportunity for mastery		Stigma
Poor coping outcomes		Individual
		Institutional

Mediating Factors
Public policy
Social support

Adaptive Responses

Health Promoting		Health Damaging
Sense of well-being		Depression
High perceived self-efficacy		Anxiety
High self-esteem		Low self-esteem

FIGURE 8.1

Adaptational model of poverty. Source: Adapted from Elizabeth Pesznecker (1984), "The Poor: A Population at Risk," Public Health Nursing 1(4); 237–49.

Homeless Children

The research on homeless children is limited, but the data that are available suggest that homelessness is not an experience to which one can adapt positively. Wright and Weber (1987) reported that 16% of the homeless children have various chronic physical disorders, double the rate among patients in the general population. Asthma, anemia, and malnutrition were among the most common. In the same study, many common acute pediatric problems were reported at inordinately high rates (upper respiratory infections, skin ailments, gastrointestinal problems, ear infections, eye disorders and dental problems). Data from Bellevue Hospital in New York City revealed that 50% of homeless children living in welfare hotels had immunization delays (Acker, Fierman, and Dreyer 1987).

Homeless infants living in welfare hotels in New York City had an infant mortality rate of 24.9 per 1,000 live births in 1985. This was over twice the overall city rate of 12.0/1,000. Pregnant women living in welfare hotels in New York City were twice as likely to give birth to low-weight infants as were women living in the "city projects" (Chavkin et al. 1987).

However, the effects of homelessness are even more profound on the mental health of the children. Bassuk and Rubin's (1987) study of children in Massachusetts shelters found that 47% of preschool children were delayed in at least one area of language, gross motor, fine motor, and personal/social skills and development. One-third of these children demonstrated problems in more than two areas. Almost half of the school-age children showed depression and anxiety, with the majority voicing suicidal ideation. The children were also noted to have sleep problems, shyness, withdrawal, and aggression. Gewirtzman and Fodor (1987) reported that children in families left homeless after fires often exhibit these symptoms as well as isolation, disorientation, confusion, grief, psychosomatic complaints, and regression. These problems are similar to those found in children of migrant workers and refugees and have been described as manifestations of post-traumatic stress disorder (PTSD) (Eth and Pynoos 1985). PTSD is a reaction to some kind of psychological trauma and, until recently, was described mostly among war veterans. A psychologist in New York City reported that PTSD is the most common diagnosis among homeless children that she encounters (J. LeClair, personal communication, May 15, 1989).

Shelter life is stressful and shameful, compounding the children's problems. All schoolchildren are sensitive to dressing below peer standards, but homeless children may also face discriminatory remarks made by teachers and classmates, making them a "minority within a minority" (Gwirtzman and Fodor 1987). Poor attendance and truancy are major problems for this population. School attendance among ten year-olds to sixteen year-olds at the Martinique Hotel, the largest welfare hotel in New York City, was less than 40%. In one study, 43% of the children had failed at least one grade; 24% were in special education classes; 50% were failing (Bassuk and Rubin 1987).

Children without parents in New York City fare worse than do homeless children with parents. Instead of being placed in individual foster homes, these children increasingly are housed in congregate shelters—dormitory-like facilities that have recently been critically exposed and condemned in a study by the Public Health Interest Consortium of New York City (Brooklyn Health Action Committee 1989). Unsanitary conditions, spoiled food, blatant fire and safety hazards, and inadequate staffing predominate in these facilities. The "orphans" are shuffled from shelter to shelter, their emotional needs are ignored, and they endure conditions that are often debilitating and sometimes life-threatening. The study reports that in one review of childhood immunizations, only 22% of the children were adequately immunized. Some of the children are HIV-positive and are at great risk for communicable diseases that easily spread in the congregate facilities:

> The children in the shelters then are in profound psychological distress, and the custodial care they receive fails to lessen their pain. The harm to these children goes beyond their immediate suffering, however. It extends to their long-term emotional development. (p. 10)

The data on homeless children suggest that predominant responses of homeless children to their experience with poverty are ones that Pesznecker categorizes as health damaging. The future for these children may be short-lived and without much hope for a better life. Longitudinal studies are needed to examine the long-term effects of a childhood experience with homelessness and the extent to which homelessness is an experience that precludes health-promoting responses to poverty.

Homeless Mothers

There is a paucity of research on the health problems of homeless mothers. They are a neglected population. Andrea Berne's experience suggests that the mothers wait for health care until they are so acutely ill that they need emergency treatment. They may not seek health care for themselves since they tend to view themselves as the least important person in the household. Their schedules may also preclude attendance at clinics.

When the homeless mothers are seen, as they were in the Health Care for the Homeless Demonstration Project from June 1985 to September 1987 (Wright and Weber 1987), it was confirmed that they suffer from most physical disorders at higher rates than do the general population. In addition to numerous chronic illnesses, the rate of tuberculosis among the homeless exceeds that of the general population by a factor of twenty-five to perhaps several hundred. Anecdotal reports from public health nurses in New York City suggest that AIDS is increasingly prevalent among homeless families and progresses more rapidly in these poor women. The overcrowded conditions of shelters and welfare hotels clearly impact on the health of the homeless mothers, as does inadequate diet, substandard bathing facilities, and multiple chronic stressors.

It is evident that these same stressors contribute to the mental health problems of homeless mothers, although there is little research in this area as well. The research that has been done coincides with studies of poverty that repeatedly describe an increase in mental health problems, particularly anxiety and depression, with increasing poverty (Belle 1982; Dohrenwend and Dohrenwend 1974; Hollingshead and Redlich 1958). Bassuk's (1986) study of eighty-two families in fourteen Massachusetts shelters reported that the majority of the mothers had a limited number of relationships, with 43% reporting no or minimal support, and 24% seeing their children as their major emotional support. Of the eighty-two families, eighteen were being assessed for potential child abuse. As children, one-third of the mothers had suffered physical abuse, while one in every nine were victims of sexual abuse. The mothers' histories showed a significant amount of major family disruption, loss of parents, lack of work skills, and residential instability (Bassuk, Rubin, and Lauriat 1986). The data suggested intergenerational aspects of family disruption and emotional difficulties. Another study estimated that 24% of homeless families in New York City were victims of domestic violence (Victim Services Agency 1989).

Homeless mothers need to be distinguished from another subgroup of the homeless, the homeless mentally ill. Homeless mothers are not psychotic any more frequently than is the general population, and the etiology of their homelessness lies in poverty rather than a combination of poverty and mental illness. Bassuk's (1986) study did find 71% of homeless mothers had personality disorders; however, both advocates for the homeless and Bassuk herself criticized this finding as being an exaggeration of the degree of psychopathology. The diagnostic labels do serve to indicate severe functional impairment and the need for help.

Substance abuse is one of the health-damaging responses with which some of these mothers may have to cope, although documenting the prevalence of the problem and whether it is antecedent to or a product of homelessness are difficult. The study of the foster children in New York City (Brooklyn Health Action Committee 1989) identified parental drug abuse as "the single biggest underlying factor in child abuse and neglect" (p. 34) that results in children being removed from their families. Bassuk (1986) found 10% of the mothers to be substance abusers, while New York City public health nurses have estimated that between 80% and 90% of the mothers in some shelters use crack. Crack, which has intensified the problem of drug abuse because of its high potency and rapidly addictive qualities, has become a cause of homelessness in New York City, as addicts use money for the drug instead of housing. Other health and mental health problems are expanded with substance abuse, and one would suspect that some of the character disorder problems seen in Bassuk's study were drug related.

As with homeless children, the data suggest that homelessness is a correlate of poverty that overwhelms the physical and emotional resources of homeless mothers. Pesznecker (1984) noted that poverty involves an interplay between environmental and individual factors. The poor encounter more stressors, especially surrounding money, social isolation, stigmatization, and parenting, all of which can be exacerbated by homelessness. Coping positively with this multiplicity of persistent stressors becomes increasingly difficult, particularly if one is repetitively unable to change them. Depression, anxiety, and feelings of powerlessness readily ensue. Under Pesznecker's model, the mental health problems of homeless mothers are most appropriately viewed as health-damaging responses to harsh environmental conditions that breed demoralization, hopelessness, and despair. The model also suggests points of intervention that can foster health-promoting responses to homelessness.

Health-Care Services for Homeless Families

Access to health care has been a major problem for homeless families (Institute of Medicine 1988). For example, a survey of sheltered children in Seattle revealed that 59% of the children had no regular care provider. The same group used emergency rooms at a rate of two to three times the rate of the general pediatric population in the United States (Miller and Lin 1988). Although substance abuse appears to be a growing problem among homeless mothers, there is a paucity of drug treatment programs in the United States, particularly those that provide long-term treatment with a family focus.

Three traditional approaches that have been used to provide health-care services to homeless families are the traditional out-patient department (OPD) or clinic, on-site services, and comprehensive outreach.

The Clinics

Ambulatory care for the poor is generally delivered in clinics. While funding from the national government and a nationwide grant from a private foundation have resulted in some outreach services to homeless families, most continue to lack access to anything except emergency room care. This has resulted in a woeful lack of prenatal care for homeless women who then arrive at the emergency room in labor and are at greater risk for maternal and infant morbidity and mortality (Chavkin et al. 1987).

Even homeless people who do have access to routine health-care services often have difficulty negotiating the system. Families are usually sheltered outside their neighborhood of origin so that they are unfamiliar with and apprehensive about new health-care providers. For families that are moved multiple times, it is difficult, if not impossible, to establish a stable relationship with a primary provider. Many hospital clinics have long waits for appointments, lack continuity of care, and often are understaffed. There have been many reports of families with "hotel addresses" being treated poorly. The clinic staff may blame the homeless for lack of immunizations and records and missed appointments, labeling them "non-compliant." In addition, families often do not keep appointments because of fear of being reported to the Child Welfare Bureau for neglect and/or abuse related to being homeless. For these reasons, the clinic system increases the stressors and stigma with which homeless families must cope and fosters health-damaging responses such as anxiety, low self-esteem, and low motivation.

On-site Services

In some settings, visiting health teams have set up shop. The goal of many of these projects is to mainstream the families into existing clinics. While this is conceptually pleasing and congruent with the goal of establishing coordinated comprehensive care for all, this approach has limitations. The efforts of two or three health providers on site are inadequate to offset the stress and stigma of this extreme level of poverty. On-site providers have become frustrated by some of the same problems that the families are up against with the system as it presently exists, as they try to refer the families to existing services. There are transportation problems, delays in getting appointments, and inadequate care. "Homeless providers" fall victim to the same discrimination that the homeless themselves face. The level of effort is inadequate to make a significant difference, but it is often used by politicians to demonstrate that they are "doing something" when, in fact, they are not. On-site services are too often a Band-Aid approach to the health problems of homeless families.

Comprehensive Mobile Outreach Services

One model program has enough resources to mitigate some of the effects of the poverty that underlies homelessness. The New York Children's Health Project has expanded on the concept of on-site services by providing comprehensive pediatric care with mobile medical units to children living in hotels and shelters in New York City. This project works collaboratively with the public health nurses and city social workers who are on-site at the hotels five days a week doing intake and case finding. The public health nurses visit the families as they enter the system and take an initial health assessment. They identify children in need of immunizations, mothers in need of prenatal care, and a wide variety of other acute and chronic health-care needs. By knocking on doors, they attempt to cross the impenetrable boundary that exists between the family and the outside world.

Acute and chronic medical problems are diagnosed and treated by nurse practitioners and physicians. School, day-care, and camp forms and Women Infants and Children's Program (WIC) certifications are frequently completed by the nurses, which has made an enormous impact on enrollment in such programs. In addition, nurses discuss routine health maintenance issues such as growth and development and nutrition as well as strategies for hotel living.

This project essentially provides "middle-class" pediatric health care to the poorest of the poor. Because of the intensive supports built into the program, there is a 70–80% compliance rate, which is comparable to middle-class compliance. The project demonstrates the mitigating effects that public policy and social support, the mediating factors in Pesznecker's model, can have on the ongoing stressors confronting homeless families.

Designing Effective Interventions for Homeless Families

This is not to suggest that comprehensive health services for the homeless are the magic tonic for the problems of homelessness. These families have an enormous number of problems, of which health problems are only one small part. Indeed, nursing interventions with homeless families must reflect an understanding of the connections between health and other life and societal conditions. Pesznecker's Adaptational Model of Poverty reflects this understanding. It also is distinguished from most poverty frameworks that actually "blame the victim"—an approach that is contrary to nursing's view of health as a human-environment interaction (Mason 1981). Her model provides direction for interventions with homeless families that address both the individuals and families and the environment and society.

Pesznecker's model suggests that homeless families can best be assisted through strategies that empower them to develop the skills and self-esteem to recognize and act on opportunities for moving out of homelessness and poverty as well as to cope more positively when those opportunities are not present. Approaching the homeless mothers and children with caring and respect is prerequisite to countering the stigmatizing attitudes they face in other encounters with society. Homeless families also need tangible and intangible support to cope with the multiple stressors in their lives. Such supports range from adequate public assistance and shelter subsidies to a network of friends and professionals who provide both mental and material support during times of crisis. In many cases, homeless families are removed from their community of origin and may be moved through a variety of communities during their experience with homelessness. Maintaining relationships with friends or providers becomes almost impossible. Such support systems could be maintained and developed if each community were required to have a plan for families in need of emergency housing.

Health-care providers have tended to view psychotherapy as a necessary intervention for homeless families, particularly given the mental health problems outlined earlier. Pesznecker's model suggests that stress management training may be an instrumental intervention. Support for this proposition is evident in two stress-reduction projects with women in the United States and Canada who were on public assistance (Resnick 1984; Tableman et al. 1985). Unfortunately, these approaches are seldom included in the health and social services that are available to homeless families.

Several model projects such as the Henry Street Settlement House in New York City and Trevor's Place in Philadelphia provide safe, clean shelter and supportive, on-site services to families. These supportive services include twenty-four-hour, on-site staff, day care, after-school tutoring, job training for mothers, assistance with entitlement, and assistance with relocation. These projects have found that the mental outlook of both parents and children improves dramatically under these stable conditions. Children start attending school again; grades and behavior improve. This approach to homelessness both increases coping options and provides some stability so that referrals for self-help groups, stress reduction techniques, or traditional psychotherapy services for the homeless who have major functional psychiatric disorders can have some hope for success.

Most health-care services for the homeless are really secondary and tertiary prevention. True primary prevention of homelessness demands social policies that call for:

- Affordable housing;
- Education and job training;
- Meaningful work at an adequate wage;
- Adequate levels of public assistance for families that cannot sustain themselves including adequate shelter allowances;
- Accessible and adequate child care;
- Access to health prevention and promotion including education about preventing pregnancy and substance abuse and coping with stress;
- Drug treatment on demand.

And if homelessness on an international level is considered, nursing's advocacy for primary prevention of homelessness would include efforts to promote world peace and improved means for resolving intranational and international political disputes.

Nurses can influence and shape policies that deal with homeless families through political advocacy. The American Nurses' Association has included homelessness among the issues it advocates in Washington, D.C., and many other state nurses' associations have done likewise. In New York City, the local district nurses' association adopted a position on homelessness that calls for affordable housing, adequate temporary shelter, and accessible health-care services.

If the nursing community is committed to primary prevention for homeless women and children, then we must participate in the debate regarding whether or not housing is a human right (Burns 1988) and recognize the connections between the health of homeless women and children and the broader social, economic, and political issues of our times. Such a perspective demands that we also understand that we truly are one world community and that these connections extend beyond geographic boundaries. We challenge the nursing community worldwide to join together in calling for conditions and policies that are health sustaining instead of health damaging, that are supportive and nurturing of families, and that make housing a basic human right, without which one cannot ensure health.

Endnote
Imagine You Are Homeless

Imagine you are a thirty-three-year-old woman with three children. Your apartment burned down six months ago. You and your children had been living with your sister in her cramped apartment until she had another baby, and now there simply is not enough room for everyone.

You sleep in your car at night. During the day, you walk the streets with your children trying to find an apartment you can afford. Finally, you go to the department of social services to try to find shelter for the night and are told that your children may have to be placed in foster care if a place cannot be found for all of you. Knowing that the foster care system in this city is unreliable and sometimes unsafe, you agree to spend the first night in an overcrowded warehouse-type shelter, where you end up sleeping on the floor.

You and your children have no privacy here. Many of the children and adults have colds, and you hear that tuberculosis has been an increasing problem among the homeless. When the opportunity arises, you agree to move into one of the single-room occupancy hotels that the city is using to house homeless families "temporarily." That temporary shelter becomes your home for thirteen months.

The temporary shelter consists of one ten by ten foot room. You have no kitchen, no refrigerator, no stove or cooking facilities. There is one bed for you and your three children.

You pull the mattress off the bed at night to make room for all of you to sleep and then pull the sheets off the bed in the day to eat on the floor.

You use running water to keep your baby's milk cool, and you do the dishes in the tub where you bathe and store things.

There is no place for your children to play, no place to sit, no place to do homework. When they try to play in the hall, they are approached by drug dealers and sometimes even pimps.

This is what life is like for you and your children. Imagine the gradual dissipation of your own and your children's self-esteem and the isolation and depression that eventually overwhelm you. Imagine having a future without space, without privacy, without hope.

References

Acker, P., Fierman, A. H., and Dreyer, B. P. (1987). "Health: An Assessment of Parameters of Health-Care and Nutrition in Homeless Children (abstract)." *American Journal of Diseases of Children* 141: 388.

Bassuk, E. (1986). "Homeless Families: Single Mothers and Their Children in Boston Shelters." In *The Mental Health Needs of Homeless Persons: New Directions for Mental Health Services*, edited by E. Bassuk. San Francisco: Jossey-Bass.

Bassuk, E., and Rubin, L. (1987). "Homeless Children: A Neglected Population." *American Journal of Orthopsychiatry* 57:(2); 279–86.

Bassuk, E., Rubin, L., and Lauriat, A. (1986). "Characteristics of Sheltered Homeless Families." *American Journal of Public Health* 76; 1097–1101.

Belle, D. (1982). *Lives in Stress: Women and Depression*. Beverly Hills: Sage.

Brooklyn Health Action Committee. (1989). *Inexcusable Harm: The Effect of Institutionalization on Young Foster Children in New York City*. New York: Public Interest Health Consortium of New York City.

Bureau of the Census. (1985). *Money Income and Poverty Status of Families and Persons in the United States: 1984*. Washington, D.C.: The U.S. Government Printing Office.

Burns, L. S. (1988). "Hope for the Homeless in the U.S.: Lessons from the Third World." *Cities* 5: 33–40.

Bustuttil, S. (1987). Houselessness and the Training Problem. *Cities* 4; 152–158.

Chavkin, W., Kristal, A., Seabron, C., and Guigli, P. (1987). "The Reproductive Experience of Women Living in Hotels for the Homeless in NYC." *New York State Journal of Medicine* 371: 10–13.

City of New York Human Resources Administration (October 1986a). *A One-day "Snapshot" of Homeless Families at the Forbell Street Shelter and the Martinique Hotel*. New York: The Administration.

City of New York Human Resources Administration. (October 1986b). *Characteristics and Housing Histories of Families Seeking Shelter from HRA*. N.Y.: The Administration.

Clines, F. X. (October 22, 1987). "For Poor, Bed and Breakfast at $34 Million a Year." *The New York Times*: 3.

Dionne, E. J. (April 17, 1989). "Poor Paying More for their Shelter." *The New York Times*; A18.

Dohrenwend, B. S., and Dohrenwend, B. P. (1974). *Stressful Life Events: Their Nature and Effects*. New York: John Wiley and Sons.

Eth, S., and Pynoos, R. (1985). *Post-traumatic Stress Disorder in Children*. Washington, D.C.: American Psychiatric Association.

Gewirtzman, R., and Fodor, I. (1987). "The Homeless Child at School: From Welfare Hotel to Classroom." *Child Welfare* 66(3): 237–45.

Hollingshead, A. B., and Redlich, F. C. (1958). *Social Class and Mental Illness: A Community Study*. New York: John Wiley and Sons.

Hope, M., and Young, J. (August 1987a). "Homelessness in Austria Rising, Although Social Programs Help." *Safety Network* 4(12): 2.

Hope, M., and Young, J. (December 1987b). Housing Privatization in Hungary—Will It Cause More Homelessness? *Safety Network* 5(3): 2.

Institute of Medicine. (1988). *Homelessness, Health, and Human Needs*. Washington, D.C.: National Academy Press.

Mason, D. (1981). Perspectives on Poverty. *IMAGE* 13: 82–85.

Miller, D. S., and Lin, E. H. B. (1988). Children in Sheltered Homeless Families: Reported Health Status and Use of Health Services. *Pediatrics* 81(5): 668–73.

Molnar, J. (1988). *Home is Where the Heart Is: The Crisis of Homeless Children and Families in New York City.* New York: Bank Street College of Education.

Patton, C. V. (1988). *Spontaneous Shelter: International Perspectives and Prospects.* Philadelphia: Temple University Press.

Pesznecker, B. (1984). "The Poor: A Population at Risk." *Public Health Nursing,* 1(4): 237–49.

Ramachandran, A. (1988). "International Year of Shelter for the Homeless." *Cities* 5: 144–62.

Report of the Committee on Legal Problems of the Homeless. (1989). *The Record of the Association of the Bar of the City of New York* 44(1): 33–88.

Resnick, G. (1984). "The Short and Long-term Impact of a Competency-based Program for Disadvantaged Women." *Journal of Social Service Research* 7(4): 37–49.

Schmitt, E. (December 26, 1988). "Suburbs Cope with the Steep Rise in the Homeless." *The New York Times*; 1.

Smith, S. (1989). "People without Land." *American Journal of Nursing* 89(2); 208–9.

Tableman, B., Feis, C. L., Marciniak, D., and Howard, D. (1985). "Stress Management Training for Low-income Women." *Prevention in Human Services* 3(4): 71–85.

Tennison, D. C. (April 25, 1983). "Homeless People Grow Numerous in Europe, Despite Welfare States." *The Wall Street Journal* 80: 1ff.

Thomas, J. (October 7, 1985). The Homeless of Europe: A Scourge of Our Time. *The New York Times.*

United Auto Workers of America. (1985). *Building America's Future.* Detroit: UAW.

Victim Services Agency. (1989). *The Screening and Diversion of Battered Women in the New York City Emergency Housing System.* New York: The Agency.

Wright, J. D., and Weber, E. (1987). *Homelessness and Health. New York: McGraw-Hill.*

CHAPTER 9

Health Needs of Infants and Children in Homeless Families in Houston, Texas

Kim Evans

Abstract

Parents and their children now constitute approximately 35% of America's homeless. Data on the actual health status of these children have been minimal. This study reviewed 401 records that reflected all pediatric clients (through age fourteen) served during the first nine months of the Health Care for the Homeless project in Houston, Texas, in 1988. The sample was dominated by minority infants and children who were five years of age or less and who had been homeless for less than one month. Three hundred and forty (85%) were seen by the health-care teams and had complete medical data. Respiratory diseases were diagnosed in 42.9% of the sample and the need for immunizations in 38.4%. Significant numbers had skin disease (17.94%), ear disease (16.76%), and gastrointestinal disease (14.4%). The average number of diagnoses per child was 1.85. These findings will enable local health-care and social service agencies to plan better methods for prevention and treatment of illness in this special population.

Children comprise a significant subset of today's homeless population because of the increasing number of homeless women, who primarily have two to three dependents. The National Association of Community Health Centers (1989), recently reported that families and children now constitute approximately 35% of the homeless and are considered its fastest growing segment; 54% of children in these families are under five, and 50% are members of ethnic minorities.

Few data exist regarding the specific health needs of the most vulnerable segment of the homeless—infants and children. Before the needs can be adequately addressed, they must be identified and documented. The primary purpose of this study was to describe the prevalent health needs of infants and children of homeless families in

Houston who used shelter clinics in 1988. The secondary purpose was to determine any associations between selected demographic factors and health needs.

Definitions

The Stewart B. McKinney Homeless Assistance Act of 1987 is the source of this study's operational definition of homeless: Homeless individuals include someone who is (1) lacking a fixed, regular, and adequate nighttime residence, or (2) having such a residence that is a shelter designed to provide temporary accommodations, an institution providing temporary residence, or a place not designed or regularly used as a sleeping accommodation. Pediatric clients are operationally defined as all infants and children through age fourteen.

Method

This study employed a descriptive research design, implementing a retrospective chart audit. The sample consisted of 401 charts that reflected all pediatric clients served during the first nine months of the Health Care for the Homeless (HCH) project in Houston (March 28, 1988–January 4, 1989).

Setting

The HCH project was developed in response to needs in the community and funds were provided by PL 100–77, the Stewart B. McKinney Homeless Assistance Act. The project is administered by the local public hospital district. Health-care teams are based at several local shelters, two of which house mostly women and children. The teams consist of occasional volunteer physicians, a nurse practitioner, a social worker who provides case management, and an eligibility worker who assists clients in establishing eligibility for the public hospital district system and other entitlement programs. Medical evaluation and treatment are performed according to protocols approved and supervised by the project director, a physician. The HCH project in Houston was initiated March 28, 1988.

Forms and Data

Each client seen for a health need had two forms entered into his chart. The "Contact Form" (Figure 9.1) provided demographic information, and the physical examination form (Figure 9.2) provided a diagnosis for each visit. Some clients made several visits. Information from these forms in pediatric charts was encoded and computerized.

Harris County Hospital District

Health Care for the Homeless

Contact Form

DEMOGRAPHIC INFORMATION

SEX: 1-MALE	RACE/ETHNICITY	EDUCATION	BENEFIT STATUS (MEDICAL)	EMPLOYED
2-FEMALE	1-WHITE	1-GRADE SCHOOL	1-MEDICARE	1-YES
	2-BLACK	2-SOME H.S.	2-MEDICAID	2-NO
MARITAL STATUS	3-HISPANIC	3-H.S. GRD.	3-VA BENEFITS	
1-SINGLE	4-ASIAN	4-VOC./TECHNICAL	4-PRIVATE INS.	VETERAN
2-MARRIED	5-AM. INDIAN	5-SOME COLLEGE		1-YES
3-DIVORCED	8-OTHER	6-COLLEGE GRD.	BENEFIT STATUS (LIVING)	2-NO
4-SEPARATED	LIST _____	7-NONE	1-FOOD STAMPS	
5-WIDOWED			2-SOCIAL SECURITY	
8-OTHER	CHILDREN		3-WELFARE	
	2-NO		4-SSI	
HOW LONG	1-YES		7-NONE	
HOMELESS _____	HOW MANY _____		8-OTHER _____	
	WITH YOU? 1-YES			
	2-NO			

PRESENTING PROBLEM(S): _____

_____

PROBLEM TYPE (CHECK THOSE WHICH APPLY)   CLIENT APPEARED

___ MEDICAL	___ FAMILY DYSFUNCTION	___ DRUNK	___ DIRTY OR UNKEMPT
___ ELIGIBILITY	___ SITUATION CRISIS	___ UNDER INFLUENCE	___ SHABBILY DRESSED
___ MENTAL HEALTH	___ ENTITLEMENT	OF DRUGS	___ CARRYING PERSONAL
___ MENTAL	___ LEGAL	___ SERIOUSLY ILL	BELONGINGS
RETARDATION	___ INFORMATION AND	___ CONFUSED	___ LUCID AND ALERT
___ ALCOHOL/	REFERRAL	___ INCOHERENT	___ NEAT AND CLEAN
SUBSTANCE ABUSE	___ OTHER _____		
___ EMPLOYMENT			

REFERRALS AND COMMENTS
  2-NO
  1-YES

IF YES, TO: _____

COMMENTS

SIGNED: _____ ___ NP ___ RN ___ DENTIST ___ SOCIAL WORK

                               ___ MENTAL HEALTH ___ ELIGIB. ___ OTHER

FIGURE 9.1
Harris County Hospital District, Health Care for the Homeless Contact Form

Harris County Hospital District

AGE _____ SEX _____ RACE _____

WT _____ HT _____ FOC _____

T _____ P _____ R _____ B/P _____

ON THE ITEMS BELOW PLEASE USE THE FOLLOWING KEY

__✔__ = NORMAL OR NO FINDINGS __X__ = ABNORMAL __0__ = NOT DONE/NOT PERTINENT

GENERAL APPEARANCE _____ MENTAL/EMOTIONAL STATUS _____ ACTIVITY/DEVELOPMENT _____

HEAD ____ EYES ____ PUPILS ____ E.O.M. ____ FUNDI ____ EARS ____ CANALS ____ T.M.'S ____

NOSE ____ MUCOSA ____ SEPTUM ____ MOUTH ____ MUCOSA ____ GUMS ____ TEETH ____ TONGUE ____ THROAT _____

NECK ____ TRACHEA ____ THYROID ____ LYMPH NODES ____ CAROTID PULSES ____ VEINS ____

CHEST ____ SYMMETRY ____ EXPANSION ____ BREASTS ____ NIPPLES ____ LUNGS ____ PP&A ____

HEART ____ P.M.I. ____ SIZE ____ RHYTHM ____ SOUNDS ____

ABDOMEN ____ TENDERNESS ____ LIVER ____ SPLEEN ____ KIDNEYS ____ MASSES ____

BACK ____ SPINE ____ MUSCULATURE ____ DEFORMITY ____

MALE ____ PENIS ____ PREPUCE ____ URETHRA ____ TESTES ____ HERNIA____

FEMALE ____ VULVA ____ URETHRA ____ VAGINA ____ CERVIX ____ UTERUS ____ ADNEXA ____

ANUS ____ INSPECTION ____ RECTAL DIGITAL EXAM ____ PROSTRATE ____ OCCULT BLOOD ____

EXTREMITIES ____ EDEMA ____ PERIPHERAL PULSES ____ LYMPH NODES ____

NEUROLOGIC ____ CRANIAL NERVES ____ REFLEXES ____ SENSORY ____ MOTOR ____ COORDINATION ____ GAIT ____

ABNORMAL MOVEMENTS ____

SKIN ____ HAIR ____ NAILS ____

DESCRIPTION OF ABNORMALITIES: _____

_____
_____
_____
_____
_____
_____

DATE _____

FIGURE 9.2
Harris County Hospital District

For encoding diagnoses (health needs), a modification of the International Classification of Disease (ICD) codes, based on that used by Wright (1985) in New York City, was used to maximize comparability with other epidemiological data. Two categories were nonspecific: the category "physical examination" provided for record of routine exams with findings all within normal limits; the category "symptom" was used when there was no accompanying diagnosis, for example headache. Descriptive statistics, frequencies, percentages, and chi-square tests were used to summarize the demographic variables and health needs.

Results

The sample consisted of 401 charts representing 401 pediatric clients seen at two shelters—the Star of Hope Women's Center (SOH) and the Salvation Army Family Residence Center (SA). Of the 401 charts, 14 (4%) had incomplete medical data and 44 (11%) were seen for eligibility purposes only. Three hundred forty (85%) were seen by the health-care team and had diagnostic assessments.

Total charts reviewed	401	(100%)
Incomplete medical data	14	(4%)
Eligibility only	44	(11%)
Charts analyzed	340	(85%)

Sample

Table 9.1 shows basic demographic data for the sample. Missing data resulted in variable sample sizes for each characteristic. There were approximately equal numbers of boys and girls. Three-fourths were of ethnic minority groups. Minorities included Black, Hispanic, and Asian. The majority of the sample were preschool-aged children (55.30%), which, when added to those less than one year of age (21.19%), represented 76.49% of the sample.

Information about the length of time homeless and the length of time in Houston was more limited and in each case reflected less than half of the total sample. The largest percentage (81.76%) had been homeless less than one month. Time in Houston was more variable, but the majority (64.77%) had been in Houston less than three years. A majority (59.10%) were seen at the SOH center. Rates of missing data from other parts of the contact form were too high to warrant reporting.

Educational status became more meaningful when compared with the children's ages (see Table 9.2). Ten preschool-aged children had attended kindergarten. Forty-seven school-aged children had records of grade school attendance, and one had a record of high school attendance. It is important to note, however, that the data forms were not specific as to past or current schooling.

TABLE 9.1
Demographic Characteristics of Infants and Children
of Homeless Families in Houston

Characteristic	Number	Percent (%)
Gender (N = 400)		
Male	197	49.25
Female	203	50.75
Race (N = 387)		
White	95	24.55
Black	223	57.62
Hispanic	66	17.05
Other	3	0.78
Age (N = 387)		
< 1 year	82	21.19
1–5 years	214	55.30
6–10 years	65	16.80
1–14 years	26	6.72
Education of child (N = 175)		
Grade school	57	32.57
High school	1	0.57
None	117	66.85
Time homeless (N = 59)		
< 1 month	130	81.76
1–6 months	28	17.61
1–2 years	1	0.63
Time in Houston (N = 176)		
< 1 month	28	15.91
1–6 months	20	11.36
6–12 months	25	14.21
1–2 years	22	12.50
2–3 years	19	10.80
> 3 years	62	35.23
Site (N = 401)		
Star of Hope	237	59.10
Salvation Army	164	40.90

TABLE 9.2
Comparisons of Age and Education of Children
of Homeless Families in Houston (N = 175)

Age	Education		
	Grade school	High school	None
< 1 year			30
1–5 years	10		86
6–10 years	34		1
11–14 years	13	1	

NOTE: Grade school for the age group 1–5 represents kindergarten.

Discussion

Approximately three-fourths of the sample of infants and children of homeless families in Houston were less than five years of age and were ethnic minorities. These findings are similar to those reported by the U.S. Conference of Mayors (1986) and the National Association of Community Health Centers (1989).

Educational status was not differentiated as to past or current, making it impossible to determine the effect of homelessness on school attendance. Data regarding time homeless and time in Houston may have contained errors due to inaccurate client recall and/or embarrassment in disclosing such information. The data suggest that homeless women with dependent children are relatively new to the Houston area and had sought the services of established shelters within the first weeks of homelessness.

In summary, the sample was dominated by minority infants and children under five years of age who had been homeless less than one month.

Health Needs

The health-needs distribution pattern is shown in Table 9.3. Respiratory infections were diagnosed in 44.12% of the sample, and the need for immunizations in 38.24%. Significant numbers had skin disease (18.24%), ear disease (16.76%), and gastrointestinal disease (14.41%). A tuberculosis (TB) skin test was reported to have been given to 61 (17.94%) of the children. Up to four diagnoses per child were included in the data analysis. Disease categories were recorded only once per child, for example, if a child came in twice for an ear infection, it was listed only once in the data base. The average number of diagnoses per child was 1.85. The majority of children (78.9%) had one or two diagnoses (see Table 9.4).

Diagnostic categories were plotted against gender, race, age, time homeless, and time in Houston. Respiratory diseases were significantly higher among white and black children as opposed to Hispanic children ($p < .05$). The need for immunization was found to be significantly higher among children aged five years or less ($p < .01$). The number of diagnoses assessed per child (1–4 more) was plotted against the same demographics, with none showing any statistical significance. Further details of diagnoses by category are provided in Table 9.5.

Discussion, Health Needs

The findings from this study document actual health needs found among the infants and children of homeless families in Houston. As in the reports of Adler and Drew (1988) and Miller and Lin (1988), respiratory and ear diseases were common in this population. Because upper respiratory tract infections are the most commonly

TABLE 9.3
Health Needs of Infants and Children of Homeless Families in Houston (N = 340)

Disease/Health need category	Frequency	Percent (%)
Respiratory diseases	150	44.12
Immunizations	130	38.24
Skin diseases	62	18.24
TB skin test	61	17.94
Ear diseases	57	16.76
Gastrointestinal diseases	49	14.41
Physical exam	22	6.47
Trauma	21	6.18
Symptom	14	4.12
Eye diseases	13	3.82
Parasitic diseases	9	2.65
Urinary tract diseases	8	2.35
Childhood diseases	6	1.76
Teeth/mouth diseases	6	1.76
Hernia	6	1.76
Nutritional diseases	6	1.76
Foot diseases/disorders	3	0.88
Musculoskeletal diseases	3	0.88
Cardiovascular diseases	3	0.88
Neurologic diseases	2	0.59
Pregnancy related	2	0.59
Gynecological diseases	1	0.29
Sexually transmitted diseases	1	0.29

NOTE: Percentages are based on the number of patients, not on the number of diseases; therefore percentages equal more than 100.

TABLE 9.4
Number of Diagnoses Assessed per Child (N = 340)

Number of Diagnoses	Number of children	Percent (%)
1	147	43.3
2	121	35.6
3	43	12.6
4 or more	29	8.5

diagnosed illnesses among young children (Dershewitz 1988), their frequency in this sample is not unexpected. The significantly higher incidence of respiratory disease in the white and black subsets is most likely a reflection of the larger number of children of these races that had both the diagnosis of respiratory disease and their race documented. Ear disease, particularly otitis media, is also a common illness in children. It accounts for one third of office visits to pediatricians (Macknin 1988). Respiratory and skin diseases are also commonly found among homeless adults (Brickner et al. 1985).

As others have (Acker et al 1987; Adler and Drew 1988; Alperstein et al. 1988),

TABLE 9.5
Description of Diagnoses by Categories

Respiratory diseases: primarily colds and pharyngitis; tonsillitis, pneumonia, asthma, bronchitis
Immunizations: DPT, OPV, MMR; two requests for flu vaccine
Skin diseases: rashes, lesions, tinea, dermatitis, dry scalp, impetigo, wart, blisters, herpes
TB test: PPD used (readings not charted)
Ear diseases: otitis media, one case of dislodged tubes
Gastrointestinal diseases: diarrhea, gastroenteritis, constipation, encopresis
Physical Examination: normal exams
Trauma: hematoma, contusion, human bite, laceration
Symptom: fever, headache
Eye disease: conjunctivitis, vision problem
Parasitic diseases: lice
Urinary tract diseases: dysuria, urinary tract infection
Childhood diseases: chicken pox
Teeth/mouth diseases: thrush, caries
Hernia: inguinal, umbilical
Nutritional diseases: underweight, anorexia
Foot diseases/disorders: swollen foot, blisters, ingrown toenail
Musculoskeletal diseases: infected ingrown toenail, sore legs
Cardiovascular diseases: murmur
Neurologic diseases: epilepsy, seizure
Pregnancy related: pregnancy test
Gynecologic diseases: vaginitis
Sexually transmitted diseases: gonorrhea, chlamydia

NOTE: Descriptors were entered into the data base along with the encoded disease category for only the initial diagnosis of each client; therefore, these descriptors reflect the initial 340 of the total 634 diagnoses.

this study found a large percentage of children of homeless families who had immunization delays. The need for immunization is more frequent among the children five years of age or younger because routine immunizations are recommended from two months through four to six years, leaving only a tetanus diphtheria (Td) to be repeated every ten years throughout life (Rennels 1988). Not only is the risk of communicable disease higher in this population of children, but it also extends to the families and contacts around them, thereby posing a real public health risk.

Tuberculosis is a communicable disease; crowded living conditions (for example, shelters for the homeless) only increase its risk to the public's health. Attempts were made to screen every child over age one year who was seen in the HCH clinics. One of the HCH nurse practitioners reported that approximately 75% of the skin tests were read by the HCH teams and, of those read, approximately 5% were positive; subsequent chest films on this subgroup were negative. With Houston's childhood tuberculosis case rate several times the national average (U.S. Department of Health and Human Services 1989; City of Houston Health Department, personal communication, October 10, 1989), the lack of the disease in this sample is surprising but may be due in part to the fact that most had lived in Houston less than three years. The importance of documented follow-up of children receiving TB skin tests must not be underestimated.

In Houston the HCH project is beginning to meet the health-care needs of the homeless. Access to health care is greatly enhanced by the presence of health-care teams in the shelters. Continuity of care, however, remains a problem, because families are often nomadic. The HCH teams have gone out to the streets occasionally to inform the homeless of the HCH program. As they go to their clients, become their friends, and allow trust to build, the homeless will be even more receptive to their services.

Children of homeless families are spending their critical years of growth and development in unstable environments, placing them at risk for health problems and compromised potential.

With a holistic approach to health care, nurses can well serve this special population of children. In addition, by becoming politically and socially active in the search for solutions to the crisis of homelessness, nurses can influence not only these special lives but also the future of our nation.

References

Acker, P. J., Fierman, A. H., and Dreyer, B. P. (1987). "An Assessment of Parameters of Health Care and Nutrition in Homeless Children." *American Journal of Diseases in Children 141: 388.*

Adler, J. and Drew, L. *(January 1988). Saving the Children. Newsweek*; 58–59.

Alperstein, G., Rappaport, C., and Flanigan, J. (1988). "Health Problems of Homeless Children in New York City." *American Journal of Public Health* 78(9): 1232–37.

Brickner, P. W., Scharer, L. K., Conanan, B., Elvy, A., and Savarese, M., eds. (1985). *Health Care of Homeless People.* New York: Springer.

Dershewitz, R. A. (1988). "The Common Cold." In *Ambulatory Pediatric Care*, edited by R. A. Dershewitz, 666–68. Philadelphia: J. B. Lippincott Company.

Macknin, M. (1988). "Acute Otitis Media." In *Ambulatory Pediatric Care*, edited by R. A. Dershewitz, 361–65. Philadelphia: J. B. Lippincott Company.

Miller, D. S., and Lin, E. H. (1988). "Children in Sheltered Homeless Families: Reported Health Status and Use of Health Services." *Pediatrics* 81(5): 668–73.

National Association of Community Health Centers, Inc. (1989). *Health Care for the Homeless: Background Paper.* Washington, D.C.: National Association of Community Health Centers, Inc.

Rennels, M. B. (1988). "Immunizations." In *Ambulatory Pediatric Care*, edited by R.A. Dershewitz, 50–59. Philadelphia: J. B. Lippincott Company.

Stewart B. McKinney Homeless Assistance Act of 1987 (PL 100–77).

U.S. Conference of Mayors. (1986). *The Continued Growth of Hunger, Homelessness and Poverty in America's Cities: 1986, a 25-city survey.* Washington, D.C.: U.S. Conference of Mayors.

U.S. Department of Health and Human Services, Centers for Disease Control. (1989). *1987 Tuberculosis statistics in the U.S.* (HHS Publication No. CDC 89–8322).

Wright, J. D. (1985). *Health and Homelessness in New York City.* Research Report to the Robert Wood Johnson Foundation. Amherst: University of Massachusetts, Social and Demographic Research Institute.

CHAPTER 10

Providing Quality Child-Care for Homeless Children: A Descriptive Study of the Seattle Experience

Nancy L. Stokley

Abstract

The unique needs of children and staff in two high-quality child-care programs for homeless children in Seattle are discussed from the public health perspective of child-care nurse consultants.

This population has critical need for immunization, acute care, and well-child examination services. Many need a therapeutic child-care environment and referral to mental health services. A high percentage are in need of developmental services, especially speech therapy.

In each area obstacles were overcome including barriers to accurately assessing children, the expense and inconvenience of services, "noncompliant" family issues, and staff burnout.

Caregivers who work with homeless children often despair of providing services that could impact on the overall conditions of the children and adopt an informal policy of resignation. If medical support services are not readily accessible, there is a reluctance to raise many basic issues with parents such as immunizations and well-child exams. Despite public health nursing support, referrals of the children are lost in the survival crisis of the family. Similarly, services need to be available for at least a year after the family becomes housed, or the identified needs of the children will not be met in many cases. Continuous case management is important to ensure follow through by the parent. Staff who work directly with these children need specialized training and ongoing support.

On the positive side, comprehensive, quality child-care services to homeless children can affect their lives significantly. And when the children prosper, the entire family benefits accordingly.

The Child-care Team of the
Seattle-King County Public Health Department

Since 1978, the Seattle-King County Public Health Department has funded public health nurses to function as child-care nurse consultants. This program was well-received by the community and grew to a current funding level of $500,000. Funds came from the City of Seattle General Fund, the city Department of Human Resources, and the King County Current Expense Fund. The program had 1.5 FTE (Full-time equivalent) nutritionists, 1.5 FTE clerical support persons, and 7 FTE public health nurses working to serve roughly 650 centers in the city and county area. They provided support to child-care centers by advising directors on health-related policies, and provide a wide variety of staff in-services on topics such as safety and risk management, infant stimulation, stress reduction, back safety, first aid, CPR, communicable disease, developmentally appropriate curriculum, positive discipline, self-esteem, sexual and physical-abuse detection and reporting, and other topics as requested by staff to meet their particular needs. They coordinated screening services for children in dental, vision, hearing and developmental and behavioral concerns, and made referrals as appropriate. They assessed individual children of concern and were available to meet with parents when concerns arose.

The nurses who worked on the team were public health nurses with a strong background in pediatrics. Our clientele was the population of children who were in licensed child care, and the population of adults who worked in child-care centers. We were not only improving the health of individuals, but our work was population-focussed. Our aim was to raise the quality of child care for all children.

In the past two years, two licensed child-care centers which serve homeless children emerged. (Unlicensed respite care was often available at some shelters, but these two programs were virtually unique in the country in attempting to provide fully licensed care for homeless children.) The needs of these programs were both more intensive and more extensive than those of regular child-care centers.

Morning Song and Our Place Child-care Centers

Morning Song is a child-care center serving the homeless population that is housed in the Seattle Emergency Housing complex adjacent to the child-care site. Families are housed in apartment units and may stay up to six weeks while awaiting permanent housing. The average length of time that a child attends the child-care program is thirty days. At this writing, Morning Song is licensed for twenty children, ages one month to six years, with a total annual operating budget of $153,000. In operation since March 1988, the program is funded by the Federal Office for Substance Abuse Prevention, with the goals of interrupting the family pattern of violence and substance abuse and minimizing their effects on the children.

Our Place Day Care, operating since 1986 under the Catholic Community Services agency, has a $134,000 annual budget and is licensed for twenty children, one to seven years old. The children are bused to the program from five different shelters throughout the city. Families are housed in a variety of arrangements in these five shelters, where maximum length of stay varies from two weeks to three months. Average length of stay in the child-care program is twenty-five days.

In comparison to other child-care settings, the homeless centers have required increased attention to the following needs and problems.

Physical Health Needs of Children Served

In the state of Washington, licensing requirements include provisions that children's immunizations be up to date and that children receive at least one physical exam every year. While this is sometimes a time-consuming requirement for child-care directors to meet, it is certainly feasible. Statewide, 90% of the children enrolled in licensed child-care centers are up to date in their immunizations, according to a survey completed in 1989. The assistance of nurse consultants usually is requested in areas such as drafting policies, parent letters, training staff to complete immunization reports accurately, and the like. But meeting these minimum licensing requirements has been extremely difficult for both homeless child-care programs. A survey of 1989 health records is shown in Table 10.1

During the time that the children attended the child-care centers, Our Place was able to immunize twenty-two children, having the services of a health-care provider on site once a week. This brought their overall immunization compliance level up to 58%. The remaining fifty-three children were not brought up to date on immunizations because of lack of parental permission to complete the immunization schedule, or children were lost to follow-up because of to the transience of the population served. Physical exams were done on thirty-six children, bringing compliance in this area to 100%.

Morning Song children did not have on-site health services but were referred to existing community clinics for immunizations, physical exams, and acute health care as needed. A nurse referred the families to one of three clinics within a two-mile radius of the child-care and housing site and provided bus fare. In the opinion of the child-care staff, this added inconvenience proved overwhelming to this population. The staff were repeatedly frustrated in their attempts to update immunizations, and to secure pertinent medical care and information about the children.

In addition to physical exams and immunizations of children, acute illness was problematic for both centers. The health-care provider for Our Place estimated that there was at least one child acutely ill on 40% of her weekly visits. Those statistics are shown in Table 10.2

Anecdotally, a similar incidence of acute illness affected the children at Morning Song, but referral to outside services was more difficult for the staff to facilitate

TABLE 10.1
Immunizations and Physical Examinations

	Our Place Children Enrolled ($N = 128$)	%	Morning Song Children Enrolled ($N = 104$)	%
At time of enrollment:				
Immunizations complete	53	(41%)	34	(33%)
Immunizations incomplete	58	(46%)	63	(60%)
Parents say "yes" but no written history	17	(13%)	7	(6%)
Physical exam in past year	81	(78%)	No Data	
Physical exam over a year ago	19	(14%)	No Data	
Parents don't remember	28	(22%)	No Data	

TABLE 10.2
Reported Illnesses

	N
Upper respiratory infections	49
Positive strep cultures	11
Scarlet fever	4
Acute otitis media	7
Gastrointestinal problems	12

TABLE 10.3
Mental Health Needs

	N
Severe depression	2
Burns	2
Suspected sexual abuse	2
Reported emotional abuse	3
Possible or reported physical abuse	2

and statistics were not kept. Staff problems that resulted from the children's health problems will be discussed in the following section.

Emotional Health Needs of Children

The health-care provider at Our Place documented the emotional health needs of children in 1989 (see Table 10.3).

It was the opinion of the physician's assistant who collected these statistics that these numbers were considerably lower than the actual cases of abuse and neglect among these children. Additional training in recognizing and treating mental health concerns was requested.

Morning Song did not collect statistics but described the effects of homelessness on the children as including developmental delays, for example, children unable to speak at age three, lack of social and play skills, lack of experience with sitting down to eat, older children playing parent to younger siblings, and children experiencing many losses (friends, home, and possessions). As part of their goal of minimizing the traumatic effects of substance abuse on the children, Morning Song provided the services of a play therapist on site.

Child-care nurse consultants found that emotional and behavioral concerns crop up with distressing regularity in all child-care centers, such as a child who is "acting out," "seeking negative attention," "too aggressive," and the like. At the homeless centers, the problems were much worse. Often severely withdrawn children refused to talk or interact at all. When angry behaviors surfaced, they were severe and prolonged.

It often took weeks for children's true abilities and developmental level to emerge, as they gradually learned that this was a safe place with predictable routines and plenty to eat. It was rewarding for staff to see a child gain the confidence to move into a housekeeping corner to play and make believe like any normal child, except that the game played was often not "house," but "moving."

A developmental screening test was done, as time permitted, on children at Our Place. When initial testing showed delays, staff were informed, and some special attention was focussed on those areas while the child was in care. Retesting was done on these children before they left the program, and they generally showed significant improvement. But there were many children for whom the staff recommended referral to developmental programs once the family was stabilized.

Problems with Appropriate Referrals and Follow-up for Identified Problems

It is now clear that families in need of basic survival requirements such as food, clothing, and housing cannot prioritize a routine immunization for their child, especially when accomplishing it requires a bus trip. Many of the health-care needs of the population at Morning Song were "appropriately referred," but, in fact, the services were never pursued and received for the children; witness the high statistics of incomplete immunizations previously noted. Similarly, at both sites, referrals due to concern over children's emotional needs, developmental delays, dental work, etc., were at times considered, and then postponed or shelved indefinitely by staff as unrealistic, given the situation within the family unit at the time.

Through no fault of the staff involved, it was simply true that a child who would be a clear focus of concern in a middle-class child-care center did not stand out from the group at a homeless center. In order to realize the benefits of a child-care program for homeless children, service must continue long after the family has stabilized.

At the present time, there is little provision at either site for the follow-up of children after they leave the child-care setting. Some services for parents, such as mental health counseling, drug and alcohol treatment programs, and prenatal care continue after the family is relocated and stabilized. But the children need follow-up as well. Increased case management services to families in transitional housing are necessary so that referrals for services to the children may be acted upon after other more basic survival needs have been met.

To summarize appropriate identification and referral of health needs of children: Because of the high turnover rates of children, and families under extreme stress, frequent on-site visits by a health-care provider are necessary if minimum licensing standards are to be met in child-care centers for the homeless. Identification of underlying emotional and developmental needs should be done only after the child has had a few weeks to adjust to the new environment. Referrals should be made after the family situation has stabilized, thus an extensive program of family follow-up must be in place to realize effective referral of problems identified.

Increased Training Needs of Staff

Typically, child-care centers required frequent training sessions because of the high turnover of staff (40% annually nationwide). While director's concerns varied it was possible to anticipate training needs and prepare some relatively standardized in-service workshops for child-care staff. The most requested programs of the Seattle King County Health Department were on risk management, communicable disease prevention, and behavior management. These programs very often did NOT meet the needs of homeless children's caretakers without substantial modification. To illustrate:

1) Extreme programmatic instability and turnover. In the past year, both programs have changed location, and one has also experienced two new directors and a change in the parent agency. In this year, every staff member at Our Place has left the program. This instability increased the already high staff stress levels.

Under these conditions priorities for in-service topics change rapidly. The program must achieve some level of programmatic and staff stability before staff can assimilate new information or effectively solve problems. In this respect, they were just like the families they serve, who prioritized their survival needs over routine immunizations.

Staff in both programs reported great frustration in their jobs, even under the best of conditions. They were working with traumatized children, had only a short time to bond with them and saw improvements, and then lost them as parents moved on. Grieving was an everyday part of the job and was simply too much for many caretakers. Most who stayed adopted a "one-day-at-a-time" mentality and fortified themselves with the belief that a single contact with a child CAN make a difference.

2) Efforts at routine communicable disease control were complicated by sev-

eral factors, including the high rates of serious illness in the children and difficulties in obtaining convenient medical care, as detailed above. But there were additional factors in homeless children's lives to consider. A normally housed child, sent home ill from school, can look forward to an afternoon of extra attention from mother, perhaps a visit with the doctor, some chicken soup, and a long nap. Knowing this, most child-care workers eagerly embrace the concept of sending sick children home. The job of nurse consultants was to train them in recognizing the appropriate symptoms and to bolster their assertiveness skills in confronting parents in order to enforce a consistent policy.

However, these children were being sent back to parents who were on the streets all day. Most shelter operators at the time frowned on any excuse to stay in the shelters during the day. Out of concern for the children, the staff at Our Place initially refused to apply the recommended exclusion policies. In spite of high illness rates among themselves as well as the children, staff members continued to accept and care for ill children. Clearly, the usual approaches were useless in this situation.

At this point, the public health nurse made the decision to intervene directly with the shelter operators, on behalf of her clients. Both the children and the child-care providers themselves needed an advocate for their health. The nurse called the child-care licensor and enlisted her support. Then, she approached the shelter operators. She presented the recommended exclusion policy of the Seattle-King County Health Department for ill children with communicable diseases. She spoke of the needs of ill children for increased rest and support from family members. She argued that sick children had a right to be cared for by their parents in a sheltered environment, and that child-care workers had the right and duty to refuse to care for ill children.

The shelter managements initially responded with the rationale behind their policy, but they rather quickly capitulated to our arguments and reversed it. Since then, they continued to allow parents with ill children the luxury of a sheltered bed during the daytime hours. The child-care workers began enforcing a reasonable exclusion policy which protected their own health as well as that of the children in group care.

In addition, the staff and public health nurse advocated with the Health Care for the Homeless program to obtain on-site services of a health-care provider to treat acute illnesses quickly. (The provider in this case was a physician's assistant, but could also be a pediatric or family nurse practitioner.) Since then, communicable disease problems at Our Place have been minimal and manageable.

The other child-care center, Morning Song, had families housed in their own apartment-style units, so they could easily send children back to their transitional housing if the child was ill. Their frustrations centered on the lack of an on-site practitioner. At this writing, they were engaged in data collection to document the failure rate of the referrals that were made for immunizations, physical exams, and acute care needs. Then the health department joined them in advocating for increased funding for on-site practitioner services.

Working with these centers has been extremely rewarding. The staff often were determined to overcome all obstacles and were extremely dedicated to the well-being of the children and their families. Great progress was made in stabilizing both programs and achieving minimum standards in intake procedures. The centers worked together and learned from each other's difficulties and successes. The gaps in services necessary to really impact on these children's lives positively were being addressed. Specifically, Seattle now has a Homeless Children's Network, which is a planning group for comprehensive child-care services for homeless children. In the next few years, hopes were to greatly expand available services for these children in crisis. We hoped to provide care for infants through school age and articulate with the school's programs to meet the developmental needs of children from birth to eighteen years. Medical, psychological and emotional needs will be assessed, and services to meet these needs after the family has been stabilized in housing are being planned.

One of the mothers who used Our Place child-care at a time of crisis in her life now sits on the Advisory Board. She chose the theme for the first open house to increase public support of the program. "We are celebrating our children," she said, "and they are all our children." Public health nurses are proud to be a small part of this process.

References

Alperstein, G., Rappaport, C., and Flanigan, J. (Sept 1988). "Health Problems of Homeless Children in New York City," *American Journal of Public Health* 78, no. 9:1232–1233.

Bassuk, E., and Rosenberg, L. (July 1988). "Why Does Homelessness Occur? a Case-Control Study," *American Journal of Public Health* 78, no. 7: 783–788.

Calugas, C., Lagerlund, L., Parker, L., Pascua, C., and Nelson, E. (Winter 1989). "Shelter from the Storm: Assessment of a Need for Day Care for Infants of the Homeless," U.W. Nursing Students Community Project.

Emergency Housing Coalition, December 15, 1988. Press release. Seattle, WA.

Erickson, J., and Wilhelm, C. *Housing the Homeless*, State University of New Jersey, Center for Urban Policy Research, New Brunswick, N.J. 1986.

Gewirtzman, R. and Fodor, I. (May–June 1987). "The Homeless Child at School: From Welfare Hotel to Classroom," *Child Welfare* 66, no. 3.

Goldberg, K., and Montague, W. (April 22, 1987). "Shelter Kids—Homeless Children Posing Special Problems for Educators, Policymakers, Social Workers." *Education Week* 6, no. 30.

Hudson, G. E. (Nov. 30, 1988). "Shelter from the Storm: A Day Care Center for Seattle's Homeless Children."

Kyle, J., ed. "Programs that Work at the Local Level." National League of Cities, 1986.

Layzer, J., Goddson, B., and DeLange, C. (March/April 1986). "Children in Shelters." *Children Today*, 15, no. 6: 6–12.

McConnell, P. (Feb. 16, 1989). "Learning the Hard Lessons of Life: Homeless Kids are Tough Test for City Schools." *Seattle Post-Intelligencer*; p. 1.

Phillips, M. Kronenfeld, D., and Jeter, V., 1986. "A Model of Services to Homeless Families in Shelters," Housing the Homeless (ed. by J. Erickson and C. Wilhelm). New Brunswick, N.J.: State University of New Jersey Center for Urban Policy Research, p. 322–334.

Public Technology, Inc., "Caring for the Hungry and Homeless—Exemplary Programs," sponsored by Emergency Food and Shelter National Board Program, 115–17.

Toelle, M., and Kerwin, S. (Sept.–Oct. 1988). "Children in Transition," *Children Today* 17 no. 27–31.

Weingarten, P. (Oct. 8, 1987). "Homeless Children Plead: 'When Are We Going Home?' " *The Seattle Times*; B1.

Wells, A. S. (Feb. 22, 1989). "Effort to Reach Homeless Students Puts Increasing Strain on Schools," *The New York Times*; 25.

CHAPTER 11

Model for Assessment of Homeless Children

Martha J. Kemsley
Juanita K. Hunter

Abstract

The health-care needs of homeless children vary from common short-term illnesses to long-term developmental and behavioral problems. A model for screening and assessment of children in homeless shelters was developed by the staff of the Nursing Center for the Homeless at the School of Nursing at the University at Buffalo at New York. The model provides a framework for nursing intervention that maximizes the expertise of the community health nurse and pediatric nurse practitioner.

Recent findings that families with young children are the fastest growing component of the homeless population have yet to raise the social conscience of society about the long-range consequences of this contemporary problem. It has been estimated that families comprise 35% of the homeless nationally and more than 50% in some cities (American Academy of Pediatrics 1988; Damrosch et al. 1988). Studies have found that more than half of homeless children are under six years of age (Bassuk and Rosenberg 1988; Miller and Lin 1988; Parker et al. 1991). Of significant concern is the prediction that single women with children will soon represent the majority of the homeless population in the United States.

Lack of affordable housing and increasing poverty are considered the primary causes of homelessness in the United States today (Wood 1989). Indeed, one in five children live in poverty with the ratio even greater for children under the age of five years (National Association of Community Health Centers, 1991). Additionally, personal crises such as divorce and family violence may precipitate homelessness, thus increasing the number of single women with children.

The impact of homelessness on children is significant and far-reaching. Life in a shelter is anxiety provoking, noisy, and stressful. Few shelters can afford professional staff to meet the needs of homeless children. The unpleasantness associated with unexpected departure or eviction from their homes disrupts normal routines and may result in behavioral manifestations of increased aggression, withdrawal, disturbed eating and sleeping patterns, and regressive behaviors. Children are frequently separated from their friends, schoolmates, and usual sources of recreation when relocated into homeless shelters. Many homeless children, often witness to and/or victims of family neglect/violence, feel responsible for the family disruption.

Communal shelter life may include new rules, restricted physical space, and lack of adequate exercise and diet, thus creating additional problems for the child. The often nutritionally inadequate meals provided in shelters, frequently high in carbohydrates, cholesterol, fat, and salt, vary from none to one a day. Fast foods and junk foods are common to these children's diets (Bass et al. 1990; Wright 1991). Limited storage place in the shelter and access to refrigeration prevents the parents' participation in supplemental food programs such as Women Infants and Children's Program (WIC).

The health problems of homeless children are similar to those of other children from low socioeconomic backgrounds: dental problems, anemia, lead poisoning, and visual problems. They lack access to health care, particularly preventive care (Arnstein and Alperstein 1988), and are more frequently exposed to communicable diseases, upper respiratory infections, and passive smoking. Head lice, scabies, and ringworm are common in this population and spread quickly among children in shelters (Wood et al. 1990; Parker et al. 1991).

Studies have documented that homeless children have increased incidences of developmental delays, emotional problems, and learning difficulties (Bassuk and Rubin 1987; Lewis and Meyers 1989, Parker et al. 1991).

The Nursing Center for the Homeless at the School of Nursing at the University at Buffalo has provided services to a segment of the homeless population of the city of Buffalo, New York, since January 1988. The project is supported in part by the Special Project Grants Program in the Nursing Education Practice Resources Branch, Division of Nursing, U.S. Department of Health and Human Services, Public Health Service, Health Resources and Services Administration, Bureau of Health Professions Administration, Grant # 5010 60003-04. The center is based upon a nurse-managed model. The services provided by the center include health assessment and nursing interventions, counseling, health education, social work, transportation, and referral. Services are provided at four sites, two of which are specifically for women and children and families. The Nursing Center has provided specific services to children since November 1989. The staff for the children's component includes community health nurses, pediatric nurse practitioners, a social worker, a psychiatric/mental health nurse, and a physician consultant.

The goal of the services is to provide on-site health services to the sheltered children and to promote positive health behaviors. The objectives are to screen all children for acute and communicable illnesses, evidence of abuse/neglect, growth and developmental delays, behavioral problems, and health education needs.

The Nursing Center for the Homeless was established with a conceptual model of differentiated nursing practice utilizing a community health nurse and nurse practitioner. As the children's service system evolved, it became apparent that the skill and collaboration of both nurse providers were needed to meet the multiple needs of homeless children and their families. Thus, it became important to distinguish between the specific functions of the community health nurse and pediatric nurse. Focusing on populations at risk and the improvement of personal and environmental health, community health nurses emphasize health through concentration on the wellness end of the wellness-illness continuum (Williams 1991). The practice is general, comprehensive, and not limited to a particular group or diagnosis, with emphasis on continuity of care. Community health focus is especially needed when addressing the needs of homeless children (Stanhope 1988).

Pediatric nurse practitioners use the nursing process in providing direct and indirect nursing services to children and their families in the specific areas of health promotion, illness prevention, and health restoration. They manage actual and potential health problems, which include common diseases and responses to disease. Pediatric nurse practitioners promote the psychological, physical, and developmental well-being of the child through an ongoing relationship with the child and the child's family. Consultation and referral occur as needed as does collaboration with other health professionals (American Nurses Association 1991).

Within this context, the Nursing Center staff developed a model for screening and referral of homeless children. The model was developed as a framework for providing care and maximizing the expertise of the community health nurse and pediatric nurse practitioner.

The model is presented in Table 11.1. As can be seen in column 1, differentiation among well children, children with physical complaints, and children with behavioral concerns is made. In column 2 sources of health care or lack thereof are identified. In column 3 assessments made are identified, and in column 4 interventions based upon the previous information are presented.

This model has been found useful in providing guidelines for screening the health status of the homeless children seen by the staff of the Nursing Center. Specifically, the community health nurse can complete the initial screening, identify health problems requiring further investigation, and triage for those situations most suited to the skills of the pediatric nurse practitioner. The pediatric nurse practitioner examines those children with definite physical symptoms, complaints, or developmental or behavioral concerns and provides the mother and child with health assurance, diagnosis, and treatment as indicated or referral as necessary. Both nurses provide parent/child education and follow up. The community health nurse adds the skill of interdisciplinary collaboration common to working with clients in communities in addressing the issues related to linkage of homeless children to the broader health-care system. It is recognized that the child is part of a larger unit, the family, whose immediate and long-term needs for safety, housing assistance, education, occupational training, and employment must be addressed.

TABLE 11.1
Procedure for Health Screening in Children's Clinic

Presentation	Source of Care	Assessments	Interventions
Well Child (no complaints)	Regular source of health care	Health Screen –growth and development –S & Sx of infection –S & Sx of abuse/neglect –Health History	Health Education –nutrition –safety –parenting –shelter effects (CHN or PNP)
Well Child (no complaints)	No regular source of health care	Health Screen as above Physical Exam (PNP)	Health Education Reinforce importance of regular care
Child with physical complaints	Regular source of care	Health Screen Hx specific to complaint Physical Exam (PNP)	Management and and treatment of Sx (PNP) Refer to PMD if needed
Child with physical complaints	No regular source of care	Health Screen Hx specific to complaint Complete Physical Exam (PNP) Schedule appointments (PNP or CHN)	Management and treatment of SX (PNP) Refer to primary care source
Child with Behavior Problems –frequent crying –temper tantrums –withdrawn, does not talk or communicate –bizarre behavior –physical attack on others		Health Screen Hx of stated behavior Complete Physical Exam (PNP)	Health education Parent/child Refer to appropriate resource when indicated (e.g., PMD, pediatric consultant, family counseling) (PNP or CHN)

CHN–Community Health Nurse
PNP–Pediatric Nurse-Practitioner

S & Sx–Signs and Symptoms
Hx–History
PMD–Private Medical Doctor

The desired outcomes of these activities are optimal growth and development and decreased mortality, morbidity, and disability for all children.

The importance of health-maintenance services for all children, which include routine screening, preventive health care, and health promotion activities, is accepted as a vital component in maintaining a healthy society. The objectives of preventive heath care of children are: 1) promotion of health and prevention of disease through health assessment, health education, and immunizations; 2) early detection and treatment of disease through health history, screening, and physical exam; and 3) guidance in the psychosocial aspects of child rearing (Hoekelman 1987). Concerted attention is needed to implement these objectives with homeless children. Indeed, the future of society is dependent upon the health and well being of today's children.

References

American Academy of Pediatrics, Committee on Community Health Services. (1988). "Health Needs of Homeless Children." *Pediatrics* 82; 938–40.

American Nurses Association. (1991). *Professional Certification–1991 Certification Catalogue*. Kansas City, Mo: American Nurses Credentialing Center.

Arnstein, E., and Alperstein, G. (1988). "Homeless Children and Families: Health Concerns." *Feelings and Their Medical Significance*. 30; 1. Ross Laboratories.

Bass, J., Brennan, P., Mehta, K., and Kodzis, S. (1990). "Pediatric Problems in a Suburban Shelter for Homeless Families." *Pediatrics* 85; 33–38.

Bassuk, E. L., and Rubin, L. (1987). "Homeless Children: A Neglected Population." *American Journal of Orthopsychiatry* 57; 279–86.

Bassuk, E. L., and Rosenberg, L. (1988). "Why Does Family Homelessness Occur? A Case Control Study." *American Journal of Pediatric Health* 78; 783–88.

Committee on Health for Homeless People, Institute of Medicine. (1988). *Homelessness, Health, and Human Needs* 2–14. Washington, D.C.: National Academy Press.

Damrosch, S. P., Sullivan, P. A., Schoeller, A., and Gaines, J. (1988). "On Behalf of Homeless Families." *MCN* 13; 259–63.

Hammersley, M. (Sept. 25, 1989). "Public School Officials Say 62% of Pupils are Existing in Poverty." *Buffalo News*: B–1.

Hoekelman, R. (1987). *Pediatric Primary Care*. St. Louis: C.V. Mosby.

Jefferson, J. (Sept. 30, 1991). "America's Poor Number 33.6 Million." *Buffalo Evening News* A–6.

Lewis, M. R., and Meyers, A. F. (1989). "The Growth and Development Status of Homeless Children Entering Shelters in Boston." *Public Health Reports* 104(3): 247–50.

Miller D. S., and Lin, E. H. (1988). "Children in Sheltered Homeless Families: Reported Health Status and Use of Health Services." *Pediatrics* 81; 668–73.

National Association of Community Health Center (1991). Access to Community Health Care, 6. Wash. D.C.

Parker, R., Rescorla, L., Finkelstein, J., Barnes, N., Holmes, J., and Stolley, P. (1991). "A Survey of the Health of Homeless Children in Philadelphia Shelters." *American Journal of Diseases in Children* 145; 520–26.

Stanhope, M., Lancaster, J. (1988). *Community Health Nursing*. St. Louis: C.V. Mosby.

Williams, C. (1991). "Community Health Nursing—What Is It?" In *Readings in Community Health Nursing*, edited by B.W. Spradley 87–94. Philadelphia, Pa.: J. B. Lippincott.

Wood, D. (1989). "Homeless Children: Their evaluation and treatment." *Journal of Pediatric Health Care* 3, 194–99.

Wood, D., Valdez, R., Hayashi, T., and Shen, A. (1990). "Health of Homeless Children and Housed, Poor Children." *Pediatrics* 86; 858–66.

Wright, J. (1991). "Children in and of the Streets." *American Journal of Diseases in Children* 145; 516–19.

Considerations in the Design, Implementation, and Evaluation of a Homeless Project in Nursing

CHAPTER 12

Role of Clinical Nurse Specialist in Homeless Populations

Martha J. Pituch
Mary A. Kiplinger

Abstract

The role of the clinical nurse specialist as practitioner, educator, consultant, and researcher in working with homeless populations is explored. Three clinical nurse specialists assigned to homeless centers describe the establishment and implementation of on-site nursing clinics for homeless individuals and families. Health-care problems presented by clients are reviewed, including the nursing diagnoses developed. Faculty practice is addressed, including the benefits and problems encountered as clinical nurse specialists in a nursing clinic for the homeless.

This chapter will be of interest to clinical nurse specialists and others establishing a primary nursing clinic for homeless individuals and families.

The role of the clinical nurse specialist has been described in a variety of nursing settings; however, it has not been clearly defined for the specialty of nurses working with the homeless population.

The clinical nurse specialist is defined as a graduate of a master's degree program in nursing, with a major in a clinical specialty. The practice is based on advanced knowledge of nursing theory, bio-psycho-social theory, and research. The primary role components have been classified into that of practitioner/therapist, teacher, consultant, and researcher (Hamric and Spross 1989). This chapter will describe the role of three clinical nurse specialists, two of whom are prepared in community health nursing and one in psychiatric/mental health nursing, practicing in shelters serving homeless families in Toledo, Ohio. It will address their roles as practitioner/therapist, teacher, consultant, and researcher. A brief description of the centers in which the nursing role is carried out is provided.

Two of the clinical nurse specialists (Anderson and Pituch) are assigned to St. Paul's Community Center/Shelter, which offers comprehensive on-site services providing more than 3,700 nursing encounters to homeless adults annually. The nursing clinic, located in the center, has been in operation for six years. It was developed as a clinical site for undergraduate and graduate students in community health and psychiatric/mental health nursing at the Medical College of Ohio School of Nursing. For the past three years it has served as a faculty practice site, which extends the clinic service to five days per week and provides evening and weekend call service. Nursing faculty are identified as part of the staff of the center and participate in staff meetings and decisions made there. A portion of the faculty salaries is supported by McKinney Grant Funds, the additional support by in-kind services of the college.

The Toledo Community Service Center is a shelter/center for homeless families. Formerly a YMCA, it has been renovated to provide temporary housing for an average of thirty families. It provides comprehensive services to families, including a preschool program. The nursing clinic, which began approximately two and a half years ago, operates five days per week. McKinney Grant Funds supply the salary for one nursing position and for equipment and supplies for the clinic. The nursing clinic is staffed by a master's prepared clinical nurse specialist (Kiplinger) and serves as a clinical placement for undergraduate and graduate nursing students at the Medical College of Ohio School of Nursing.

The nursing clinics in both centers are staffed entirely by nurses but are integrally linked with other agencies in the homeless health-care network, including services related to medical care, mental health and substance abuse, dental and tertiary emergency care, prescription service, transportation service and outreach. The Cordelia Martin Health Center, a primary-care health center, serves as the coordinating body of the homeless network. Protocols for practice in an expanded nursing role are approved by the medical staff at the Cordelia Martin Health Center.

The goal of the nursing clinic program is to promote the health and well-being of homeless individuals and families by increasing their self-care skills. Each of the clinical nurse-specialists utilizes Dorothea Orem's Self-Care Deficit of Nursing theory as a framework for practice. The staff feels that the self-care framework is particularly appropriate to the homeless clients they serve, as it promotes self-reliance and dignity. They have found that most clients can and do assume responsibility and accountability for their health if they are assisted in practicing self-care methods, and if the expectation of self care is clearly defined. The role between client and nurse becomes one of a partnership in health. The clients become able to identify their strengths and limitations in self-care and can seek and use the assistance of the nurse and other health-care providers more appropriately and effectively. As a result of the growth in the clients, the staff find that clients develop increased self-esteem and become their own self-care agents. Some even become teachers of self-care to other clients. Those who use the nursing clinic become one of the major referral sources for new clients. Nursing diagnoses are structured in the self-care format.

A major assumption of the Self-Care Deficit Theory of Nursing is that each individual has the potential for developing skills for self care. If there is a deficit or deficiency in the client's ability to carry out needed care due to lack of knowledge, motivation, or ability, then nursing's role is to assist the client toward self care. In the nursing clinic serving homeless individuals or families, the appropriate nursing systems are supportive/educative (that is, teaching the client about self care), or partially compensatory (where the nurse does for/or acts for the client until he is able to act alone).

Nursing service is provided to clients in the clinic and other community settings. Clinic services include physical and mental health assessment and counseling; treatment of minor illness, utilizing expanded nursing skills and emergency care; referral, and health teaching with emphasis on self care. "Home visits" are made to clients living in single room occupancy hotels (SRO's) or group homes if necessary. Where possible, follow-up "home visits" also are made to clients who leave the shelter to assure continuity of care. Clients are accompanied to health-care visits, emergency room visits, and out-patient surgery as necessary. If clients are hospitalized, they are visited or phoned daily. The nursing students play a vital role in these extended services.

Practitioner Role

Upon admission to the shelter/center, clients are given a complete physical and mental health assessment, which incorporates the universal, developmental, and health deviation self-care requisites described by Orem. Special attention is given to a drug and sexual history. The client's ability (adult or parent, if child) to carry out self-care is then determined. If there is a deficit in the client's knowledge, motivation, or ability to carry out the needed care, then the nurse provides an appropriate educative/supportive or partially compensatory nursing system.

The type and amount of teaching is determined from the client assessment. Clients are instructed about health habits that promote wellness, how to assess their own health, and instruction on how to treat emergencies and minor illness. Emphasis is placed on assisting the clients(s) to use the health-care system appropriately by identifying when and where to seek health care, how to make and cancel appointments appropriately, and how to talk to health-care providers, so that they are empowered to take charge of their health. They are instructed in how to carry out prescribed treatments and about the proper administration of prescription and over-the-counter medications. They are given a copy of easy-to-understand instructions related to the action and side effects of medications. Clients are taught appropriate ways to protect themselves from the elements, and, if they lack appropriate clothing, the nurse works with their caseworker in securing it. Instruction on proper foot care and wound care is provided. Once they have been instructed, they then come to the clinic and carry out their own care, with supervision by the nurse.

If medical or related care is required, appropriate referrals are made. After the visit, the client reports to the clinic, and the medical regimen is reviewed with the client to assess his/her understanding of it and ability and intention to carry it out. Clients are then asked to report to the nurse periodically to determine the effectiveness of the treatment.

Personal counseling is an integral part of the nursing service. Clients often present themselves to the clinic for physical reasons; however, after assisting them with the presenting problem, it is found that they really needed someone to confide in and relate to. Clients are frequently alienated from their families and loved ones and have no close friends. Many come from dysfunctional family systems, may have experienced severe physical and psychological abuse, and have acquired coping behaviors that are incompatible with appropriate social functioning. Their mistrust of people and the "system" has resulted in their being closed to sharing feelings and themselves. The nursing staff use counseling techniques to help the clients work through some of their problems and to take responsibility for their behavior. Developing self-esteem is a major component of the counseling role. The nurse also often assists the clients in identifying the need for more extensive counseling and in linking them to an appropriate mental health or drug counseling center. Many clients report to the nursing clinic daily to get a hello, a smile, a handshake, or a hug. For many of the clients, the clinic staff serves as a surrogate family and an "anchor."

A partially compensatory nursing system is required when clients lack the ability to carry out self care and require more assistance from professionals. Some clients with chronic conditions such as diabetes, hypertension, or chronic lung disease are routinely monitored. Blood sugars and blood pressures are taken and recorded, and the results are given to the clients to present on medical visits. A few of the clients with chronic obstructive pulmonary disease (COPD) come in regularly for a "pulmonary toileting."

If clients have difficulty in using the health-care system because of alienation, confusion, or fear, the clinical nurse specialist or designate accompanies the client on the first health-care visit to outside agencies and acts as an advocate/mentor for the client. Once the clients have established relationships with these providers, they are able to continue with the care, including making and keeping appointments. Close coordination is provided between other health-care providers and the staff at the nursing clinic. For clients who are severely mentally disabled, the nurse and/or the caseworker will accompany the client to each outside health visit. If the client requires hospital emergency care, surgery, or admission to the hospital, the nurse or designate accompanies the client. During the hospitalization, the client is called or visited regularly.

Group health screenings are conducted quarterly for hypertension, anemia, cholesterol, blood glucose, and sickle cell anemia. This has provided an excellent method for case finding. The screening is provided through the service of a mobile unit of one of the local hospitals.

Teacher Role

Health instruction is provided both to individuals and groups of clients. Group health sessions are held weekly in the center, and all clients are invited to participate. The educational sessions range from thirty minutes to one hour and focus on health problems and issues common to the population. Educational programs on health-related topics also have been presented to the staffs in the centers. Giving clinical instruction to students enrolled in the baccalaureate and master's degree programs is an integral part of the clinical nurse specialist's role. Approximately twenty students per quarter are assigned to the two shelters. The clinical nurse specialist provides clinical supervision and mentorship to the students.

Consultant Role

Consultant activities of the clinical nurse specialist are numerous, both within the shelter and with outside agencies. Major functions have been to interpret the clinical nurse specialist role and services of the nursing clinic and networking with other staff. The clinical nurse specialist takes an active role in planning and evaluating agency programs. Daily conferences are held with caseworkers to coordinate client care within the agency. The clinical nurse specialist participates in multiagency staffings for selected clients and works collaboratively with the local school district to provide integration of students into the educational system. Serving as an agency representative on interagency committees is also a part of the nursing role. Nurses in the respective shelters act as consultants to each other.

Researcher Role

Through the care of the clients in this special population, many nursing questions evolve that are appropriate for further study. The research questions range from simple to complex. A recently completed research study, *Health and Self-care of the Homeless,* identified self-care practices of the homeless and facilitated the development of appropriate nursing interventions for the population. Orem's Self Care Deficit Theory of Nursing provided the framework for the study. Health assessment forms have been developed, tested, and revised to meet the needs of this special population and a resource directory has been developed to promote better collaboration and referral. Additional research studies are being planned to answer the questions raised in nursing practice. Several grants have been obtained through the Ohio Minority Coalition on Health to conduct special programs in the shelters on hypertension and family violence.

In conclusion, the clinical nurse specialist possesses the sophisticated use of clinical knowledge, systematic assessment and intervention, independent clinical decision making, and accountability that are required to provide care to the homeless. Through education and experience, the caregiver is able to view the client from a holistic and health-oriented perspective, incorporating education, consultation, and research as a part of the role. The use of the Self Care Deficit Theory of Nursing as a framework for practice has proved invaluable with the homeless population. When clients are assisted in and expected to take responsibility for their health, they are accountable and responsible and feel better about themselves.

References

Note: The authors wish to acknowledge the contribution of Judith Anderson, MSN, assistant professor, Medical College of Ohio School of Nursing in the development of the Clinical Nurse Specialist Role in the homeless population in Toledo, Ohio.

Hamric, A. and Spross, J. (1989). The Clinical Nurse Specialist in Theory and Practice. New York; Grune and Stratton.

CHAPTER 13

Essentials of Establishing an Outreach Health-Care Unit for the Homeless

Catherine L. Hopkins

Abstract

The Outreach Health Care Unit (OHCU) at the Homeless Services Network (HSN) and its other locations is a unit of the Center for Nursing Research and Clinical Practice, Lienhard School of Nursing, Pace University, Pleasantville, New York. It provides nurse-managed primary health-care services to the homeless families of Yonkers, New York. Family nurse practitioners, in collaboration with a family practice physician, provide primary health services to this high-risk population. The OHCU also serves as a clinical site for undergraduate and graduate nursing students and practice medical residents.

The OHCU is unique in several ways. At the HSN services are initiated from a centralized Coordinated Services Center which functions as a central intake, assessment, and referral site for homeless families in Yonkers. In nursing the role of the health-case manager is seen as a strategy of the advanced practitioner of nursing and could reflect any of several areas of clinical specialization. The nurse practitioner works closely with the other team members in designing a complete care plan. This model in interdisciplinary collaboration enhances access through immediacy of professional action from team members in helping high-risk individuals and families with multiple needs.

Community-based, nurse-managed primary care can be more responsive to the homeless. It emphasizes the autonomy and comprehensive nature of professional nursing and the effectiveness of interdisciplinary relationships. Access to clients and management of care can provide a sound basis for nursing research in practice. Key factors in establishing a health-care unit are: documentation of need, ensuring financial viability, professional liability, prescriptive privileges, and quality assurance. These will be discussed in relation to the development and implementation of the OHCU at its various locations.

Description of the Settings

In December 1985, under the auspices of the Westchester County Department of Community Mental Health, several community agencies met to discuss the development of a network of health and human service delivery systems for homeless families. As a result of this and subsequent meetings, the HSN was established in January 1987 as a demonstration project to provide centralized and coordinated services to meet the complex physical, social and health needs of homeless families living in Westchester County. The HSN is a consortium of both private and public agencies that collaborate and actively participate in providing a comprehensive and integrated service delivery system for homeless families who are living in motels and emergency housing. These agencies include Pace University's Lienhard School of Nursing, Center for Preventive Psychiatry, Student Advocacy, Westhab, Westchester Department of Social Services, the Sharing Community, the Yonkers Youth Connection, and others.

The HSN functions as a central intake, assessment, and referral site for homeless families housed in Yonkers and throughout Westchester, Putnam, Dutchess, and Rockland Counties. When a family presents to the HSN, a social worker does an intake assessment. Based on the data collected during the intake interview, the social worker makes referrals to the various providers in the Network. The services offered by the different agencies include provision of physical and mental health care, social services case management, housing education and advocacy, school/student advocacy, tutoring, parent-child therapeutic play groups, preschool programs for four-year-olds, and hot lunches.

The service providers meet weekly to discuss the individual needs of each family. Thus, there is an interdisciplinary approach to families with very complex problems.

The Sharing Community is a private, not-for-profit organization formed in 1983 to meet the critical needs of the homeless and hungry in southwest Yonkers, the most economically depressed quadrant in Westchester County. The establishment of the program was an outgrowth of efforts by community leaders, advocates, service providers, business leaders, and clergy.

The Sharing Community currently operates the largest shelter and the largest soup kitchen in Westchester County. The Emergency Shelter Program provides service-intensive accommodations for sixty homeless persons each night. While at the shelter, the guests are assisted with immediate and long-term needs by a professional staff of social workers, nurses, a substance-abuse counselor, and a housing specialist. Some of the beds each night are reserved for people seeking emergency shelter after Department of Social Services "business" hours.

The Soup Kitchen at the Sharing Community provides a free, nutritionally-balanced midday meal to approximately 230 people daily, 365 days per year. It is the only meal of the day for many of the soup kitchen guests; for all of them it is their main meal. Through a contract with the Westchester County Department of

Community Mental Health and other sources of support, the guests at the soup kitchen receive other services as well. The social workers assist guests with issues ranging from crisis intervention to employment, transportation, substance abuse, eviction, entitlements, clothing, food pantry referrals, medical and detoxification referrals, and interpersonal and general counseling.

The Model of the Outreach Health-Care Unit

The OHCU is a nurse-managed clinic operated by the Center for Nursing Research and Clinical Practice, Lienhard School of Nursing, Pace University, which provides primary health-care services to the homeless. It provides nurse-managed primary health-care services to homeless families and single men in Yonkers, New York. The OHCU at the HSN offers services to homeless families, and the OHCU at the Sharing Community offers services to homeless men who are shelter guests of the Sharing Community. Both clinics operate within a larger organization, providing numerous services to homeless people.

Initially, nursing faculty and nursing students were to provide health screening and health education to families enrolled in the HSN several mornings a week. After providing such services during the first two months of operations, a Health Needs Survey was made. It contained questions pertaining to the clients' sources of primary health care, perceived health status, attitudes toward health care and health-care providers, and the clients' self-assessment of level of wellness. The need for primary health-care services was identified as the greatest presenting need.

As funding became available, a family nurse practitioner began providing primary health-care services in collaboration with a family practice physician. The nurse practitioners are master's-prepared and either American Nurses' Association (ANA) certified or eligible for ANA certification in family health. Nurse practitioners are well trained and experienced in caring for clients with acute, self-limiting, as well as chronic illnesses. Nurse practitioners are also well trained in providing health case management, health education, and community health services to the clients of the OHCU.

The nurse practitioners at the OHCU each have a formal letter of agreement between themselves and the consulting physicians that delineates the nurse practitioner's and physician's roles and responsibilities at the OHCU. In New York State, on April 1, 1989, nurse practitioners were granted prescriptive authority as long as a formal agreement between the nurse practitioner and physician exists and there are mutually agreed upon protocols. The protocols in some cases were written by the nurse practitioners and supplemented with published protocols. The consulting physicians review and sign the protocols yearly.

The OHCU provides services Monday through Friday, 8:30 a.m. to 5:00 p.m.

Services offered at the health-care units include health histories; physical examinations; gynecological services; family planning; care of acute, self-limiting illnesses; well-child care; health education; and counseling and referrals.

Financial Resources

The OHCU is supported financially by federal funding, private charitable contributions, and revenues. In June 1987 a grant application entitled "Innovative Health-Care Services for the Homeless" was submitted to the Special Project Grants Program in the Nursing Education Practice Resources Branch, Division of Nursing, U.S. Department of Health and Human Services, Public Health Service, Health Resources and Services Administration, Bureau of Health Professions Administration and in October 1987 funding was received in the amount of $539,900 for a three-year period. The purpose of the grant is to "demonstrate methods to improve access to nursing services in non-institutional settings through support of nursing practice arrangements in communities." Specifically, the project objectives are:

1. Expand access of homeless families to an innovative model of integrated nurse-managed health-care services in the community.
2. Develop a model nursing practice site for collaborative education of nursing, medical, and other professional students.
3. Document the health-care needs and available services to improve access to services to the homeless.
4. Document the cost of community-based primary health-care services managed by nurses.
5. Evaluate and modify the project through an ongoing process of obtaining and utilizing feedback to effect the desired change.

This funding has allowed for the expansion of the OHCU by increasing the range of services, increasing the number of client encounters, and allowing for further collaboration with other agencies. One such agency is St. Joseph's Medical Center, which operates a family health center and is located several blocks from the OHCU. St. Joseph's applied for and received a Certificate of Need so that the OHCU is a part-time extension clinic of St. Joseph's Family Health Center. St. Joseph's Medical Center is responsible for billing services for the OHCU. This arrangement has enabled the practitioners to receive payment for health-care services through Medicaid reimbursement. Primary health-care services are provided fifteen hours a week, and the remaining time is spent offering support groups, workshops, health screening, and Women Infants and Children's Program (WIC) sign-ups.

In May 1988 St. Joseph's Hospital and the Lienhard School of Nursing jointly submitted a grant application to the New York State Department of Health to replicate the OHCU at the Sharing Community. Funding was received in the amount of

$197,000. Recently, a second request was submitted to the Department of Health, and an additional $150,000 was received for the second year.

Quality Assurance

Several methods are utilized to assess the quality of primary care provided at the OHCU. In conjunction with St. Joseph's Medical Center, a quality assurance program has been developed which includes a monthly schedule of chart reviews. The results of the chart reviews are then presented to the health-care providers of the OHCU (nurse practitioners and physician consultants) and then the ambulatory care committee of St. Joseph's Medical Center. The director of the OHCU is a member of the ambulatory care committee, which meets monthly. This committee is the liaison between the hospital's medical board and its outpatient departments.

Professional Liability

Professional liability insurance for the nurse practitioners, nurses, and student nurses is maintained by Pace University. The university is reimbursed for the cost of this insurance through the health-care units' grant funding and revenues. Professional liability insurance for the director of medical consultation, the physician consultants, medical students, and residents is maintained by St. Joseph's Medical Center. Pace University and St. Joseph's Medical Center provide copies of such insurance policies to each other annually to ensure such coverage.

Educational Setting

The project is seen as an opportunity to further involve nursing students in community service through clinical exposure at the HSN. Students' learning experiences at the HSN vary greatly from in-hospital experiences.

The OHCU also serves as a clinical site for medical students and family practice medical residents from St. Joseph's. Family practice medical residents have used the OHCU as a clinical site for their community medicine rotation.

Families also are assisted in their contacts with other providers of health care, and an active relationship among many social service agencies allows for the integration of other physical and psychosocial needs.

CHAPTER 14

Homeless Families in Westchester: A Case Study in Individual, Social, and Professional Ethics

Strachan Donnelley
Lillie M. Shortridge
Bruce Jennings

Abstract

This chapter presents the results of an ethics roundtable program held on October 19, 1989, at Pace University, analyzing the ethical challenges in providing health care for homeless families. The participants of the roundtable were faculty, staff, and consultants of Pace University and the Hastings Center. The participants were from Pace University's Lienhard School of Nursing, School of Law, Dyson College of Arts and Sciences, the Michaelian Institute for Suburban and Urban Governance, Center for Applied Ethics, and Center for Nursing Research and Clinical Practice. Participants from the Hastings Center presented a model for analysis of ethical concerns and assisted in the analysis of the case study.

The current realities were presented first, including the known number of homeless families, health problems, difficulties in service delivery, and strategies being implemented to address the health-care needs. Several vignettes of situations creating conflict in providing care and the analysis by the ethics roundtable participants will be discussed.

The ethical challenges were analyzed by the participants considering individual, social, and professional ethics. Our moral obligations as individuals, citizens, and health-care professionals were discussed.

Homelessness in America is a national tragedy. The estimates of the numbers of homeless people range from 300,000 to more than 2 million with families representing the fastest growing subgroup among the homeless (Institute of Medicine 1988). In addition to all the problems related to lack of shelter itself, the homeless experience more health problems than the population as a whole (Institute of Medicine 1988), some of which may have contributed directly or indirectly to the person's becoming or remaining homeless. To address issues related to the health care of homeless families, Pace University and the Hastings Center held a day-long, multidisciplinary conference in October 1989 on Health Care for Homeless Families: The Ethical Challenge. Pace University is a liberal arts university with campuses in Westchester County (Briarcliff Manor, Pleasantville, and White Plains) and New York City. The Hastings Center, which is located on the Briarcliff Manor campus, is an independent research and educational institution that examines ethical issues in medicine, the life sciences, and the professions.

The aim of the conference was to gain a brief but systematic overview of the plight of homeless families in Westchester County and of the health-care professionals that serve them. The conference participants examined the social, economic, political, and health-care dimensions of this pressing local problem. Further, they explored how best ethically to address and analyze this moral failure of contemporary American society. What ought to be our practical ethical responses, both as individual citizens and as a political community, to homelessness in Westchester County and elsewhere?

Participants from the Hastings Center staff included bioethicists with backgrounds in political science, philosophy, medicine, and the law. Fifteen Pace University faculty and students came from the Lienhard School of Nursing, the Dyson College of Arts and Sciences, the Michaelian Institute for Suburban and Urban Governance, the School of Law, the Center for Applied Ethics, and the Center for Nursing Research and Clinical Practice. The Pace participants included nurses, public policy and health policy analysts, a computer professional, a lawyer, and an economist.

According to data prepared by the Westchester County Department of Social Services (1989) and Westchester County Commission on the Homeless (1988) and to the participants' own professional experiences, there are roughly 4,300 homeless people, including 930 families and 1,800–1,900 homeless children in Westchester County. Contrary to popular misconceptions, only 10% of these homeless were deinstitutionalized from mental institutions. The majority, 57%, were evicted from rental units or houses or driven from overcrowded homes of relatives. Many have or had jobs. Many are black or Hispanic, female, and adolescent.

The conference participants discussed the social, economic, and political forces that work against those struggling "on the margin" to keep homes and jobs. These obstacles include the gentrification of Westchester County, the failure of the wealth of the county and nation to "trickle down" to those most in need, and the growing gap between the American rich and poor, with a diminishing middle class. During the 1980s there were federal cutbacks of 75% in housing subsidies, leaving insufficient low-income housing in Westchester County, even while rents and the costs of housing rapidly increased. An average Westchester home now costs $300,000 ($90,000 down payment). Thirty thousand rental units were lost to gentrification and new restrictive zoning practices (Bernstein, et al 1990; Bowie et al. 1990).

Governmental responses to the plight of the homeless and potentially homeless are uncoordinated and irrational, if well-intentioned, a crazy quilt of laws and regulations. For example, public assistance and shelter allowances in Westchester County are about $390 per month. This support is insufficient by half, given rental costs. Yet, for those evicted from their homes, the costs of emergency housing or shelter in motels can run more than $100 per night and $3,000 per month. Further, though the county has responsibility for taking care of the homeless, it does not have the authority or resources to build public housing.

These and other systemic social and political realities have a decisive impact on the personal lives of homeless families. Homeless families are disenfranchised and "dismembered." They lose their citizen rights—for example, the right to vote or to serve on juries. They are often forced from their neighborhoods and local communities, "moteled" elsewhere, in or out of Westchester County, with children often taken long distances by taxi back and forth to their schools, at great public expense.

This severe dislocation of homeless families from their home communities typically leads to, or exacerbates, personal or individual disintegration. Health-care providers report the numerous, often severe, health and personal or mental problems of homeless families, who, moreover, have difficulty in gaining access to health-care services and in responding adequately to the services when provided. There is a high incidence of patterns of sexual or physical abuse among both parents and children (38% of homeless families). Children often have difficulties or are "problems" in school. The daily crises and "marginalized" life precipitated by homelessness typically make health care a low priority or difficult to pursue regularly (Halbach and Shortridge 1989).

The situation puts particular strains on health-care providers, creating a set of ethical dilemmas. These health-care professionals face the same system of uncoordinated and underfunded health-care and social services as their homeless clients/patients, and the clients themselves, pressured by their circumstances, are often difficult, uncooperative, or even dangerous. While trying to help clients negotiate "the system," professionals may face a client's noncompliance with medical regimes, drug abuse, and even stealing or selling of medical resources. This poses decisive challenges to professional integrity and an unequivocal advocacy of client/patients, with ensuing personal and professional "burnout."

There is a corresponding pattern of inadequate access of the homeless and their families to legal redress and the courts and a failure of client responsibility with respect to legal professionals. Within this crisis situation, health is not and often cannot be a priority.

With all these problems facing homeless families and their professional providers, their plight only masks the wider reality of America's poor and socially disadvantaged, who are caught within an economic, social, and political system that at crucial junctures is marked by inequality and injustice.

What should we do? How ought we to respond ethically? The reality of homeless families in Westchester County and elsewhere fundamentally challenges us to rethink our understanding of individuals and communities, and how they are, or ought to be, related to one another. In particular, both our moral response as individuals and our public policy response as a society to the challenge of homelessness in our midst needs to be informed by a clear and systematic conceptual framework. Without such a framework, it is likely that policy will be reactive and ad hoc in character, incrementally responding to particular crises or pressure groups, but without systematically addressing the underlying causes of homelessness and without a firm sense of the goals our public policy ought to serve.

Two different conceptual frameworks are available for us to use in facing public and health policy in response to homelessness. The first draws from our country's liberal and constitutional tradition and focuses on the concept of individual rights. An alternative conceptual framework, also deeply rooted in American political culture historically, is one centered on notions of membership, civic equality and respect, and community. We believe that the resources of both these conceptual frameworks will be necessary in order to fashion proper responses to the problem of homelessness in the future. The liberal rights framework, while politically and ideologically powerful, will not be sufficient as a conceptual vocabulary to express all of the meanings and purposes we should strive to articulate in our social response to homelessness. As a supplement, therefore, to the liberal rights tradition, communitarian notions also must be drawn upon, clarified, and developed as the public conversation continues.

Consider first the liberal rights tradition. America and the liberal political and ethical ethos that undergirds its social institutions place a high, if not overriding, value on the human individual. Individuals are understood as independent of, if not isolated from, one another in the pursuit of a personally good life. Our tradition makes much of individual "negative" and "positive" rights (or liberties). Negative rights are our protection against coercion or interference by the state or other people, in our legitimate pursuit of life, liberty, happiness, and self-determination. Positive rights morally (and legally) establish our claims on the state or others to provide what is minimally necessary to pursue a life of self-determination and noninterference by others. (For a classical discussion of negative and positive liberty, see Berlin 1969) Such claims might be made for minimally adequate housing, food, health care, education, or opportunities for employment (Berlin 1969).

Taken alone, the notion of a positive right would be sufficient morally to condemn our society's treatment of the homeless and would require practical policies of social welfare and services. Yet is this liberal individualism enough? Certainly the notion of positive or welfare rights remains very controversial in the post-Reagan era. But is it even theoretically adequate to the ethical and political task?

An inadequately conceived individualism can imply adversarial social or "free marketplace" relations, where the individual's negative rights and liberties are pitted against the positive rights of others, with inevitable concrete or practical clashes. For example, the homeless have a right not to be interfered with and to perch over hot-air vents or in other public places. Yet businesses have the right to pursue their enterprises without undue obstruction, and commuters have the right to reasonably pleasant and safe public transit systems. The mentally impaired, the socially disadvantaged, and the homeless ought to have minimally decent care facilities, but "not in my backyard," which infringes upon a resident's pursuit of negative liberty and noninterference. Such clashes of citizen rights have become commonplace in our daily newspapers.

Surely such socially adversarial relations between independent individuals and such intermixtures and clashes of positive and negative liberties leave something important out of account. As individuals, we are not all that independent or isolated. We are essentially involved with one another in a bewildering variety of ways. We are communal individuals, essentially interdependent, socially requiring cooperation as much as competition. This has particular importance for ethics and for our understanding of ethical harms and obligations. The homeless are not merely politically "disenfranchised," losing individual positive and negative liberties. They become socially "dismembered." They are ripped out of their neighborhoods, local communities, and familiar webs of lives, at great personal cost. This is decidedly an evil or harm visited upon these individuals, who do not usually live independent existences, alone and by themselves. If our liberal moral and political traditions cannot account for or include this, so much the worse for the liberal traditions.

In short, in theory and practice we need to move to a renewed sense of moral community life. With respect to the poor, disadvantaged, and unfortunate, who could be (and may become) any one of us, we need to move from an attitude of "they are them" to "they are us." We need to re-enfranchise and "re-member" those on the community's margins. We need a renewed sense of mutual communal responsibilities, obligations, and opportunities to go along with our political and ethical commitment to vigorous individuality.

Homeless families provide a particularly instructive case from this new or renewed ethical perspective. How can we break the cycle of disenfranchisement, dismemberment, and misfortune, the perpetuation of an underclass, at great cost both to society and the individuals involved? How can we support a responsible and respected reintegration into vigorous community life? This ethical imperative evolves as the central ethical concern for families as fundamental and necessary units of human, social, and political life. The health and well-being of human communities, its families, and its individuals go hand in hand. This is the deep ethical challenge, for both theory and practice, posed by homeless families in Westchester County and elsewhere in America.

References

Berlin, I. (1969). "Two Concepts of Liberty." In *Four Essays on Liberty*. New York: Oxford University Press.

Bernstein, A. J., Mitchell, D. H., Banks, R. B., Dhir, A., and Rippy, E. (1990). *Addressing the Problem of Homelessness in Westchester County*. White Plains, N.Y.: Skadden, Arps, Slate, Meagher, and Flom and McKinsey and Company, Inc.

Bowdler, J. E. (1989). "Health Problems of the Homeless in America." *The Nurse Practitioner* 13: 47–51.

Bowie, J. M., Mitchell, D. H. Bernstien, A. J., and Banks, R. B. (1990). *Addressing the Problem of Homelessness in Westchester County: The Legal Analysis*. White Plains, N.Y.: Skadden, Arps, Slate, Meagher, and Flom.

Halbach, J. L., and Shortridge, L. M. (1989). *Outreach Health Care Unit, 1988–89 Report*. Pleasantville, N.Y.: Center for Nursing Research and Clinical Practice, Lienhard School of Nursing, Pace University.

Institute of Medicine's Committee on Health Care for Homeless People. (1988). *Homelessness, Health, and Human Needs*. Washington, D.C.: National Academy Press.

Westchester County Commission on the Homeless. (1988). *Westchester Homeless Data*. White Plains, N.Y.: Housing Office, Westchester County Department of Social Services.

Westchester County Department of Social Services. (September 22, 1989). *Number of Homeless Families, Children and Singles, August 1989*. White Plains, N.Y.: Westchester County Department of Social Services.

Mental Health
and the Homeless

CHAPTER 15

Is Mental Health Care a Priority Need of Homeless People?

Barbara Cross

Abstract

Most community caregivers and researchers can generally agree that mental health services should be offered to approximately one-third of the homeless population. Few studies have systematically examined the process by which the homeless gain information about mental health services or if they consider mental health care a priority need in their lives.

In March 1988, the Homeless Network of Allegheny County conducted a field research study which surveyed the homeless in Pittsburgh regarding their current needs for community services (including mental health care), how they learned about the availability of community human services, and how they prioritized their needs for community services. Questionnaires were distributed to twenty target facilities in the inner city, largely soup kitchens and shelters that served the homeless. Twelve facilities returned the questionnaires which indicated that the homeless identified shelter, food, clothing, and jobs as their primary needs. Most homeless people learned of community services from other homeless people or shelter workers. Mental and physical health care were listed as a low priority need.

After obtaining basic needs (food, shelter, income), homeless people may be less stressed and more amenable to referral to mental health services. Increased sensitivity to the perceived needs of the homeless would suggest that, other than in emergency situations, community caregivers should defer referral to mental health services until after these basic needs are met. This study also suggests that the process of mental health referral should be through persons who have formed attachments with the homeless, such as shelter providers, outreach workers, and mental health "field" case managers.

While community caregivers and researchers can generally agree that mental health services should be offered to approximately one third of the homeless population, few studies have systematically examined the process by which the homeless gain information about mental health services and whether they consider mental health care a priority need in their lives.

In January 1989 the Homeless Network of Allegheny County, Pittsburgh, Pennsylvania, conducted a field research study to identify the needs of the homeless (Table 15.1). The Homeless Network was a "grass-roots" movement started in March 1988 by several human-service professionals who were interested in advocating for increased services for the homeless in Allegheny County. The Homeless Network and other community coalitions for the homeless were concerned that the existing services for the Pittsburgh homeless were not as adequate as the local politicians had indicated to the general public. This field research study was the first of its kind in Allegheny County in that it asked the homeless people to identify the gaps in service delivery in relation to their perceptions of their basic needs.

In order to assess the needs of the homeless population, the Homeless Network needed to be able to access them. As is well known, the homeless are often a disenfranchised group that has been difficult to engage in any formal system, even if the outcome will benefit them. For this reason, there were many barriers to completing such a study.

The greatest barriers anticipated were acceptance and distribution of the survey. In order to access the homeless population, it was vital to get the cooperation and support of the shelter management and workers. A brief, friendly cover letter was written to solicit the help of the shelter workers. This letter announced the survey and outlined directions for its dissemination, completion, and return to the Homeless Network. The survey was specifically designed to allow the individual to complete the twelve questions quickly and confidentially, while gathering some basic demographics to compare and validate the state and national statistics on homelessness in the study area. The homeless people were to complete the survey themselves unless special assistance was needed from one of the shelter workers. The surveys were hand carried by outreach workers or mailed approximately one week prior to the designated time of data gathering to decrease the possibility of the surveys' being lost or destroyed. Due to limited monies and resources of the shelters, self-addressed, stamped envelopes were supplied to increase the number of surveys returned.

The Homeless Network decided to focus the survey on twenty facilities that had long histories of servicing the homeless. These facilities consisted of shelters for both men and women and were located in or near the inner-city area of Pittsburgh. Over a one-month interval (January 1989), when shelter occupancy is usually at or over capacity, twelve of the facilities returned 181 surveys, or 41% of the total distributed.

In order to continue the enhanced relationship with the homeless population and shelter community, the survey results were tallied, and a follow-up report was sent

TABLE 15.1
Homeless Survey (Developed by Homeless Network)

1. ARE YOU CURRENTLY LIVING ON THE STREET? (CIRCLE ONE) YES / NO

2. LAST SHELTER YOU STAYED: _____

3. HOW LONG HAVE YOU BEEN HOMELESS?
   _____ DAY _____ WEEKS _____ MONTHS _____ YEARS

4. WHERE DID YOU GET THIS QUESTIONNAIRE? _____

5. WHICH SERVICES HAVE YOU USED? (CHECK ALL YOU HAVE USED.)
   _____ SHELTER   _____ MEDICAL SERVICES
   _____ SOUP KITCHENS   _____ DETOX (DRUG OR ALCOHOL)
   _____ CLOTHING   _____ MENTAL HEALTH
   _____ FOOD BANKS   _____ OUTREACH WORKERS
   _____ WELFARE   _____ JOB BANKS
   _____ SOCIAL SECURITY   _____ OTHER _____

6. WHICH SERVICES DO YOU NEED? (CHECK ALL YOU NEED.)
   _____ SHELTER   _____ MEDICAL SERVICES
   _____ SOUP KITCHENS   _____ DETOX (DRUG OR ALCOHOL)
   _____ CLOTHING   _____ MENTAL HEALTH
   _____ FOOD BANKS   _____ OUTREACH WORKERS
   _____ WELFARE   _____ JOB BANKS
   _____ SOCIAL SECURITY   _____ OTHER _____

7. HOW DID YOU FIND OUT ABOUT THE SERVICES YOU HAVE USED?
   (CHECK ALL YOU HAVE USED.)
   _____ SHELTER WORKERS   _____ SOUP KITCHEN
   _____ OUTREACH WORKERS   _____ OTHER (NAME SERVICE)
   _____ OTHER HOMELESS PEOPLE _____

8. CHECK ALL THE HOMELESS SERVICES OR PROGRAMS YOU HAVE
   HEARD OF OR USED.
   _____ URBAN LEAGUE
   _____ CITY HOUSING AUTHORITY
   _____ COUNTY HOUSING AUTHORITY
   _____ HOUSING ASSISTANCE PROGRAM
   _____ OTHER (LIST SERVICE) _____

9. AGE _____ RACE _____ SEX _____ (OPTIONAL)

10. WOULD YOU BE INTERESTED IN HELPING TO START A HOMELESS
    SELF-HELP GROUP IN ALLEGHENY COUNTY? (CIRCLE ONE) YES / NO

11. IF YES TO #10, HOW CAN YOU BE REACHED? _____

12. OTHER SUGGESTIONS: _____

TABLE 15.2
Homeless Survey Results

Living on the street:	28%		
Recently in shelter:	78.5%		
Length of Homelessness:	< One Week	7%	
	1–3 Weeks	32%	
	4–52 Weeks	36%	
	> One Year	25%	

Services Used:

Shelters	78%	Job Banks	19%
Welfare	75%	Outreach Workers	16%
Soup Kitchens	62%	Detox Services	15%
Clothing	50%	Mental Health	13%
Medical Service	43%	Social Security	12%
Food Banks	23%	Other	7%

Services Needed:

Shelters	67%	Other	14%
Soup Kitchens	61%	Social Security	13%
Clothing	46%	Outreach Workers	13%
Job	41%	Mental Health	9%
Welfare	34%	Detox Services	8%
Medical Service	29%		

Source of Information

Shelter Workers	56%
Outreach Workers	15%
Other Homeless People	36%
Soup Kitchen	28%
Other	27%

Recognition of Services:

Urban League	52%
City Housing Authority	46%
County Housing Authority	40%
Housing Assistance	13%
Other	24%
Interest In Self-Help Group:	49%
Contact Requested for Group:	44%

Other Suggestions: 13% Responded

—"Need Transportation"
—"More Twelve Step Programs"
—"Need More Mental Health Recovery Groups"
—"Support Group for the Homeless"
—"Training Programs"
—"Jobs and Job Coaching"
—"Active Involvement with Government Agencies"
—"More Federal Funding"
—"Decrease Alcohol Availability"
—"Cleaner Shelters"
—"Aid Should be Connected to Willingness to Help Oneself"
—"Let the Trickles Trickle Up"

to all of the shelters in Allegheny County regardless of participation. Other political and community leaders also were sent a report of the survey findings in an effort to advocate for more services for the homeless.

The survey results (Table 15.2) supported state and national figures in terms of average age and sex characteristics. The average age of the homeless surveyed was 37.5 years. The group most affected by homelessness was the black male. Sixty-five percent of respondents were 25–45 years old. Twenty-nine percent indicated that they were currently living on the street. Some 78.5% of the respondents indicated that they had lived in shelters at some time.

The length-of-homelessness question was included to give the Homeless Network a sense of how long the homeless population had been dealing with living without a permanent residence. The survey indicated 36% of the respondents had been homeless for four to eleven months. Seven percent had been homeless for less than one week. In all, 93% had been homeless for one week or longer. It was clear from this survey that the long-term housing needs of this population were not being met.

The homeless population responded that their priority needs were shelter (67%), food (61%), clothing (46%), and jobs (41%). Other needs had less priority to the respondents. The lowest needs were for psychiatry (9%) or detoxification from drugs or alcohol (8%).

Unlike many other communities in 1989, Pittsburgh did not have a peer support group for homeless people. Support often came from other homeless people in informal settings such as drop-in centers or at a local soup kitchen or in more organized groups such as alcoholic rehabilitation programs. From our survey, 49% of the respondents were interested in starting a self-help group. Forty-four percent were willing to list their names and locations so they could be contacted to join a group. Six months after this survey, a self-help group called "Self Help and Friends" was started by an unemployed steel worker who was working in a local shelter for homeless men.

Finally, the survey inquired about how the homeless found out about services. They received their information from other homeless people or from soup kitchen staff 28–56% of the time and from outreach workers only 15% of the time. Outreach workers were defined as trained professionals from varied backgrounds such as medical, religious, mental health, and drug and alcohol counseling who would frequent locations where the homeless could be found to engage them in services.

The Homeless Network survey indicated that the basic needs of homeless individuals still remained unmet in the Pittsburgh area. The shelter and soup kitchen system is not adequate to solve the difficulties of the homeless, but they can lay the foundation for contact to resolve the individuals' misfortunes. Often, a well-meaning shelter worker will too quickly move the homeless individual into accepting services that he or she is not able to handle. In order to have appropriate referrals to services, care must be taken to provide a proper assessment of the individual's perceptions and goals. Increased sensitivities to the perceived needs of the homeless would suggest that in the majority of cases, community caregivers should first focus on meeting the more basic needs of shelter, food, and clothing. The mentally ill homeless are no exception to this process. As the philosophy of Maslow's Hierarchy of Needs reminds us, one must have basic needs met before being ready to move to a higher plane and progression towards self-actualization. In such a demanding state as homelessness, for varied reasons, very few people are ready or willing to accept mental health counseling when their basic human needs are not being satisfied. Often, their behavior to survive is viewed as inappropriate when mental health assistance is being offered by an untrained helper. The mentally ill are generally more amenable to referral to mental health care after their basic needs are met. This survey also suggests that referral of homeless people including the mentally ill population should be initiated by individuals with whom they have developed relationships.

Care must be taken to assure that the shelter or outreach worker does not jeopardize the homeless person's trust, and that referrals are made only to those services that the individual desires to guarantee successful completion of goals and progression towards strengthening of the individual's ability to survive, heal, and self-actualize.

CHAPTER 16

Predictors of Homelessness in the Severely Mentally Ill

Marilyn A. Davies
Barbara Cross

Abstract

This retrospective study examined the risk factors associated with homelessness in 100 severely mentally ill patients discharged into the community from an acute-care psychiatric facility. Subjects included 50 patients who were homeless and 50 patients who were not homeless and matched on diagnosis, sex, race, and income variables. Risk factors for homelessness included sociodemographic characteristics, mental health history, history of residential instability, criminal activity, severity of mental illness at discharge, and social support from family.

Introduction

The percent of mentally ill who are homeless at any given time is relatively small (5–10%); however, over the course of a chronic mental illness, many persons may experience homelessness (Hatfield et al 1984; Lamb 1984). The mentally ill homeless are also a major challenge to caregiving systems (Tessler and Dennis 1989). Over the past ten years, epidemiologic research which has investigated the prevalence or correlates of homelessness among the mentally ill has been largely descriptive (Bachrach 1984; Lamb 1984; Milburn et al 1984; Fischer et al 1986; Santiago et al. 1988; Susser et al 1989). Despite methodological differences in definitions of homelessness, sample selection, diagnostic criteria, and methods of screening, this first generation of epidemiologic research has provided relevant data on which to base future research efforts (Tessler and Dennis 1989).

Descriptive studies implicate several risk factors for homelessness among the mentally ill. These include lack of income, unemployment, unavailability of low-cost housing (Baxter and Hopper 1981; Bassuk 1984), residential instability (Chafetz and Goldfinger 1984; Appleby and Desai 1987; Lipton et al 1988; Drake et al 1989), social disaffiliation (Segal et al 1977; Fernandez 1983; Bassuk et al 1984; Nordstrom and Berglund 1974), and criminal activity (Lamb and Grant 1982; Fischer and Breakey 1986; Belcher and Tooney 1988). For example, studies of homeless persons consistently show that many of those with mental health problems have been hospitalized in a psychiatric facility within the year prior to the study. In Baltimore, Fischer and colleagues (1986) found that one-third of fifty-one homeless had a previous psychiatric hospitalization; three-fifths of these reported an inpatient episode within the previous year. Likewise, Benda and Dattalo (1988) report that 30% of their homeless persons in Richmond, Virginia, had been hospitalized in a psychiatric facility, and, of these, 50% reported this occurrence within the past year. Our own studies indicate that rates of psychiatric hospitalization within the past year were 20% for residents of a single room occupancy (SRO) hotel (Davies et al 1987) and 23% for shelter residents (Bromet et al 1985).

Studies of patients with schizophrenia, a large subgroup of the homeless mentally ill (Arce et al. 1983; Kaufmann 1984; Lipton et al 1983), demonstrate the complexity of the homeless process. Many schizophrenic patients reduce their social networks and jeopardize their living arrangements while they are hospitalized (Cohen and Sokolovsky 1978; Denoff and Pilkonis 1987). Both factors could increase their risk for homelessness. Outcome studies indicate that housing change occurs with remarkable frequency among deinstitutionalized patients trying to survive in the community (Lamb 1984; Caton and Goldstein 1984) and that homelessness is more likely to occur for those patients with unstable living conditions. Caton and Goldstein reported that over the course of one year, 50% of their sample of deinstitutionalized patients changed their living arrangements at least once, while 21% changed their living arrangements two or more times. These researchers found that episodes of homelessness "are more likely to occur among patients whose living arrangements are unstable" (p. 763). Data collection at three-month intervals indicated that rehospitalization was a significant predictor of a change in living arrangements. In a more recent, prospective, one-year follow-up study of 187 after-care patients, Drake and colleagues (1989) found that predominantly homeless persons were more likely to return to the hospital, compared with the occasionally homeless and those with stable housing.

Recent research in homelessness indicates that many homeless persons have limited social resources and that socially isolated persons have increased risk for homelessness. Fernandez (1983) identifies the absence of a stable support system as the core deficit of homelessness. Segal, Baumohl, and Johnson (1977) studied a breadline over the course of one year. They report that these individuals were not adept at making friends, had widely varying relationships with their families, lacked skill in managing interpersonal relations necessary for "dealing" and successful street living, and were judged by other persons as "incapable of appropriate association" (p. 390). Using clinical contacts as points of entry into formal social networks, these researchers also found that these disturbed street people lacked social resources with community service institutions and lacked "starter materials" (living arrangements, Social Security income) required of serviceable clients by agencies.

Methods

The subjects for the study were inpatients at Western Psychiatric Institute and Clinic (WPIC), Pittsburgh, Pennsylvania, between August 1987 and July 1988 (a randomly selected year), and met the following criteria: 50 patients who were known to the Base Service Unit as homeless and 50 nonhomeless patients who were matched for diagnosis, sex, race, and income. Subjects were defined as "homeless" versus "non-homeless," a dichotomous rating which was selected to afford comparability and consistency with other research projects reported in the literature. We selected the definition used by the Ohio Department of Mental Health (Roth and Bean 1986) in their state psychiatric hospital survey. This definition was applied to a sample quite similar to our sample (i.e., psychiatric patients), and the types of living arrangements in the definition accurately reflect those that are available in the Pittsburgh community.

Three trained nurse clinicians, blind to homelessness status, reviewed the inpatient medical records of these 100 subjects regarding the presence of variables of interest. Based on an extensive review of the literature related to correlates of homelessness, twenty risk factors for homelessness included sociodemographic characteristics, mental health history, history of residential instability, criminal activity, severity of mental illness at discharge, and social support from family. All factors were operationally defined. If no information was documented regarding a specific variable, it was recorded as missing data.

Results

Frequency distributions and measures of central tendency for all independent variables indicated that the sample was predominantly male (60%), young (31.5 years $\pm$ 6.25), and unemployed (80%). The clinical composition, in terms of diagnostic categories, was essentially 50% with a primary diagnosis of schizophrenia or schizoaffective disorder and 30% with "other disorders" which included atypical psychosis, adjustment disorders, and personality disorders. Since WPIC does not admit persons with a primary diagnosis of alcohol or drug abuse who are referred to another facility, these persons are not represented in this sample. However, subjects in this study could carry a secondary diagnosis of alcoholism or drug abuse.

Using a t-test for the continuous variables and chi-square analysis for the

TABLE 16.1
Measures of Association for Homelessness Risk Factors*

	Homelessness			
	Yes	No	X^2	P
History of residential instability				
Yes	26	4	20.54	.0001
No	4	19		
Legal status (admission)				
Involuntary	10	5	0.51	NS
Voluntary	23	18		
Self-damaging behavior				
Yes	18	9	0.25	NS
No	15	14		
Noncompliance				
Yes	16	12	0.93	NS
No	14	11		
Use of illegal drugs or alcohol				
Yes	17	15	0.80	NS
No	15	8		
Criminal activity				
None	12	10	4.8	NS
Misdemeanor	11	2		
Felony	10	11		
Vague plans for future				
Yes	13	4	3.10	NS
No	20	19		
Not fully recompensated (at discharge)				
Yes	18	10	0.66	NS
No	15	13		
Leaving without permission				
Yes	1	5	4.9	.03
No	32	18		
Residential plans (at discharge)				
Tenuous	21	2	20.93	.0001
Stable	8	20		
Family support				
Good	5	15	16.23	.0003
Marginal	17	· 5		
None	11	2		

*1 df for chi-square analysis

categorical variables, group differences were explored on eleven independent variables that had demonstrated variability within the sample. Using p<.05 as the criterion for significance, there were no significant differences on age or age at onset of psychiatric illness. The results of the chi-square analysis for categorical variables (Table 16.1) indicated that the two groups were very similar in variables related to their mental health history. History of residential instability, discharge status, and family support emerged as being significantly different for the two groups. These differences are in the expected directions. At discharge, homeless patients tended to have tenuous plans for their living arrangements. They also had marginal or no family support during their hospital stay as compared to the non-homeless, who tend to have good support, as demonstrated by process. Interestingly, only one homeless person left the inpatient facility without the permission of the treatment team, whereas five non-homeless subjects left without permission.

Next, logistic regression was used to test the relative contribution of specified variables to differences between the two groups, the most parsimonious logistic regression equation comparing homeless and nonhomeless included the variables of residential instability (entering first) and family support. These factors demonstrated a predicted probability of .85 (S.E. .25) as compared to the observed proportion (.88) of homelessness.

Discussion

This study indicates that, prior to discharge, inpatients can be assessed for their "risk for homelessness" and that the occurrence of homelessness in the post-discharge period is predictable and, therefore, potentially preventable. Few published studies present a multifactorial model for predicting homelessness in the seriously mentally ill (Levine 1984; Milburn et al 1984; Fischer and Breakey 1986; Farmer 1989). Future epidemiologic research on the mentally ill homeless should validate identified risk factors and determine which ones are modifiable. These modifiable risk factors would then become a focus of intervention for the prevention of homelessness in the mentally ill (Hough 1982; Hatfield et al 1984, Lamb 1984).

Pragmatically, if certain "at-risk" mentally ill patients are identified, they could be the focus of targeted interventions that could prevent or impede the drift to homelessness. This subgroup of severely mentally ill persons may be more accessible and receptive to attention, time, and resources of the caregiving system because they are actively engaged in mental health treatment and "connected" to a caregiving system. They may be willing, able, and/or open to seeking and obtaining help for their overwhelming life condition.

References

Appleby, L. and Desai, P. (1987). "Residential Instability: A Perspective on System Imbalance." *American Journal of Orthopsychiatry* 57:515–24.

Arce, A., Tadlock, M., Vergare, M. J., Shapiro, S. H. (1983). "Psychiatric Profile of Street People Admitted to an Emergency Shelter." *Hospital and Community Psychiatry* 34:812–17.

Bachrach, L. L. (1984). "The Homeless Mentally Ill and Mental Health Services: An Analytical Review of the Literature." *The Homeless Mentally Ill,* edited by R. H. Lamb. Washington, D.C.: American Psychological Association.

Bassuk, E.L. (1985). "Research Perspectives on Homelessness: A Response to the APA Recommendations on the Homeless Mentally Ill." *Psychosocial Rehabilitation Journal:* 4:31–34.

Bassuk, E.L., Rubin, L., Alison, L. (1984). "Is Homelessness a Mental Health Problem?" *American Journal of Psychiatry* 141(12):1546–50.

Bussuk, E. (1984). "The Homelessness Problem." *Scientific American* 251:40–45.

Baxter, E. and Hopper, K. (1981). *Private Lives/Public Spaces Homeless Adults on the Streets of New York City.* New York: Community Service Society.

Baxter, E. and Hopper, K. (1982). "The New Mendicancy: Homeless in New York City." *American Orthopsychiatric Association* 52:393–408.

Belcher, J. R. (1988). "Defining the Service Needs of Homeless Mentally Ill Persons." *Hospital and Community Psychiatry* 39: 1203–5.

Belcher, J.R., and Tooney, B.G. (Spring 1988). "Relationship between the Deinstitutionalization Model, Psychiatric Disability and Homelessness." *Health and Social Work*; 145–53.

Benda, B.B. and Dattalo, P. (1980). "Homelessness: Consequence of a Crisis or a Long-term Process?" *Hospital and Community Psychiatry* 39:884–86.

Bromet, E., Schulz, S.C., and Schulberg, H.C. (Spring 1985). "Mental Illness Among the Homeless in Allegheny County." A report submitted to Allegheny County MH/MR Board. Pittsburgh, Pa.

Caton, C. and Goldstein, J. (1984). "Housing Change of Chronic Schizophrenic Patients: A Consequence of the Revolving Door." *Social Science and Medicine* 19:759–64.

Chafetz, L. and Goldfinger, S.M. (1984). "Residential Instability in a Psychiatric Emergency Setting." *Psychiatric Quarterly* 56:20–34.

Cohen, C.I. and Sokolovsky, J. (1978). "Schizophrenia and Social Networks: Ex-patients in the Inner City." *Schizophrenia Bulletin* 4:546–60.

Davies, M. A., Munetz, M. R., Schulz, S. C., and Bromet, E. J. (1987). "Assessing Mental Illness in SRO Shelter Residents." *Hospital and Community Psychiatry* 38(10):1114–15.

Denhoff, M. S. and Pilkonis, P .A. (1987). "The Social Network of the Schizophrenic: Patient and Residential Determinants." *Journal of Community Psychology* 15:228–44.

Drake, R. E., Wallach, M. A., and Hoffman, J. S. (1989). "Housing Instability and Homelessness among Aftercare Patients of an Urban State Hospital." *Hospital and Community Psychiatry* 40:46–52.

Farmer, M. (1989). Personal communication. Conference on Homelessness and Mental Illness Towards the Next Generation of Research Studies Conference. Bethesda, Md.

Fernandez, J. (1983). "In Dublin's Fair City: The Mentally Ill of No-Fixed Abode." Lecture on Conference on Homeless. Dublin.

Fischer, P.J. (1988). "Criminal Activity among the Homeless: A Study of Arrests in Baltimore." *Hospital and Community Psychiatry*, 38:46–51.

Fischer, P.J. and Breakey, W. R. (1986). "Homelessness and Mental Health: An Overview." *International Journal of Mental Health* 14:6–41.

Fischer, P.J., Shapiro, S., Breakey, W.J., Anthony, J.C., and Kramer, M. (1986). "Mental Health and Social Characteristics of the Homeless: A Survey of Mission Users." *American Journal of Public Health* 76:519–24.

Gelberg, L., Linn, L. S., and Leake, B. D. (1988). "Mental Health, Alcohol and Drug Use, and Criminal History among Homeless Adults." *American Journal of Psychiatry* 145: 191–96.

Hatfield, A. B., Farrell, E., and Starr, S. (1984). "The Family's Perspective on the Homeless." In *The Homeless Mentally Ill. A Task Force Report of the American Psychiatric Association*, edited by H. R. Lamb. Washington, D.C.: 279–301.

Hough, R.L. (1982). "Psychiatric Epidemiology and Prevention—An Overview of the Possibilities." In *Psychiatric Epidemiology and Prevention: The Possibilities*, 1–28. Los Angeles: Neuropsychiatric Institute.

Kaufmann, C. C. A. (1984). "Implications of Biological Psychiatry for the Severely Mentally Ill: A Highly Vulnerable Population." In *The Homeless Mentally Ill*, edited by R. H. Lamb. Washington, D.C.: American Psychiatric Associates.

Lamb, H.R. (1984). "Deinstitutionalization and the Homeless Mentally Ill." *Hospital and Community Psychiatry* 35(9):899–924.

Lamb, H. R. and Grant, R. W. (1982). "The Mentally Ill in an Urban County Jail." *Archives of General Psychiatry* 39:17–22.

Levine, I. S., Lezak, A. D., and Goldman, H. H. (1986). "Community Support System for the Homeless Mentally Ill." In *The Mental Health Needs of Homeless Person*, edited by E. L. Bassuk. Washington, D.C.: Jossey-Bass 27–42.

Levine, I.S. (1984). "Service Programs for the Homeless Mentally Ill." In *The Homeless Mentally Ill. A Task Force Report of the American Psychiatric Association*, edited by H. R. Lamb. Washington, D.C. 173–200.

Lipton, F. R., Michaels, P., and Sabatine, A. (1986). "Characteristics and Service Needs of the Homeless Mentally Ill." In *Treating the Homeless: Urban Psychiatry's Challenge*, edited by B. E. Jones. Washington, D.C., American Psychiatric Press.

Lipton, F. R., Nutt, S., and Sabatine, A.: (1988). "Housing the Homeless Mentally Ill: A Longitudinal Study of a Treatment Approach." *Hospital and Community Psychiatry* 39:40–45.

Lipton, F. R., Sabatine, A., and Datz, S. E. (1983). "Down and Out in the City: The Homeless Mentally Ill." *Hospital and Community Psychiatry* 34:817–31.

Milburn, N. G., Watts, R. J., and Anderson, S. L. (1984). "An Analysis of Current Research Methods for Studying the Homeless." Final Report. Washington, D.C.: Institute for Urban Affairs and Research, Howard University.

Nordstrom, G. and Berglund, M. "Successful Adjustment in Alcoholism: Relationships between Causes of Improvement, Personality, and Social Factors." *Journal of Nervous and Mental Disease*, 1986; 1974:664–668.

Roth, D. and Bean C. J. (1986). "New Perspectives on Homelessness: Findings from a Statewide Epidemiological Study." *Hospital and Community Psychiatry* 37:712–719.

Santiago, J. M., Bachrach, L. L., Berren, M. R., and Hannah, M. T. (1988). "Defining the Homeless Mentally Ill: A Methodological Note." *Hospital and Community Psychiatry* 39 (10):1100–1102.

Segal, S. P., Baumohl, J., and Johnson, E. (1977). "Falling Through the Cracks. Mental Disorder and Social Margin in a Young Vagrant Population." *Social Problems* 24:387–401.

Susser, E., Conover, S., and Struening, E. L. (1989). "Problems of Epidemiologic Method in Assessing the Type and Extent of Mental Illness among Homeless Adults." *Hospital and Community Psychiatry* 40:261–65.

Tabachnick, B. G., and Fidell, L. S. (1983). *Using Multivariate Statistics*. New York: Harper and Row.

Tessler, R., and Dennis, D. (1989). "What Have We Learned to Date? Assessing the First Generation of NIMH-Supported Research Studies." Presented at Homelessness and Mental Illness Towards the Next Generation of Research Studies Conference, Bethesda, Md.

CHAPTER 17

The Department of Veterans Affairs' Program for the Homeless Chronically Mentally Ill Veteran

Marilyn R. Englert

Abstract

Veterans have always been a part of the homeless population. In 1987 the Homeless Chronically Mentally Ill (HCMI) Veterans Program was established by an act of Congress to address the needs of homeless veterans.* The program operates at forty-five Veterans Affairs (VA) sites throughout the nation and provides a broad range of services including: outreach, assessment and treatment, referral and advocacy services, and brief residential treatment at non-VA facilities under VA contracts. The HCMI Program is the largest integrated program in the country that serves the homeless.

> "Homelessness is often the final stage in a lifelong series of crises and opportunities, the culmination of a gradual disengagement from supportive relationships and institutions." (Bassuk 1984)

Homelessness is not new, and veterans have always been part of the homeless population. Robertson (1987) described the homelessness of veterans during several periods, including the past decade. After the Civil War thousands of Americans were homeless, and several depressions in the late 1800s forced more Americans to live on the road, migrating throughout the country. At that time no government relief existed, and there were few private charities. In 1932 approximately 20,000 homeless World War I veterans staged a demonstration in Washington, D.C., to de-

---

* A special thanks to Rosemarie Burke whose support and guidance has been instrumental in the development and operation of the Buffalo HCMI Program and Linda Frisman whose technical skills were so valuable in the writing of this chapter.

mand government help. At present between one third and one half of homeless men are estimated to be veterans, many from the Vietnam era.

In February 1987 Congress enacted legislation (Public Law 100-6) which established the Homeless Chronically Mentally Ill (HCMI) Veterans Program, a national initiative designed to reach out and provide medical and psychiatric treatment to homeless veterans suffering from psychiatric and substance abuse disorders. This program is under the leadership of Dr. Paul Errera and Dr. Robert Rosenheck and has been in operation at Department of Veterans Affairs (VA) Medical Centers located in twenty-six states and the District of Columbia since May 1987. It is the largest integrated treatment program for the homeless chronically mentally ill in the United States. More than 30,000 homeless veterans have been seen thus far (Rosenheck et al. 1991). At first, there were two clinicians, usually a nurse and a social worker, at each of forty-three sites. There are now forty-five sites with an average of three clinicians per site.

Rosenheck et al. (1991) list the services provided by the program. They include:

1. Outreach services in shelters, soup kitchens and on the streets;
2. An assessment of needs and direct treatment by HCMI staff and at VA Medical Centers;
3. Referral and advocacy services;
4. Brief residential treatment at non-VA facilities, under VA contracts.

Over the past five years each HCMI site has developed its own unique program. Sites differ on the number and backgrounds of clinicians, the geographic area, the population density of the area, the availability of community resources, the size of the host VA Medical Center, the level of support given by the hospital and community, and the types of cases encountered. The broad diversity of settings and clinicians has not changed the main goal of the program: to assist homeless veterans in breaking the cycle of homelessness by helping them participate in therapeutic medical and psychiatric programs and obtain and maintain a safe and stable living environment (Rosenheck et al. 1989).

Outreach

An important component of any program serving homeless populations is outreach, because many homeless persons feel alienated from the large, impersonal organizations such as hospitals. In order to link with such systems their trust must be won gradually through a process of engagement. The reclamation of these homeless individuals can only begin where they are—in the streets. For that reason "nurses and other professionals need the freedom and flexibility to move beyond the traditional modes of treatment" (Abdellah 1986). "White uniform" or traditional hospital approaches will not work.

When the HCMI program was established, the idea of reaching out to veterans in community settings was identified as a key concept. It was not reasonable to expect homeless people who have high rates of mental illness and substance abuse to initiate linkage with established services. HCMI workers were encouraged to make contact with homeless veterans at shelters, soup kitchens, and on the streets. Perhaps just as important, hospitalized, "hard-to-place" veterans were not to be served by the program, as these individuals already had the services of hospital staff. Limiting HCMI entry to outreach effectively targets the resources of the program to the truly underserved.

To engage the homeless through outreach, one must do more than physically leave a comfortable office. One must also leave behind attitudes that foster the notion that the homeless are unworthy of services or that they are totally responsible for their plight. Professionals who work with homeless veterans have an attitude of positive regard. Their genuine concern and caring for the homeless individual are evident. The initial contact and the building of trusting relationships are fostered and nurtured through consistency, honesty, and empathy. Although outreach needs to be aggressive, it cannot be threatening. Mutual acceptance is one of the keys to effective outreach.

In Buffalo, New York, a marketing approach is used to link with the homeless. The homeless are thought of as service consumers. Just as in marketing other commodities, the services provided need to be made known to prospective customers. Posters and brochures are placed in areas the homeless frequent. In soup kitchens the outreach team goes from table to table, informing prospective clients about the program. At the shelters HCMI workers stand before the group and discuss various topics of interest such as: locations of soup kitchens, accessing public benefits, housing, and treatment. They provide hand-outs that reinforce the steps that need to be taken to access various services as well as handouts that list local hospitals, substance abuse treatment programs, housing opportunities, employment opportunities, etc. These handouts are available to all homeless persons, not just veterans.

As the program at Buffalo matures and becomes more widely known among the homeless, some of the homeless veterans are contacting its office. Yet it is important that outreach activities continue, so that those who are most isolated can be served.

Assessment and Treatment

Reaching out is only the beginning step in providing services for the homeless. After making contact, an assessment is done. A staff member uses a fifty-one-item questionnaire that provides basic information. It covers eight general areas: veteran description, military history, living situation, medical problems, substance abuse, psychiatric status, employment status, and interviewer observations. Copies of this form are sent to the Northeast Program Evaluation Center, where statistical information from all the sites is compiled. Table 17.1, which is reprinted from the 1991 annual report of the HCMI program, lists descriptive characteristics of veterans seen in the program.

HCMI assessments require a holistic approach. Staff consider not only medical and psychiatric needs, but the need for income, food, clothing, and shelter. As one might expect, the homeless themselves are mainly concerned with problems related to lack of material resources and personal and physical protection. Their concerns about social, medical, and psychological problems are generally secondary. Ball and Havassy in 1984 reported a serious mismatch between the kinds of services that community mental health systems traditionally provide and the kinds of services the homeless population feel they need. Simply put, "You can't sell dishes to a man who has no food." Some programs won't even accept a person unless he or she can pay for treatment and has a permanent residence. For many of the homeless, even modest charges make treatment prohibitive. The Buffalo study indicates that 43% of the homeless veterans seen by them have incomes of less than $100 per month; nationwide 54% have incomes of less than $100 per month. Fortunately most of the services of the VA Medical Center are free. Program staff assist veterans to access available services at the VA Medical Center, and for unmet needs they refer and advocate for them with community agencies. To bridge the gap in usable services, clinicians must be very knowledgeable about what resources and services are available in the area and how to access them.

In Buffalo the HCMI staff is equipped with a lap-top computer with a modem. In the community this computer can be hooked to a phone and provides access to some patient records including: appointments, diagnosis, lab reports, and prescriptions. This resource is very valuable in making assessments and providing follow up.

Referral and Advocacy

Accessing treatment and services for the homeless may be the most difficult task of the homeless outreach worker. The clinician must in essence be a resource directory. No single source lists all the services needed by the homeless veteran; agencies continually change staff, phone numbers, and policy. By gathering information about local agencies and updating it regularly, clinicians can make effective referrals. Knowledge of the system narrows the gaps and increases the potential for successful outcomes.

Many other agencies seem to require extensive documentation for each client. The homeless have difficulty keeping track of such papers and may not even have identification. Items necessary for agencies to process benefits applications such as identification and names and addresses of past and present health-care professionals must be assembled prior to filing for these benefits if the homeless are to get

TABLE 17.1
Characteristics of Intakes Completed in Fiscal Year 1987–1988
(N = 10, 529) and in Fiscal Year 1989–1990 (N = 8,623)

	Fiscal Year 1987–1988, 1st year	Fiscal Year 1989–1990, 3rd year	Percentage Change (%)
Demographics			
Age (mean)	42.6	41.9	−0.7
+ Gender:			
Male	98.6%	98.1%	−0.5*
Female	1.4%	1.9%	0.5
+ Race:			
White	58.3%	53.4%	−4.9***
Black	33.6%	41.5%	7.9***
Hispanic	6.7%	4.0%	−2.7***
Other	1.4%	1.1%	−0.3
#Marital status:			
Married	3.6%	4.3%	0.7
Were married	62.8%	62.8%	0.0
Never married	33.6%	32.9%	−0.7
Residential Status			
+ Current residence:			
Own apartment	7.7%	4.4%	−3.3***
Intermittent with family/friends	9.2%	11.2%	2.0*
Shelter	47.6%	39.7%	−7.9***
No residence/ institution	35.5%	44.7%	9.2***
+ Homelessness:			
< 1 month	24.9%	25.3%	0.4
1–5 months	29.0%	34.7%	5.7***
6–11 months	14.1%	13.3%	−0.8
12–23 months	10.8%	9.7%	−1.1**
24 months or more	21.2%	17.0%	−4.2***
Public support/employment			
+ Public support			
Service Connected: Psychiatric	4.6%	5.5%	0.9*
Service Connected: Medical	8.6%	9.3%	0.7
Non-service connected pension	6.0%	4.8%	−1.2***
Non-VA disability	10.7%	11.0%	0.3
Other public support	21.0%	20.2%	−0.8
#Usual employment: past 3 years			
Full time	30.5%	31.7%	1.2
Part-time regular	33.8%	26.7%	−7.1***
Student	1.2%	0.5%	−0.7***
Retired/disabled	8.4%	14.9%	6.5***
Unemployed	24.4%	25.8%	1.4

TABLE 17.1 *continued*

	Fiscal Year 1987–1988, 1st year	Fiscal Year 1989–1990, 3rd year	Percentage Change (%)
Program entry/clinical status			
+ How program contact initiated:			
Outreach	56.8%	54.2%	2.6
Non VA homeless			
program	12.2%	11.2%	− 1.0
Came to VA	18.2%	26.5%	8.3***
Came to Vet Center	6.3%	2.8%	− 3.5***
Other	6.5%	5.2%	− 1.3
+ Where interviewed:			
Shelter	31.4%	31.2%	− 0.2
Street	4.1%	4.0%	− 0.1
Soup kitchen	11.5%	6.6%	− 4.9***
VAMC	30.5%	38.2%	7.7***
Vet center	4.7%	3.8%	− 0.9**
Other	17.8%	16.3%	− 1.5**
@Clinical psychiatric diagnoses:			
Alcohol dependence	55.2%	64.2%	9.0***
Drug dependence	18.4%	34.9%	16.5***
Personality disorder	18.3%	19.9%	1.6**
Schizophrenia	12.3%	12.3%	0.0
PTSD from combat	9.3%	10.0%	0.7
Affective disorder	9.3%	23.1%	13.8***
+ Past hospitalization:			
Psychiatric	33.1%	32.3%	− 0.8
Alcohol abuse	44.2%	50.7%	6.5***
Drug abuse	15.4%	26.9%	11.5***

Significance of difference between 1987/88 and 1989/90:

* $p < .05$
** $p < .01$
*** $p < .001$

NOTE: Sample sizes vary because of different rates of completion of various forms:
$N = 10, 529 (+), 3, 701 (\#), 4, 984 (@)$

From: Rosenheck et al. 1991.

appropriate determinations. HCMI workers often hand out check-off lists so veterans can assemble the required items before they make applications or to help them gather needed materials.

A veterans' benefits counselor has been assigned to the program and accompanies HCMI staff in the community several times a month. He will assist the veteran in making applications and follow them until a determination is made. This interagency networking also is important in expediting and obtaining needed services for homeless veterans.

The HCMI clinician also needs to refer veterans to sources of free or low-cost food, housing, furniture, clothing, and other essentials to establish and maintain a stable living environment.

The free literature offered by the HCMI program is not only used for promotional purposes but to simplify the referral process. The documents are very specific and give names, addresses, and telephone numbers. Some are designed as self-help guides. Although HCMI workers are willing to accompany veterans to various agencies, the feeling is that enabling them to make their own contacts empowers them and increases their self-esteem. Not only do professionals need to be advocates, but the homeless need to learn to advocate for themselves. Susscr et al. (1990) say that the homeless need to be taught to use the survival skills they have developed on the street to effectively negotiate the system. He calls this "constructive sociopathy."

In Buffalo, to enhance working knowledge of the system, the staff has networked with others who work with the homeless and with various agencies that may provide needed services. Several years ago a group for "Outreach Providers" was started for sharing information about different agencies and trying to resolve problems of the homeless.

Residential Treatment

The HCMI Program provides residential treatment on a time-limited basis (up to one year, but usually less than six months). This is funded through VA contracts at non-VA facilities. For many this intensive therapeutic support in residential facilities is necessary to interrupt the mutually exacerbating effects of psychiatric illness, substance abuse, and homelessness.

Potential community sites are inspected by a nurse, social worker, psychiatrist, and fire safety officer. The residence must meet rigid program guidelines to be eligible for an HCMI contract. Those guidelines include structural and program components as described in VA Circular 10-87-31 National set of rules and regulations. The facility must:

1.   Conform to the standards of the Life Safety Code;
2.   Provide a supervised environment that is staffed at all times;
3.   Maintain clinical records;
4.   Provide therapeutic and rehabilitative services;
5.   Support a drug/alcohol-free lifestyle;
6.   Provide support and guidance toward the goal of independent living.

Yearly formal inspections ensure that the standards are maintained.

Residential treatment facilities most often provide substance abuse counseling (at 46% of facilities), psychological counseling (41%), and social skills development assistance (36%) (Rosenheck et al. 1991). Veterans in these facilities are provided a mean of twenty-two hours of therapeutic activities weekly. Group meetings and activities are scheduled for an average of nine hours per week. Individual counseling accounts for an additional 3.5 hours.

In Buffalo, as in many other parts of the country, appropriate residential treatment facilities are scarce. In 1989–90 each HCMI site maintained contracts with an average of three facilities, and an average of 5.3 veterans were in treatment at each facility. The daily charge ranged from $10 to $96, with an average of $39. The most expensive facilities offered more intensive treatment and were better staffed.

The prime facility used by the Buffalo HCMI program is the Veterans Housing Coalition/Transitional Housing Program (VHC/THP). This facility was specifically designed to provide treatment for this group. At any one time, there are nine veterans in residence; and the per diem rate is $52.

In addition to the general services listed above, the residential treatment facility also networks with various other agencies including employment (Department of Labor, Private Industry Counsel, Office of Vocational Rehabilitation/Vocational and Educational Services for Individuals with Disabilities), housing (Housing Assistance Center, Buffalo Municipal Housing Authority, Rental Assistance Corporation, Belmont Shelter Corp.), and community health and mental health centers.

The Buffalo treatment facility is often referred to as "the launching pad." Veterans are selected for residential treatment based on their desire to change, their need, and the availability of beds and funds. The majority of the veterans placed are substance abusers. Sometimes discharge planning begins even before the day of admission. During the stay veterans are assisted in achieving financial stability through employment or application for disability benefits if they are entitled. Money management is a key issue that is discussed with the veteran and monitored. Arrangements for permanent housing are initiated. If appropriate, applications are made for low-income housing through Belmont Shelter (Section 8 certificates) and Buffalo Municipal Housing Authority. Both agencies are funded through the Department of Housing and Urban Development (HUD) and both have been extremely helpful.

To support a drug- and alcohol-free life-style, veterans participate in three or four Alcoholics Anonymous or Narcotics Anonymous meetings per week as well as on-site group and individual counseling. A breathalyzer is on site, and random urine specimens are collected at least once per week. Those persons whose urine specimens test positive for drugs or alcohol are immediately terminated from the residential program. Although no empirical data are available to judge the impact of this policy compared to imposing sanctions on residents who use alcohol and drugs, the HCMI staff has observed that the threat of eviction is an effective deterrent to substance abuse.

HCMI staff visit the facility several times per week. They provide support and act as a liaison between the veteran and hospital or other community programs when necessary. For example, HCMI staff may set up needed appointments and provide transportation to them.

When the veteran is discharged, HCMI staff assist him or her in locating furniture and other needed household items. To obtain these, the staff makes needs known in the hospital newsletter and solicits from voluntary organizations such as Amvets, the Disabled American Veterans, the Order of the Eastern Star, and Vietnam Veterans Organization. Accessing the needed items is a team effort between the hospital employees who donate and identify other donors and the homeless veterans, who usually assist in moving. The VA also provides the truck to move the furniture, and VHC provides storage for some items until they are needed. It should be noted that both veterans who are setting up housekeeping and veterans in residence have access to these resources. The goal is to have everything in place by the time a veteran is ready to leave the contract residence so that the transition to independent living is as smooth as possible.

More than half of the veterans successfully complete the residential treatment program; their average length of stay is approximately five to six months. Veterans appear to maximize their chance of successfully completing the program and maintaining a stable living environment in the community if:

- They had recently completed an in-hospital substance abuse program before entering the contract residence;
- The length of stay is long enough to get into place all the supports needed before moving to independent housing;
- They attend AA and NA meetings.

Discussion

The HCMI Veterans Program is the largest program in the country to assist the homeless. The continued dedication of hundreds of staff across the nation has resulted in numerous advances in narrowing the gap between homelessness and stable living. This progress is encouraging, but there is still much more to be done.

These two themes—comprehensiveness and collaboration—underlie the current evolution of the HCMI Program. A pilot comprehensive center for the homeless has been initiated at the Dallas, Texas, HCMI site. Special domiciliary programs for the homeless have been established at twenty-four VA Medical Centers. Other HCMI sites are developing compensated work therapy/independent housing programs. New VA collaborations include a demonstration project with the Social Security Administration and with the Veterans Benefits Administration, both of which involve outreach to the homeless and expedited claims.

Also, the VA is working with HUD to combine the VA's homeless case management with HUD's housing resources. In Buffalo, the HCMI program, Western New

York Veterans Housing Coalition, and the City of Buffalo have united to submit a Shelter Plus Care Program to HUD. This proposal would provide forty-one permanent apartments to the homeless, with Section 8 Certificates and follow-up supportive services. These demonstration projects all promise better coordination of services and more services to homeless veterans.

No quick or easy solution will solve this immense problem, because homelessness is not just a housing issue. There are still many obstacles in accessing medical and psychiatric services for the homeless. Working together, agencies need to devise plans that will assist the homeless and bridge the gaps without duplicating services. Federal, state, and community agencies also need to collaborate to develop policies and practices that will not exclude the homeless, but will embrace them.

References

Abdellah, F. G., Chamberland, J. G., and Levine, I. S. (Sept.–Oct. 1986). "Role of Nurses in Meeting Needs of the Homeless: Summary of a Workshop for Providers Researchers, and Educators." *Public Health Reports* 101, no.5 p. 494–98.

Ball, J., and Havassy, B. E. (Sept.1984). "A Survey of the Problems and Needs of Homeless Consumers of Acute Psychiatric Care." *Hospital and Community Psychiatry* 35, no.9; p.917–21.

Bassuk, E. L., Rubin, L., and Alison, L. (Dec. 1984). "Is Homelessness a Mental Health Problem?" *American Journal of Psychiatry* 141(12); p.1546–49.

Cohen, M. B. (Nov. 1989). "Social Work Practice with Homeless Mentally Ill People: Engaging the Client." *Social Work*; p. 505–9.

Kosof, A. (1987). *Homeless in America*. New York: Franklin Watts Publishing Co.

Martin, P. (Jan. 1987). "How We Help and Harm the Homeless." *Harper's Magazine*; p.36–47.

Robertson, M. (1987). "Homeless Veterans: An Emerging Problem?" In *The Homeless in Contemporary Society*, R. Bringham, R. Green, and S. White. Beverly Hills, Calif.; Sage Press.

Rosenheck, R., Gallup, P., Leda, C., Keating, S., and Errera, P. (1991). The Fourth Report on the Department of Veterans Affairs Homeless Chronically Mentally Ill Veterans Program. West Haven, Conn.: Northeast Program Evaluation Center, Department of Veterans Affairs.

Rosenheck, R., Leda, C., Gallup, P., Astrachan, B., Leaf, P., Thompson, D., and Errera, P. (Sept. 1989). "Initial Assessment Data from a 43 Site Program for Homeless Chronic Mentally Ill Veterans," *Hospital and Community Psychiatry* 40, no.9; 937–42.

Rosenheck, R., Gallup, P., Leda, C., Thompson D., and Errera, P. (1988). "Reaching Out: The Second Progress Report on the Homeless Chronically

Mentally Ill Veterans Program." West Haven, Conn.: Northeast Program Evaluation Center, Department of Veterans Affairs.

Surber, R. W. Dwyer, E., Ryan, K. J. Goldfinger, R. and Kelly, J. T. (March–April 1988). "Medical and Psychiatric Needs of the Homeless—A Preliminary Response." *Social Work*; p. 116–19.

Susser, E., Goldfinger, S. M., and White, A. (Oct. 1990). "Some Clinical Approaches to the Homeless Mentally Ill." *Community Mental Health Journal*, 26, no.5; 463–80.

Torrey, E. F.. (1988). *Nowhere To Go*, New York: Harper and Row.

SECTION 6

Innovative Approaches to Nursing Service, Practice, and Education

The Homeless Population: A Clinical Laboratory for Students in Community Health and Psychiatric/Mental Health Nursing

Judith Anderson

Abstract

This chapter explores the use of a homeless center/shelter as a clinical laboratory for undergraduate nursing students enrolled in community health and psychiatric/ mental health nursing and discusses the integration of clinical experiences and educational objectives for student experience with homeless individuals and families. Specific student learning experiences providing direct nursing care to individual clients and families, networking, and client advocacy and student-developed projects specific to the needs of the homeless are described. Also included are student reactions in working with the homeless.

For more than five years the Medical College of Ohio at the Toledo School of Nursing has used a homeless setting for a joint community health and psychiatric–mental health nursing project for undergraduate and graduate students.

Over the years we have grown from having no headquarters and only four students at a time to having more than twenty students working out of our faculty-created, faculty-run nursing clinic.

I am a psychiatric clinical nurse specialist with a background in community health and teach psychiatric–mental health nursing to senior-level undergraduate and graduate nursing students. Dr. Martha L. Pituch has had long academic and practical experience in community health and teaches advanced students. Together, we work to coordinate nursing student experiences in a community center and shelter for the homeless.

Our joint efforts began in the fall of 1984, when the plight of the homeless in our community and across the nation began to elicit grave concern. A local community

center for the homeless advertised plans to establish a thirty-bed shelter for men
and women adjacent to their center. Roles for both psychiatric and community
health nurses working with the homeless seemed evident. We approached the
center requesting a combined psychiatric and community health nursing clinical
experience for a small group of undergraduate students. Clinical activities were
coordinated to maximize the students' time. We also negotiated for our students to
assist at a once-a-week, free health clinic that came to this homeless center, as well
as establishing a small faculty practice there. Following our first year, we surveyed
those early students and were able to publish an article chronicling our initial experiences (Anderson and Martaus 1987).

Today, we share one or two undergraduate clinical groups for two quarters each
year, and, during the other quarters, serve as preceptors to our Registered Nurse/Bac-
calaureate Nursing Students who elect to have either their community health and/
or psychiatric–mental health nursing clinical experiences with the homeless. We
also have advised and supervised individual graduate nursing students from our
school in adult health, community health, or psychiatric–mental health nursing for
clinical experience, master's projects, and research field experiences.

Four years ago, the free health clinic moved out of the center to a nearby location. We were left without a health room or base, yet the health needs that we were
uncovering every day were mounting. Our personal caseloads had grown, and we
had gained the trust of the staff and of the many clients who frequented the center.
Shelter staff, in particular, had come to rely on our health assessments of all new
shelter admissions. At the same time, reimbursed practice became an expectation
for those faculty who wished to have a practice. So we intensified our search for
funds and a place to house our students.

In the interim we were able to continue our school-supported practice at the
center, and, in so doing, began what is now our nursing clinic. We still did not have
a room, but we had file space and were able to share common space and telephones
with the other workers. Everyone at the center and our school supported our efforts, but there was no money to finance us.

Finally we were able to each negotiate a 25% practice at the center as nurse/case
managers and create a 50% faculty-run nursing clinic that is occupied for the other
50% of the time by our student clinical groups. This funding is part of a large, community-based health care program for the homeless grant under the McKinney
Homeless Assistance Act of 1987. We are presently in the third year of the grant,
which is administered by a community-based health clinic and is part of a homeless
network. Through this network we now have access to clinic, emergency room, and
mental health care for our clients, as well as transportation for their appointments.

In our practice, we each spend about ten hours per week in the clinic. In addition
we also work during our quarter breaks and the summer. Our position is ideal right
now because we set our own hours and can be flexible. This is very important because we have full-time faculty appointments and are expected to carry a full-ser-
vice load at the school.

The students spend from twelve to eighteen hours per week at the center. Those spending the eighteen hours are doing the joint community-psychiatric experience, while the twelve-hour group is doing community health experience only. The students' schedules result in three full days of service at the shelter—thus our nursing clinic ends up being open full time for more than half the year.

Over the years we have learned a few things about preparing students for working with the homeless and for the culture shock they all face. We have become enculturated and thus forget how our setting seems to the first timer. Each group, however, brings us back to our early days, as we help them to work through their initial feelings. It is at such times that having a partner faculty person is invaluable as we work very closely in helping the students adjust.

In the beginning the students chose our setting themselves and, since we only had four students, we were able to be very selective among applicants. Students still select our groups; however, we no longer have the luxury of knowing who is coming. The larger group can be up to thirty students (ten students in three groups), so orientation is very different and requires other procedures.

We work together to orient the groups jointly. Ideally, we meet both groups together and talk about the experience. We use some very effective audiovisuals: videotapes that portray homelessness as a national issue, local news broadcasts that discuss Toledo's homeless problems, and a videotape of the 1989 March for Housing held in Washington, D.C. made by a student. We also have a student-created and narrated slide-tape program entitled "An Introduction to the Student Experience at St. Paul's" that helps the students visualize the setting and see and hear about the activities. Our students report that it also lessens their initial shock and allows them to see St. Paul's as a place where students and clients are relaxed, friendly, and enjoy being with each other.

We provide each student with an orientation folder that identifies the major health concerns of the homeless, tells what is expected of the student, describes the setting and expectations of all center employees, contains the mission statement of the agency, and includes a map on how to get there and where to park.

We then adjourn to St. Paul's, where the center staff provides a short orientation and students are given a tour. It works best if we then have time for the students to mingle with the clients; however, most often our time restraints preclude this.

Over the years the student groups have been consistent in how they have adapted to working with the homeless. Initially, they all feel some sort of shock. They may be repulsed by the odors, overwhelmed by the number of men, fearful of their stares, and embarrassed by inappropriate remarks made by some of the men that experience has taught us to regard as a "rite of passage" in this culture. This behavior disappears, for the most part, within a couple of weeks, and the students become more adept at handling the isolated remarks that continue. Clients also become very protective of the students.

In the beginning some students report that the client stares or tells them "stay away from me," while other students report that the same stares are indicating "that you couldn't possibly ever begin to help me." Other students report feeling immense guilt for having lived more privileged lives. Many have trouble leaving their clients' problems at the center and find they spend much time after work thinking about their clients' situations. All need help in handling their feelings and interpretations.

Some students come with biases, prejudices, fixed beliefs, and fears that hinder their ability to serve. It is not unusual for a student to have had minimal exposure to poverty, to have never before been assigned to a male patient, or talked with a black man or people who have been involved with drugs, prostitution, or other illegal activities. However, we have had no attrition, and all students appear to have become more self-confident, self-assured, assertive, self-directed, and certainly more professional. This is a result of feeling positive about their accomplishments, from having to rely on their own skills and from the good will and respect they receive from the clients.

Student activities include helping in the clinic with first aid, health screenings, and health assessment on clinic clients and new shelter admissions. They become more knowledgeable of community resources as they do primary nursing which includes finding resources for their clients and even, when indicated, visiting the client in his or her group home, apartment, or hotel room.

Assessing for substance abuse/dependence and for suicidal ideation is a common experience for each student. Interacting with hallucinating and delusional clients becomes less threatening, although still challenging, and, at times, successful. Clinical conferences are times for students to share their joys and frustrations—everyone learns from the others. Having faculty in their practice setting also allows the students to have good role models from whom to learn. Usually when I am in an interaction with a client, students either assist or observe. Students join with clients in a variety of regularly scheduled recreational and social activities including games and creative arts. Last fall the students decided to have a make-over session for the women, as they were concerned about the women who reported lack of mirrors, lost makeup, and not being able to curl their hair. The students were able to obtain donations of hair-care supplies from a nearby beauty school including shampoo, styling gel, hair spray, combs, and brushes. The students then supplied the curling irons, blow-dryers, and the makeup. It was so successful that it has been repeated each quarter since.

We now are planning to have a similar session for the men, as a result of comments we have received from the clients. The make-over session and some parties have been held toward the end of the quarter to give the students and the clients a chance to become acquainted with each other. Both sessions have been very popular; it has been remarkable to see the clients' responses. At our first makeover session we had a battered woman with early stages of Huntington's chorea who was very reluctant to come into the room. After talking with the client, the student discovered that she had not washed her hair for a long time because she found it difficult to balance herself at a sink, and her apartment had no shower or tub. Her clothes were also soaked that day, as she had walked to the center in the rain. This client was literally transformed by having her clothes dried, her hair washed and styled, and makeup applied. Later she was observed smiling in the lunch line, and she hasn't missed a make-over session since.

As part of the community health requirements, each student must do a teaching-learning project. First aid, breast and testicular self-examination, hypertension, frostbite, diabetes, cancer, AIDS, and other sexually transmitted diseases are a few of the topics that have been presented. Two students prepared a videotape for clients on frostbite that included a demonstration on how to line shoes with cardboard and pantlegs with newspaper. It also demonstrated how to insulate a cardboard box with paper and how to position the box out of the wind. For best effect, the students filmed this outside in winter. Another group prepared a notebook on the homeless shelters in Toledo that included photographs of the facilities and details regarding criteria for admission, programs offered, and other relevant information.

In closing, I would like to share with you some of the benefits of having undergraduate nursing students involved with the homeless:

1. Students are conditioned to become proactive as nurses and to understand the plight of the homeless more fully.
2. Students learn that seeing a client holistically is essential, that treating a presenting problem as they often do elsewhere may actually be a waste of time and energy. They learn to start where the client is.
3. They learn the necessity of working *with* the client in developing all goals and plans, for, if the client does not respond positively to what we are offering, then adherence probably will not occur.
4. Students also learn to be flexible and to begin wherever the client is. This obstacle has been very hard for many of the registered nurses in our registered nurse completion program and probably reflects their previous indoctrination into the health-care system's "care on *my* terms" philosophy.
5. Students also learn to routinely address suicide and to routinely elicit drug and alcohol patterns and use. Hopefully, these practices will be retained as they move on in their nursing careers.
6. Frequently interacting with hallucinating and delusional clients reduces students' fear of these clients. They also become better at reducing the hallucinating person's anxiety, are better at recognizing delusional thinking, and, most importantly, see these people as individuals with problems, people to be helped, not avoided.

I would like to close with remarks from three students from our first group: "I feel that I can sit down and talk with a depressed client and not be afraid of what he might say. I know I can handle it."

"Being put in a situation of not knowing what I was going to say [in advance], not knowing anything about the person, and having to find out all of the information on my own was a helpful experience for me. It helped me think quicker and was a challenge. I came to really enjoy it."

"I discovered that homeless people are humble, friendly, and do participate in self-care more than I thought—they really care about their health and their lives."

Reference

Anderson, J., and Martaus, T. (1987). "Combining Community Health and Psychosocial Nursing: A Clinical Experience with the Homeless for Generic Baccalaureate Nursing Students." *Journal of Nursing Education* 26 (5); 189–93.

CHAPTER 19

Testing a College-Based Nursing Model for Health Care for the Homeless

Jane C. Swart
Mary Ann Christ
Paige Gradick

Abstract

With the growth of the homeless population, nurses are being challenged to rethink and modify traditional health-care delivery systems. Nurses have responded to this challenge by designing and implementing innovative nurse clinics to meet the unique needs of the homeless. One example of an innovative clinic is the Nurse Clinic for the Homeless in Charleston, South Carolina. This clinic, supported by a grant from the Department of Health and Human Services, Division of Nursing, Special Projects, is now providing primary health care and health promotion/education services to homeless clients.

The purpose of this chapter is to share experiences in implementing, testing and evaluating a college-based nursing model for providing health care to the homeless. In particular, this presentation focuses on the following critical components of the model: case management, services, information management, cost analysis and research/evaluation. The case management model provides the organizational framework for the structure, implementation, and consistency of clinic activities. It includes assessment, intake and triage, specific services provided, referral, follow-up, and evaluation processes. Service and learning models relating to paid staff, volunteers, and student/faculty involvement in clinic activities are assessed for efficiency and effectiveness. The computerized information management system for primary care clinics implemented at the Nurse Clinic for the Homeless is described and evaluated. The system utilizes Mumps Utility Multi Program System (MUMPS) programming language and is based on public domain software. Models for monitoring costs and assessing effectiveness and for evaluating programs are included within the Nurse Clinic Model.

This project was supported in part by the Special Project Grants Program in the Nursing Education Practice Resources Branch, Division of Nursing, U.S. Department of Health and Human Services, Public Health Service, Health Resources and Services Administration, Bureau of Health Professions Administration, Grant Number 5D10NU60047, initial grant period: September 1, 1988, to August 31, 1991. At the time of this writing the project was not fully implemented and actual outcome data was limited.

Introduction

In the United States, homelessness is a persistent and pernicious societal problem. The number of homeless persons continues to escalate at an alarming rate. Actual numbers of homeless are difficult to determine for a variety of reasons and the figures vary depending on the source. For example, in 1985 the numbers of homeless reported ranged from 250,000 to 3,000,000 people without a permanent residence (Brickner et al. 1985; U.S. Department of Urban Development 1984).

The homeless population is one of the most underserved and disenfranchised groups in the country. The unmet social, economic, and health needs of this group are of growing concern to public and private sectors alike. Changes in size and composition of the homeless population can be traced to fluctuations in economic circumstances and demographic forces (Institute of Medicine 1988). Unemployment, underemployment, lack of available low-income housing, family disorganization, lack of benefits, deinstitutionalization of the mentally ill, and certain personal factors such as alcoholism and chronic substance abuse are implicated in the condition known as homelessness (Brickner et al. 1985). Efforts to alleviate the immediate problems of the homeless are typically concentrated on emergency measures to provide food, shelter, and clothing. Until fairly recently, health care has not been a part of these emergency responses (Brickner et al. 1985).

Homeless persons are particularly vulnerable to illness due to their life-style on the streets. Unfortunately, because of the difficulty that the homeless experience trying to access the health care system, they often do not seek or receive treatment for health problems until a crisis situation arises. Then the homeless usually seek health-care in one of the most expensive components of the health-care system, the hospital emergency room, for conditions that have progressed to much more serious problem states that are more difficult and costly to treat.

Problem and Need

There have always been homeless people in the world and in the United States. Relatively permanent "skid rows" exist in many large cities where homeless people congregate. For a long time such areas perpetuated a stereotype of the homeless as old, drunk, used-up men, persons marginal to society whom much of society found easy to ignore. Since the early 1980s, the growing body of literature about the homeless has shattered the stereotypes and helped homelessness in America achieve the dubious status of a household word. The topic now appears as much in the popular media as professional literature and it is recognized that the homeless are a cross section of American society, including men, women, and children of all ethnic and religious backgrounds and ages.

Nationally, 33% of the homeless are women and children, and this is the fastest growing segment of the homeless population. The literature suggests that homeless persons fall into four general and partially overlapping groups: street people, persons with chronic alcoholism or other substance abuse, people with chronic mental illness, and situationally homeless people. In shelters around the country, one may see elderly women who have raised and educated children, but whose children say no when she is left without money when her husband dies. One may also meet teenage or adult alcoholics whose parents or families have simply had enough.

Homeless individuals are subjected to the same illnesses as the general population. However, epidemiological data documents that their life-style, which includes prolonged exposure to the elements, crowded conditions and lack of privacy, poor nutrition and hygiene, and increased stress levels, predisposes them to exacerbation of chronic illnesses and puts them at risk for contracting various infectious diseases. Acute illnesses, which begin as minor problems, can become potentially life threatening and, at times, a threat to others, when they go unattended.

Health Care for Charleston Homeless

In exploring the problem of homelessness in Charleston, South Carolina, nursing faculty from the College of Nursing, Medical University of South Carolina, met with local shelter directors who discussed the plight of the homeless guests who frequented the shelters and expressed serious concern about their unmet health needs. It was through these meetings that the seeds of an idea were planted. The idea was that nurses in Charleston could take the leadership in providing access to health care for homeless people. Those seeds were nurtured over a three-year period through the involvement of College of Nursing faculty and students with the homeless and with providing health clinics at the Charleston Interfaith Crisis Ministry Helping Ourselves Meet Emergencies (HOME) Shelter. During this period the informal "Wednesday Night Clinic," initiated by the nursing school faculty and staffed primarily by nursing faculty, students, and community nurse volunteers, also attracted medical student volunteers. Medical students and faculty then implemented a Wednesday evening medical clinic as a family practice student project during the year before the start of the Nurse Clinic for the Homeless. While nursing faculty and students maintained a presence in the Wednesday clinic, primary efforts were directed toward meeting a totally neglected health problem by

providing an early morning foot clinic for homeless individuals and toward assessing overall health service needs for this population.

Needs Assessment

As the relationship developed between the shelter and College of Nursing faculty
and students, the need for more specific data about the Charleston homeless and
their health became obvious. Faculty, graduate students, and community nurses
participated in a faculty designed descriptive survey of health status and characteristics of the homeless (Malloy et al 1988). Sensitivity to the needs of the homeless increased dramatically during those interviews.

The survey, based on one hour interviews with forty-five male and five female
subjects, which equaled approximately one half of shelter guests on any given
night, described the personal characteristics, health status, and utilization of health
services of the homeless population seeking refuge in an urban shelter. Although
based on a small sample from a single shelter serving predominantly males at the
time the survey was conducted, results were consistent with those of studies conducted in other locales. The current homeless population differs greatly from the
stereotypical alcoholic, homeless older male of the past. It includes many young
men and a rapidly growing number of families, women with children, youth, and
chronically mentally ill persons. Unemployment, underemployment, and lack of
low-cost housing are perceived as root causes of the growing homelessness problem in all areas of the United States, but particularly its urban areas. Maintaining
health, while considered important, is only one of a myriad of competing priorities
for the homeless, not the least of which are food and shelter. There is also a problem
of lack of access to appropriate and affordable health-care services that adds to the
plight of the homeless, and that was a major impetus for the development of this
college-based model nurse clinic for the homeless.

A Model Nurse Clinic for the Homeless

In response to the health needs of the homeless in Charleston, several College of
Nursing faculty authored a proposal, which was funded for a three-year period, to
develop and implement a nurse-managed health-care clinic at an established shelter for the homeless. To demonstrate methods to improve access to health care for
the homeless in Charleston, the project established a free-standing nurse-managed
clinic to provide nursing services for Charleston homeless. Four objectives provided an organizing framework for the project: 1) provide nursing services to the
homeless; 2) initiate and evaluate a case management model that facilitates referral
and follow-up, improves continuity of care, and avoids duplication of health-care

services; 3) increase awareness of students, faculty and other community nurses of the multiple variables influencing health of the homeless; and, 4) determine cost of nursing services delivered to the homeless in community-based, non-institutional settings.

Interestingly enough, although not available during the original proposal development, the objectives developed for focusing the project were very consistent with recommendations made by the American Public Health Association (APHA) invitational conference on the role of nurses in meeting the health/mental health needs of the homeless. The conference, sponsored by the U.S. Public Health Service and the National Institute of Mental Health, recommended improved professional education to enable health-care providers to better meet the needs of the homeless; improvements in the system, including flexible and diverse care and reimbursement models, increased commitment and availability of low cost housing; support for community and family living initiatives that keep families intact, discharge planning and follow-up; nursing advocacy for a coordinated and comprehensive response to the health needs of the homeless with an emphasis on community-based services; and increased nursing research to address the gaps in knowledge that currently hinder the provision of services to the homeless population. The workshop groups also recommended that case management be a focus for developing model services and called for a major conference to promote a reeducative process for nurses regarding care management and to evaluate its use with different types of patients in various care delivery settings (APHA 1986).

Many of these elements, notably the emphasis on increasing access, continuity of care, case management, and education of nurses about health care for the homeless, were part of the college-based model for providing for the health needs of the homeless.

Given the demonstration nature of this project, evaluation was considered a major component. The primary goal of the evaluation plan was to measure the efficiency and effectiveness of the project's intervention in the problem of providing access to health-care services for Charleston's homeless. For purposes of evaluation, the main objectives and activities of this proposal to establish a demonstration nursing clinic for the homeless were perceived as addressing three broad goals:

I.   To improve access to health care for Charleston's homeless through the delivery of high-quality nursing services.
     Objective 1: Establish a nurse-managed clinic to provide nursing services for the homeless in Charleston.
II. To demonstrate the cost-effectiveness of a community-based nursing practice model in providing health services for the homeless.
     Objective 2: Evaluate a client case management model.
     Objective 3: Determine costs of nursing services provided for the homeless in a noninstitutional setting.

III. To increase the number of professional nurses who are prepared to work effectively with homeless persons.

Objective 4: Increase awareness of students, faculty, and other nurses of the multiple variables influencing the health of the homeless.

Evaluation Model

The model developed by the project evaluator involved systematic assessment of the linkages between the policies, goals, and objectives of the program established (the Nurse Clinic for the Homeless) and the needs, problems, and potential causes of problems that contributed to the high incidence of poor health-care utilization among the homeless. The evaluation model demanded review of both process and outcomes in the effort to ensure that appropriate data were available for staff decision making and the various constituent groups interested in the project.

Needs, Problems, and Probable Causes

The goals listed above emanated directly from the needs, problems, and probable causes of problems associated with health care for the homeless. Very briefly, there was a need to provide better access to high-quality health care for homeless persons. Both the news media and research literature have identified problems that support the existence of that need. An increase in the number of homeless in America has been documented, although the exact number varies widely in different reports. The literature also documents that this population has limited or no financial resources, lacks any strong support networks, is under or unemployed and thus rarely has employment benefits for health care, and frequently suffers from a variety of negative personal and social factors, including family violence, alcohol and drug abuse, and social disaffiliation.

These and other factors combine to make the homeless a very vulnerable population that is at risk for a wide variety of major physical and psychiatric acute and chronic conditions, as well as a myriad of other debilitating problems such as pediculosis, foot ulcers, and nutritional diseases, which are directly related to the conditions in which the homeless exist. Because homeless individuals' energies are used for marginal survival, they tend to neglect routine health care, ignore potentially serious health problems, and have difficulty negotiating the city's complex health-care systems.

When persons from this vulnerable population seek health care, they not only experience difficulty in accessing the system, but frequently come up against health-care providers whose understanding of their problems and response to their needs is less than satisfactory. Although there has been some improvement in the situation recently, many health-care providers lack any frame of reference in cultural or social diversity. Consequently they find it difficult to comprehend, much less understand, the behavior and the life circumstances of the homeless.

These factors lead the homeless to develop negative expectations and perceptions of the health-care system and health-care providers. The decreasing funds available for indigent care both locally and nationally, as well as the increasing corporatization of the American illness care system contribute to the limited treatment options available to the homeless. These circumstances reinforce the frequent frustration, bewilderment, and hopelessness that homeless persons experience as they seek to access needed health care. In Charleston, South Carolina, for example, there are no major sources of financial assistance to support health care for this population unless a medical emergency exists. Even the resources are limited, primarily to costly emergency room services. Free services by community-based, primary health-care providers are needed badly. Services that involve the client in developing skills for self care and decision making about health behaviors are an even more critical need and one that nurses especially are prepared to meet.

The act of making health services available may itself contribute to the problem, given the perception of barriers that many homeless persons have developed after repeated failures to achieve any kind of supportive or positive response from health-care providers. The Charleston Nurse Clinic for the Homeless identified several key characteristics for services that attract clients and enhance continuity of care for the homeless. Locating the Nurse Clinic on site at a shelter where a majority of homeless access food, clothing, showers, mental health and substance abuse counseling, social work services, and crisis assistance established the clinic as a part of the homeless person's daily life. It also enabled the clinic to complement and supplement already existing services and to more easily accomplish interagency and interdisciplinary referrals. Further, the chance of a client's getting "lost in the system" or "falling through the cracks" decreased substantially when close links were established among service components. Other key elements that encouraged clients to seek health care at the Nurse Clinic included the concerted effort of clinic staff to foster a trusting relationship with homeless clients, flexibility of scheduling, the comprehensiveness of primary-care services offered, and establishment of effective communication with homeless persons.

In planning services, project staff also found it important to identify and address the constraints and barriers that prevented homeless persons from obtaining the best results from the health care they received. Some deterrents to seeking proper health care were disaffiliation and lack of personal support through linkages with family, friends, or social organizations. Simple barriers often caused the greatest problems for homeless individuals. For instance, many homeless did not have access to clocks so multiple dose medication was often not feasible for these clients. Consequently, the Nurse Clinic prescribed once or twice daily medications and/or treatments whenever possible.

Often, because of elevated stress levels, mental illness, or alcohol or other substance abuse, homeless clients were forgetful and needed to be regularly reminded of referral and follow-up visits. They were reminded in numerous ways, including posting a note on the bulletin board where cots were set up nightly, reminding them through personal contact throughout the day, or by providing appointment cards. The Nurse Clinic used all these strategies to increase compliance and promote continuity of care.

Client perception, goals related to health-care, the outcomes expected by clients for both acute and chronic diseases, and how they anticipate achieving them, represents challenges for health-care providers. For example, before the provider prescribes a typical intervention for a health problem, such as elevating legs throughout the day for peripheral vascular disease, he should have a plan in place about how this can be accomplished by an individual with no home or no other priorities for the day. Prescribing medications creates a whole new set of problems stemming from difficulty in storage or refrigeration of medications, protecting supplies of medications from loss or theft, or remembering to take medications at prescribed times when you don't have a watch or your mind is wandering or focused on other priorities.

Treatment compliance and efficacy depend on the client's goals and priorities, as well as his psycho-physiological state. Health-care efforts will be futile and outcomes ineffective unless health services are tailored to the homeless and the enhancers and deterrents for the individual and the prescribed therapy are clearly articulated and addressed with the client.

Nurses are well prepared to manage many acute and chronic illnesses. They also have a strong traditional emphasis on promoting positive health behaviors, preventing complications from health problems, and facilitating the development of self-care health behaviors. The professional knowledge and skills and emphasis on caring of nursing practitioners constitute an untapped resource for meeting primary health-care needs for this vulnerable population. It was the premise of this project and the focus for evaluation that nurses can provide primary health care through nursing services. The use of case management within a nurse clinic delivery model, can maximize the use of existing health resources and produce positive health outcomes for clients.

Concisely stated, these issues related to the homeless and health care were both the rationale for program goals and objectives and the outcome variables against which program success were to be measured. The remainder of the evaluation plan dealt more specifically with the foci, methods, and instruments to be used in evaluation, as well as with plans for dissemination of findings. As mentioned previously, evaluation of this project focused on both the efficiency and effectiveness of the nurse clinic health-care delivery model in addressing the needs of Charleston's homeless.

Efficiency is concerned with system variables, that is, with program operational issues of all kinds. Thus the issue of efficiency has three-fold significance for this evaluation plan. (1) Evaluation of efficiency will provide an assessment of how well staff followed through on implementing the program activities and strategies outlined in proposal methodology. (2) Efficiency also involves cost as well as process. Therefore, assessment of efficiency will document how much it costs to provide primary care through a nurse clinic delivery model, as it describes steps, activities, and strategies that have potential value for successful implementation of similar projects by other persons in other settings. (3) In addition, evaluation of efficiency will provide a description of the significant characteristics of program operations and participants, as well as their role and influence on changes in outcome variables.

Evaluation of the *effectiveness* of this project to improve access to health care for the homeless, on the other hand, focuses on assessing outcomes. Data were generated to determine what had happened to the targeted homeless population in terms of the types and amount of health services they utilized, as well as change in their health behaviors and their perceptions of health-care providers. In addition, data were collected and analyzed to determine whether change had occurred in the attitudes and behaviors of nurses and nursing students related to the homeless, and in their feelings of satisfaction in working with nontraditional, community-based populations. Also considered were the effectiveness of a client case management model, and of a nurse clinic as a cost-effective alternative model for delivering health services for the homeless.

Key Questions

In summary, the key questions related to efficiency and effectiveness served as the focus for evaluation of a college-based model for delivering health care for the homeless include:

1. Is the nurse-run clinic reaching the targeted problem population—Charleston's homeless? (Who is being reached and who is not being reached?)
2. Is the project being implemented in the ways specified in the proposal methodology? (Are program concepts being implemented?)
3. What services are being provided and to whom?
4. What is the quality of services being provided?
5. Is the project effective in:
   a) changing availability, access to, and patterns of health-care services usage by the homeless of Charleston;
   b) demonstrating the effectiveness of a client case management model;
   c) changing knowledge, beliefs, and attitudes of nurses and nursing students toward the homeless and,
   d) demonstrating the effectiveness of a nurse clinic as an alternative model for the delivery of high-quality health-care services for the homeless?
6. Is it cost effective to provide primary health care services for the homeless through a nurse-clinic delivery model? (How does this concept of delivery compare to other options?)

The knowledge and experiences of the project authors and those from whom they sought consultation and input led to the establishment of policies by which the project translated agreed upon goals and objectives into action to address the needs, problems, and causes of problems that have been identified. Methodology outlines what should be happening regarding tasks, people, and strategies. What should occur is presented below in simplified form:

1. Delivery of health services to Charleston homeless through a nurse-managed clinic.
2. Improved access to health care for homeless.
3. Improved client tracking system, documenting increased usage of primary care services and decreased use of emergency care for non-emergency services and of hospitalizations and rehospitalizations, and improved compliance with treatment regimes.
4. Better knowledge and attitude base of professionals working with the homeless.
5. Recognition of nurse clinics as a cost-effective alternative model for delivering primary health services for nontraditional, community-based populations.

Project Development

As the nurse clinic for the homeless and the educational program for nursing professionals and students were implemented, evaluation data were collected to get a sense of what was really going on. The simplified model above was altered as new information about tasks, people, strategies and outcomes developed.

Measurement Indicators

The following measurement indicators were identified for changes in the primary outcome variables, reflected in the description of needs, problems, and causes of problems:

1. Increased use of primary health services by the homeless.
2. Increase in knowledge of the homeless about health, prevention, self-care activities, and accessing and utilizing the continuum of health-care services.
3. Improvement in perception of health-care providers by the homeless.
4. Improvements in knowledge and attitudes of nurse professionals and students related to the homeless.
5. Increased satisfaction of nurse health-care providers with their competency and confidence in working with the homeless.
6. Documentation of costs of providing primary health-care services through a nurse clinic.

7. Improvements in client case management, for example, tracking and monitoring of the homeless with respect to health status, compliance with treatment, health behaviors, self-care activities, and use of health-care system.

Specific measurement indicators for system or program variables for accomplishment of each major objective and its concomitant strategies/activities represented the key points for the formative evaluation plan. They were used in the development of quarterly evaluation reports provided to project staff and advisory committees for consideration in improving or changing objectives or methodology or adding new strategies. These reports were used to assess the efficiency of implementation strategies and planning for modifications and revision.

Evaluation Design

This project was a new model for the Charleston area for which clear comparisons did not exist and standards were not established. It was also a demonstration project involving a vulnerable and underserved population—the homeless. For these, as well as cost reasons, a true controlled experiment using comparison groups was not deemed feasible nor the most appropriate at the early stage.

The case study was used as the primary evaluation design for the overall project evaluation. Emphasis was on documentation and evaluation of what had occurred in the program, with heavy reliance on qualitative methodologies, observation, and interviews. In generating data relevant to some of the measurement indicators, such as changes in knowledge, attitudes, behaviors, etc., the case-study method was combined with a time-series design so that "before and after" program implementation comparisons could be made. In this case the group being studied was used as its own comparison since data were analyzed to compare performance at various stages to assess changes due to project activities.

An effort was made to determine if enough data were available, through local hospitals that provided indigent care, and from the preliminary clinic services offered by Colleges of Nursing and Medicine faculty, and students, to establish some comparisons between the homeless served by this project and homeless groups seeking services elsewhere in the community.

This latter design, if it proved to be viable, was to be used to determine changes and/or differences in patterns of use of health-care services, in client management patterns, and in costs of services.

Data Collection Instruments

Evaluation of this demonstration nurse clinic project involved an assessment of the degree of success in meeting each of the project's primary objectives. A GANTT chart was used to schedule collection and tallying of results and to assign people to data collection activities.* Forms developed for collecting data about clients, services, providers, and costs became part of clinic operations. Forms were completed by health-care providers and staff. Research assistants were assigned to compile data from completed forms under the direction of the project evaluator.

All instruments that had not been standardized or validated in other research studies were pilot tested to ensure that they provided reliable data of the kind intended. When appropriate, multiple measures were used to increase credibility of measurement outcomes.

The specific processes and instruments for the outcome evaluation and for use in the operation of the clinic remain were developed or finalized during the project. The types of instruments and/or data needed for evaluation purposes were identified below under each of the major objectives of the project.

Objective 1:   Provide Nursing Services to the Homeless

The evaluation of nursing clinic services required the collection of data related to characteristics of clients, characteristics of providers and services, client health-care needs, and the extent to which these needs were met through participation in the nurse clinic. It was planned that the following data collection instruments were to be used:

Homeless Client Health Profile Tool.   No instrument specifically suited to this evaluation project was found, although there were a number of standardized instruments that included items that were significant for this population. The study conducted by College of Nursing faculty, which was described earlier, provided descriptive data on Charleston's homeless. The data collection instrument used in that project were incorporated into a client profile tool that was based on published instruments and that focussed on the client's bio-psycho-social functioning, health needs, health status, demographic characteristics, health perceptions, perception of powerlessness related to health and illness, and perception of health services and health-care providers.

The instrument was developed as an intake interview schedule to be used with all clients. Subscales of the instrument were also used in the intervals designated by the time-series design to collect data to assess changes over time in some of the variables measured, notably patient perceptions, health status, and self-help activities.

Site Appraisal Review.   Again, there was no published instrument that specifically met the data collection needs for this aspect of the project evaluation.

---

* GANTT is a project management chart that matches timelines with activities. It was named after Henry Gantt, who developed it in the 1920s, and has been used etensively since that time.

However, the conceptual framework used by Lemke and Moos (1990) in their development of tools for conducting a comprehensive assessment of sheltered care settings were modified to provide a format for a site appraisal of the nurse clinic for the homeless. The four relevant domains they identified are listed as: physical and architectural resources, policy and program resources, resident and staff resources, and social climate resources. Data collected with the instrument developed included information about the location and setting of the clinic, access and financial arrangements, expectations and regulations concerning client behavior, and participation in clinic services and activities, the clinic's organizational structure and its linkages with other health-care providers and services, the services provided for clients, client utilization of services and activities of the clinic, the social relationships and perceived opportunities for growth offered within the clinic, and observer impressions of client and staff behavior/functioning.

Objective 2: Evaluate a Client Case Management Model for Noninstitutional Clients

A variety of services were established to meet the health needs of the homeless of Charleston. The unique characteristics of this population required the development of a case management model that (1) documents the characteristics of homeless clients; (2) facilitates the documentation of nursing interventions, referrals to other health providers/services, tracking, and follow-up of clients; (3) establishes quality assurance processes; and, (4) documents client outcomes. The initial conceptualization of a model of case management used in the project is depicted in Figure 19.1. Evaluation tool(s) for this objective were developed based on the final model actually put in place in the clinic.

Objective 3: Increase Awareness of Students, Faculty, and Other Nurses of the Multiple Variables Influencing the Health of the Homeless

During the project, many nurses, nursing students, and volunteers were recruited and oriented to the clinic services. Questionnaires and interview schedules were developed and administered prior to and following their participation in the educational programs and in the implementation of clinic activities and services. These instruments assessed changes in attitudes, values, and behaviors related to providing health care for the homeless, as well as knowledge about the homeless population and the major variables impacting their life-style and health behavior choices. These instruments were developed during the first few months of the project prior to the implementation of the educational component or volunteer network.

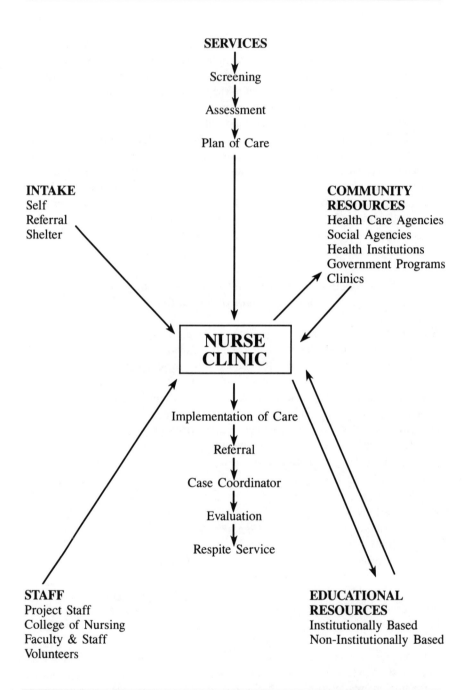

SERVICES

Screening

Assessment

Plan of Care

INTAKE
Self
Referral
Shelter

**COMMUNITY
RESOURCES**
Health Care Agencies
Social Agencies
Health Institutions
Government Programs
Clinics

**NURSE
CLINIC**

Implementation of Care

Referral

Case Coordinator

Evaluation

Respite Service

STAFF
Project Staff
College of Nursing
Faculty & Staff
Volunteers

**EDUCATIONAL
RESOURCES**
Institutionally Based
Non-Institutionally Based

FIGURE 19.1

Objective 4: Determine Cost of Nursing Services Delivered to the Homeless in a Noninstitutionalized Setting

A cost model was implemented to identify and track cost of services provided both by paid and volunteer health care providers. Included were the costs of facilities, resources, and staff activities and services. The model was oriented to tying costs to client health needs and utilized a computer based data collection process. It was based on a client classification system that stems from an assessment of acuity and on identification of the average nursing care cost per case. In determining costs, direct (salaries or their equivalent in the case of volunteers or students, equipment and supplies) and indirect expenses, as well as miscellaneous costs were included. Instruments were to be developed that would be specific to a nurse clinic for the homeless.

Objective 5: Evaluate the Overall Project

A final summative evaluation was completed that provided participant profiles and role performance data on both clients and providers. Included in the summative evaluation were assessments of (1) efficiency of the nurse clinic model in delivering health services for the homeless; (2) effectiveness of services; (3) effectiveness of volunteer training program and other components of educational program; (4) effectiveness of project in changing client and provider attitudes, beliefs, knowledge, and behaviors; (5) effectiveness of a client case management model; and, (6) cost-effectiveness of the nurse clinic model.

Project Implementation

A specific philosophy shaped the decisions related to development of the Nurse Clinic for the Homeless. This philosophy espoused the beliefs that all persons have inherent value and dignity and that they are entitled to optimal health care, a safe and therapeutic environment, appropriate treatment for health problems, and opportunities for maximizing health promotion/disease prevention and self care, regardless of their position in society or ability to seek health care for themselves.

During the initial planning phase for the Nurse Clinic, the nurse practitioner/ clinic coordinator along with faculty and student volunteers offered daily nursing services to the homeless at the homeless shelter and served as a health-care resource to the staff. Having a visible presence on site at the shelter, offering flexible hours as well as a weekly scheduled foot clinic, contributed to the rapid rapport developed between the shelter guests and the clinic. Only after a trusting relationship developed were homeless clients willing to participate in self-care, follow-up, and referral activities. Before that they would access clinic services only in the face of acute problems and would not take advantage of health promotion or prevention services. The clients were seen in their own environment, that is, on the sidewalk, in the parking lot, during soup kitchen, in the hallways of the shelter. This was non-threatening and increased the willingness of clients to avail themselves of treatment and follow-up health-care services offered by the Nurse Clinic.

A cadre of nurse volunteers helped staff the Nurse Clinic. These committed and talented individuals came from a variety of nursing backgrounds, but all had in common an interest in increasing access to health care for underserved and vulnerable persons. Given limited fiscal resources, the Nurse Clinic could not function either efficiently or effectively without these nurse volunteers. They functioned under a specific position description and assisted the family nurse practitioner/ clinic coordinator in providing hands-on care, setting up and breaking down the clinic, and provided patient education, follow-up, and referral services and activities.

Services provided by the Nurse Clinic and the scheduled availability of services varied according to client and system needs. In keeping with identified health-care needs of homeless individuals, clinic services included blood chemistries; diabetes, hypertension, and vision screening; health assessments; well baby examinations; pregnancy testing and counseling; prenatal/postpartum counseling and follow-up with community health-care services. Clinic staff also provided client advocacy, arrangement of transportation to health-care appointments or hospital services, canes, crutch tips and crutches, lotion, bandage supplies, and medications.

Project and clinic faculty and staff became adept at convincing other persons, groups, or companies to contribute supplies and services toward the health and well-being of the homeless. For example, because of contributions obtained from a mill that does business in the state and from a local discount store, clients attending the weekly foot clinic were provided with clean socks and, if needed, a certificate for a pair of shoes. Also, an optometrist contributed one night a week to provide eye examinations for persons referred from the Nurse Clinic, and, if needed, clients received a certificate donated by a local service organization that was used to obtain a pair of glasses. Lists were compiled of physicians and dentists who agreed to take a certain number of referrals per month at no cost to the homeless or to the Nurse Clinic. Three community physicians agreed to share responsibility for providing the consultation and "backup" required under state law. They worked with the clinic coordinator to develop a mutually agreeable set of clinical protocols. Once these were established and the issue of liability clarified, the physicians agreed to be available by telephone during the times that primary health-care clinics were scheduled. All clinic services were provided by the nurse practitioner, volunteer nurses, faculty, and students.

The Nurse Clinic tried not to duplicate existing health-care services that were available within the community for homeless persons, but did offer those services either not available or not accessible because of distance and transportation problems, cost of services, overcrowding of service facility, ineligibility, and/or fragmentation of services. Health education was another major component of nurse-managed health care. Disease prevention, health promotion, and teaching self care were major service components of the Nurse Clinic. Special attention was given to developing educational materials that were at an appropriate literacy level and that were relevant to the health needs and life context of the homeless.

Case Management and Data Base Management Systems

Full implementation of the evaluation model rested on final development of a case management model of health-care delivery and the computerization of a data management system. These systems were designed to accommodate the transient nature of the homeless population, problems with compliance, inadequate follow-through and feedback from community referrals, and lack of established mechanisms for collaboration among various segments of the community working with the homeless. Without effective and efficient case management and information management systems the homeless client often "falls through the cracks" of the health-care system.

The case management model of health-care delivery used within the Nurse Clinic for the Homeless included intake assessment, plan of care, monitoring, tracking, advocacy, referral, and follow-up of clients. Referred to by Zander (1985) as "second generation primary nursing," it combined the principles of primary nursing and managed care. The case manager accepted accountability for primary health care management and the outcomes of care for entire episodes of illness care or chronicity management (Center for Nursing Case Management 1988).

The Nurse Clinic for the Homeless project focussed on four concepts that frame the context of the case management model: collaboration, client care, evaluation, and resources. Collaboration provided the framework for decision making and collaborative practice; used the skills and knowledge of a variety of care providers; and established mutually agreed upon outcomes, timelines, and care processes. The project had developed a sound set of protocols for managing episodic illnesses of clients, as well as criteria for referral, that were mutually "signed off on" by the nurse practitioner/clinic coordinator and volunteer community physician/consultants. The concept of client care fostered an integrated approach; included mechanisms to obtain, negotiate, coordinate, and evaluate services across delivery systems to accomplish expected outcomes in a cost-efficient manner; and incorporated learning services for the educational needs of clients, students, and staff.

Evaluation emphasized a framework for clinic outcomes and a system for evaluation of financial outcomes. It incorporated a mechanism to determine contributions and effectiveness of care providers and to evaluate quality assurance and implementation of nursing standards. Further, it facilated identification, evaluation, and change for ineffective and inefficient management of cases and use of resources. The concept of resources promotes efficient and effective use of resources, appropriate in amount and sequence to client case type and specified outcomes. This component of the clinic required the implementation of a computerized information management system to coordinate data and decision making.

The computerized information system developed to support the health record, research, case management, and evaluation needs of the homeless project was designed around the VA FileMan software. The VA FileMan is a multiuser data base management system written in the MUMPS programming language, which currently is in use in more than 150 VA hospitals and clinics. FileMan is not only an exceptionally well-designed and flexible data base management system, but is also a "language" in itself that permits specific applications to be developed. One such application, the Indian Health Service (IHS) Outpatient Management System, was chosen for this project's health data base and research needs. The major capabilities of the system include: 1) data entry/editing and forms design; 2) report design; 3) custom menu development; 4) complex data base retrieval/queries; 5) statistical procession; and, 6) multiuser remote communication.

The Resource and Patient Management System (RPMS) of the IHS Outpatient Management System is an integrated group of automated data systems designed to operate on microcomputers located in any hospital or clinic setting. The primary objective is to integrate patient care and cost data in a single automated data processing system that collects and stores a core set of health and management data that cuts across disciplines and facilities. A typical RPMS configuration in a health facility such as the Nurse Clinic for the Homeless might include these systems: Patient Registration, Pharmacy, Maternal and Child Health, Contract Health Services, Laboratory, and Patient Care Component.

The Patient Care Component (PCC) provides for the collection and storage on local computers of a broad range of health data resulting from clinic visits as well as various referrals. It is designed to support health-care delivery, planning, management, and research/evaluation. For health professionals, the PCC is a tool that assists in providing the type of care which addresses all of a patient's known health problems and preventive health needs. Data input options include, but are not limited to, date, type and location of visit, providers of service, assessments, diagnoses and procedures, health problems and treatment plans, personal and family histories, reproductive factors, laboratory test results, and a variety of other health-related information deemed significant for the project.

Both the VA FileMan and the IHS software packages are in the public domain. Both have been thoroughly tested and have proven to be "user friendly" and powerful software systems for the management of health information. The system is being implemented on an IBM PS/2 Model 50 microcomputer located at the College of Nursing and a Zenith Supersport 286 portable lap-top computer located at the Nurse Clinic for the Homeless. Both computers have modems and communication software to support the multiuser database and research needs of the IHS software and this project.

References

APHA. (March 6–7, 1986). *Proceedings of the Workshop: The Role of Nurses in Meeting the Health/Mental Health Needs of the Homeless*. Rockville, Md.: UPHS/NIMH.

Bowdler, J. (1989). "Health Problems of the Homeless." *The Nurse Practitioner*. 14(7):44–51.

Brickner, P. W., Scharer, L. K., Conanan, B., Elvy, A., and Savarese, M. (1985). *Health Care of Homeless People*. New York: Springer Publishing Company.

Center for Nursing Case Management. (1988). Case management: Meeting the Challenge. *Definition: the Center for Nursing Case Management*. 3, 1, 1–3.

The Institute of Medicine. (1988). *Homelessness, Health and Human Needs*.

Lemke, S. and Moos, R. (Dec., 1990). Validity of the sheltered care environment scale: conceptual and methodological issues. *Psychology and Aging*. 5, no. 4, 569–571.

Malloy, C., Christ, M. A., and Roscinski, P. (1988). "A Survey of the Characteristics of the Homeless: Health Status and Needs." Medical University of South Carolina College of Nursing. Unpublished research report.

Nyamathi, A., and Shulter, P. (August 1989). "Factors Affecting Prescribed Medication Compliance of the Urban Homeless Adult." *The Nurse Practitioner*: 47–54.

U.S. Department of Health and Human Services. (1984). *Helping the Homeless: a Resource Guide*. Washington, D.C.: U.S. Government Printing Office.

U. S. Department of Housing and Urban Development. (1984). *A Report to the Secretary on Homeless and Emergency Shelter*. Washington, D.C.: Office of Policy Development and Research.

U.S. General Accounting Office. (1985). *Homelessness: A Complex Problem and the Federal Response*. Washington, D.C.: GAO.

Zander, K. (1985). "Second Generation Primary Nursing, a New Agenda." *Journal of Nursing Administration*. 15 (3):18–24.

SECTION 7

Cost Effectiveness
of Nurse-Managed Clinics

CHAPTER 20

Development of a Model Nurse-Managed Clinic for the Homeless

Bernadine M. Lacey
Beatrice V. Adderley-Kelly

Abstract

Homeless people are prone to a broad array of health problems complicated by their exposure to environmental extremes, malnutrition, and trauma. Yet, they are among those most neglected by the established health-care system due to inadequate resources and/or health insurance.

Problems of growing joblessness, unavailabity of affordable housing, addictive behaviors, broken families, and other overriding social factors underpin the health needs of the homeless men, women, and children. The problems of homeless people have grown, but the response of the health-care delivery system has lagged significantly behind. There are an estimated 2–3 million homeless persons in the United States for whom health services ought to be available.

Introduction and Background

The Howard University College of Nursing became involved with the homeless through the interest and talents of one faculty member in the spring of 1986. This interest, though present for some time, was sparked by a discussion of power and powerlessness in a doctoral program.

At that time the homeless population was increasing rapidly, and more attention was being given to this group throughout the country, particularly in the nation's capital. One of the strongest advocacy groups, the Community for Creative Non-Violence (CCNV), was exerting pressure on many powerful groups to be more responsive and to provide more services for the growing population of homeless individuals. It seemed reasonable that some answers on power and powerlessness could be obtained by talking with the CCNV, and a meeting was held between the faculty member and the leaders of CCNV in early spring 1986.

The CCNV had just acquired a large vacant building in southwest Washington, D.C. The building was to be renovated and used as a 1,400-bed shelter with a 32-bed health unit based in the lower level. During the meeting with the leaders of CCNV, the topic of the health unit was discussed. Because of the faculty member's experience in working in a variety of health units, she was asked to assist with its architectural design. The first meeting with the architect was held in late March, and consultation was provided throughout the summer.

Discussions were held between the faculty member and the acting dean of the College of Nursing about the possibility of the college faculty and students becoming involved with the homeless and the shelter. In the fall of 1986, the faculty member and the acting dean made several visits to the facility to observe the renovations and to make suggestions concerning the health unit. Through the work of the faculty member and the acting dean, an affiliation agreement for student experiences was signed between Howard University College of Nursing and the CCNV in late fall 1986. The first student began affiliation in fall 1987 after completion of the renovation.

Development of the Nurse-Managed Clinic

The College of Nursing received a three-year grant in the amount of $1,040,520 from the W.K. Kellogg Foundation in August 1989. The purpose of the grant is to improve the health of homeless people by providing education and services and by training volunteer staff. More specifically, the project will extend health promotion, maintenance, and convalescent services to the homeless men and women at the 1,400-bed Federal City Shelter for the homeless through a nurse-managed health-care delivery model involving collaboration among nurses, shelter staff, nursing educators, nursing students, and other health professionals.

In developing our nurse-managed clinic, factors contributing to homelessness and major health problems of the homeless had to be considered. Factors contributing to homelessness include: lack of affordable housing, marginal employment/unemployment, elderly on fixed incomes, deinstitutionalization of the mentally ill, and alcoholism and drug abuse. Major health difficulties include: problems of the feet; problems related to exposure to heat or cold such as hypothermia, heat exhaustion/heat stroke, burns from lying on grates, and frostbite; malnutrition; trauma; infection; G.I. disturbances including constipation and/or diarrhea; dehydration; depression/suicidal ideation; and tuberculosis.

One of the objectives of the grant is to integrate undergraduate and graduate students into the shelter environment for educational services and research opportunities. Even though the College of Nursing was particularly sensitive to the plight of the homeless, several factors either impeded or facilitated the integration of homelessness into the curriculum and clinical experiences. Those which impeded integration were mostly faculty issues and focused primarily on: concern over the safety of the homeless environment; contentment with curriculum as is; the already-overloaded curriculum; reluctance to move from traditional to nontraditional experiences; lack of established models to guide clinical experiences; lack of established protocols; unstable staffing patterns; minimal medical supports; loose organizational structure and inadequate supplies and equipment; and liability. Of all the concerns expressed by faculty, the lack of established protocols to guide clinical experiences and the loosely organized structure were the two of greatest importance. Through ongoing discussions and with strong advocacy for the homeless from the administration and several faculty members, eventually all faculty accepted the idea and became fully supportive of the project.

Factors that facilitated integration were: recognition of homelessness as a national problem; access to a "homeless power base" through a highly respected and trusted faculty member; administrative enthusiasm and support; cadre of enthusiastic and supportive faculty; positive experiences with small, high-impact projects; a plausible conceptualization of the scope of homeless involvement with education, service, and research; student satisfaction; and collegial and public recognition and approval.

The College of Nursing involvement in the nurse-managed clinic includes clinical experiences for both undergraduate and graduate students. The integration of clinical experiences into the undergraduate curriculum occurs at the sophomore through senior levels. Five of the clinical courses in the undergraduate curriculum utilize the shelter for clinical experiences. Students at the sophomore level in the course Essential Components spend two clinical days each at the shelter. One of the course objectives is used as the basis for the experience. The objective is to describe adaptive behaviors which represent how man organizes and integrates his environment to prevent disturbances of functions. This includes orientation to man's response to a homeless environment (food, shelter, sleep, rest, elimination, belonging, self-worth, etc.), and observation and interaction with homeless people, using both communication skills and interaction skills.

At the junior level two courses utilize the shelter for some of the experiences. The course, Health Assessment, was one of the first to implement a clinical experience in the shelter's 32-bed health unit. Two course objectives guided the clinical experience: demonstrate beginning skills in performing a physical examination, utilizing the techniques of observation, palpation, percussion, and auscultation; and to assess the health status of clients throughout the life span, considering sociocultural influences and other parameters that promote health as well as emphasize wellness. Students spent two clinical days at the shelter on a rotating basis. In implementing their objectives, they were expected to perform physical examinations and report and record findings; assess and analyze health status by discriminating between normal and abnormal findings and interpreting findings in light of the current homeless situation; and identify emerging health problems inherent in street living.

In the other junior-level course, Medical-Surgical Nursing, three of the course objectives were used to guide the clinical experiences: implement the nursing process with clients responding to alternatives in health status; apply the nursing process to selected client situations; and engage in activities that foster the health promotion and maintenance capabilities of clients. There were three groups of eight students each. In implementing the objectives, each group spent two to four clinical days at the shelter. The students were able to apply the nursing process to clients with altered health status such as impaired peripheral circulation, selected hormonal imbalances (diabetes), and impaired carbon dioxide-oxygen exchange. They planned and applied intervention strategies such as dressing changes, range of motion, exercises, foot care, health teaching, maintenance of a clean environment, and therapeutic communication. Health promotion activities included teaching health to individuals and small groups. Topics included managing a diabetic diet with limited and unpredictable resources; minimizing infections and burns during street living; and strategies to prevent hypothermia. Students also assisted in the design and implementation of such health-promotion activities as exercise programs and personal hygiene classes.

Two senior-level courses, Leadership and Management in Nursing and Community-Mental Health Nursing, utilized the homeless shelter for clinical learning experiences. In Community-Mental Health Nursing, several shelter experiences were incorporated into the clinical learning for the students. At first, exposure was limited to females only, but later experiences included homeless men in the health unit, the postdetoxification unit, and the general residential area of the shelter. The course objectives deemed appropriate for the experiences were: synthesizing theoretical concepts that relate to the health of the community; implementing the nursing process with individuals, families, groups, and communities adapting to different levels of stress; and functioning as a change agent when providing health care in the community. In implementing the objectives, students were able to assess the community of the homeless, identifying those factors that facilitate and impede healthy adaptation. Students were expected to conduct case findings by making rounds in the shelters and by providing comprehensive care, health promotion, and teaching activities for individuals and groups. Further, students were expected to serve as resource persons and catalysts to assist in identifying priorities for health-promotion and health-maintenance activities for the homeless community and to advocate for the homeless.

For the course Leadership and Management two objectives were used to guide the clinical experience: apply the principles of leadership and management when coordinating activities of clients and staff; and collaborate with members of the health-care team when providing a variety of services to people. In implementing the objectives, students assessed the health-care environment of the shelter, identified deficits or potential deficits related to management, and designed and implemented appropriate intervention strategies consistent with the philosophy of the shelter. They provided health-promotion classes and staff development for shelter volunteers. They also collaborated with graduate students in the design, implementation, and evaluation of health-promotion and health-maintenance activities.

The homeless experience also was integrated into the graduate curriculum in all three majors: Adult Health Nursing, Primary Family Health, and Gerontological Nursing. The integration of the shelter experience was emphasized and implemented in the administration role-development area of each of the three majors. In addition to the student's own objectives, two course objectives were used as the basis of the experience: apply selected organizational environments in relation to administrative and management theory, identifying areas requiring administrative intervention; and evaluate the impact of the nurse-managed health-care delivery model on the health status of the homeless and education of students.

The development of the nurse-managed clinic, which is an ongoing process, and the integration of the homeless experience into the curriculum have not been without problems. However, student satisfaction with opportunities to learn from the homeless and to provide care for this group was one of the major factors in facilitating the college's involvement. Also, once a significant number of faculty members were involved in positive experiences and the realization that the College of Nursing had an opportunity to make a significant contribution to a needed group and to the community, enthusiasm gained momentum throughout the college.

The College of Nursing remains involved in many other activities related to the homeless. Faculty and graduate students are performing ongoing research. Faculty, students, and staff participate in several service activities for the homeless and continue to be advocates for them. The nurse-managed clinic is functioning well, with an advisory committee and a planning committee making significant input.

This project demonstrates that a nurse-managed clinic for the homeless can be of vital and lasting benefit, not only to the clients, but to everyone involved.

Reference

Powell, D. L., and Lacey, B.M. (1989). "Taking Nursing Education to the Streets." In *Perspectives in Nursing, 1989–1991*. National League for Nursing, pub. no. 41-2281; 107–16.

CHAPTER 21

A Survey of Evaluation Approaches for Health Care in Homeless Projects

Juanita K. Hunter

Abstract

This chapter describes preliminary work prior to implementing a national survey to gather information about how homeless health-care programs evaluate their services. At the time the study was begun, there was no known national listing of providers of health care for the homeless. Efforts to identify those providers through telephone contacts, library research, and contacts with professional associations yielded some useful information. A recurring significant theme was that homeless health-care providers experience feelings of isolation and burden with the responsibility for providing care to the homeless and securing funding for those services.

Interest in the unmet health needs of the homeless population has prompted health-care providers nationwide to establish health-care services for the homeless in shelters and other sites. The State University of New York at Buffalo, School of Nursing, Nursing Center for the Homeless is one example of a nursing center approach to meet the health-care needs of this diverse population. The purpose of this project was to provide access to nursing services for the homeless population within the City of Buffalo at the City Mission. The Nursing Center was established as a demonstration project in January 1988 through funding provided by the Special Projects Grants Program in the Nursing Education Practice Resources Branch, Division of Nursing, U.S. Department of Health and Human Services, Public Health Service, Health Resources and Services Administration, Bureau of Health Professions Administration, Grant #5D1060003-03. The Center provided comprehensive, interdisciplinary services to this disadvantaged population. Those services were extended to three additional sites during a three-year project period which ended January 31, 1991. The nursing services provided included, but were not limited to, health assessment, health education, counseling, health maintenance, and referral.

The service setting has provided opportunity for faculty practice, student learning experiences, and faculty and student research. Continuity of care for the clients was improved through the establishment of a referral process and provision of client transportation which facilitated and increased follow-through with treatment regimens. Nursing staff served as client advocates and assisted in this process. Data from this project have documented that episodic care, chronic health problems, and clients' numerous social and emotional needs can be appropriately addressed within a nursing center (A Nursing Center for Homeless Persons in Buffalo). Little is known, however, about the actual cost of those services or the potential value of them to the future provision of health care for the homeless and other vulnerable populations.

Within this context, the Nursing Center and other health-care providers have attempted to address their concerns about the cost effectiveness of health care for the homeless. Cost effectiveness implies the factor of valuing human life and is more meaningful when alternative uses of resources are being compared. Rather than examining the cost-effectiveness of a nursing clinic, one would compare the cost-effectiveness of the nursing clinic as compared to X and Y. A number of limitations are placed on interventions with the homeless, and these moderate the approach for cost analysis of the programs. A number of authors have written about various methods to assess the economic evaluation of health care (Carrin 1984; Weinstein and Stason, 1977; Cantor et al. 1985; Smith and Veglia 1987). Very little is available in the literature on the evaluation of homeless projects particularly with regard to cost. Many of the articles describe the health-care needs of the homeless groups and what care is provided, but none address evaluation efforts of the programs.

The purpose of this study was to determine various approaches utilized by homeless projects to evaluate their services. The full study was based on Don Dillman's (1978) Total Design Method (TDM). Dillman's method was used as a framework to develop and implement design and survey procedures. TDM consists of a set of specific techniques that have been associated with high response rates. The use of TDM for surveys is based upon the theoretical base known as "social exchange." The foundation of this theory is that individual actions are motivated by the benefit they expect to gain or draw from others. Further, Dillman described a cost-reward balance inherent in successful surveys, if the cost to the individual is maximal and trust is established (Dillman 1978). This descriptive study was conducted among several geographic regions across the United States. Data were collected by conducting a national mail and telephone survey of facilities that provide health care to homeless groups.

At the time the study was planned, little was known about the number of providers of health care for the homeless across the country, their locations, sources of funding, or services provided. Therefore, an initial plan was developed whereby a small nucleus of providers would be identified, contacted by telephone, and asked

TABLE 21.1
Procedures, Questions for Initial Phone Survey

[Procedures for caller: introduce the Nursing Center for the Homeless, SUNY at Buffalo, its location, source of funding, services provided, and current staffing.]

Researcher says: "We are looking for people involved in primary care for purposes of networking and compiling a national listing."

Researcher then asks these questions:

Are you involved in direct patient care?

In what way do you provide primary health care?

Are you interested in networking with us?

Do you know of others we might contact?

---

for names of other providers from this group. In so doing, it was felt that the list would then grow until large enough to use as a study population. Thus, the researchers began by listing all known providers, including the May 3–4, 1990, "Homelessness: An Issue for the Nineties" conference participants. A listing of those known providers from personal contact was also completed. Next, the literature was reviewed to generate the names of authors who had written about the homeless issue. Once the list was expanded to about thirty individuals, the researchers then designed a series of questions to be asked when the research assistant, Lora Warkentin, made the initial phone calls. The purpose of these calls was to verify the names and addresses of those called and to generate other names from this group. The specific questions asked were developed to elicit that information (see Table 21.1).

If the person responded affirmatively to the questions asked, the caller then verified the name, mailing address, and phone number for the contact person. At the end of each phone call, notations were made on the contact slip, and a separate list of persons, names of agencies, and addresses was developed. On earlier calls the caller also asked if they were aware of the May 3–4, 1990, conference, "Homelessness: An Issue for the Nineties," and if they would like a brochure. A list of those sources used may be found in Table 21.2.

It soon became apparent that this process was very time consuming, and oftentimes, several calls were made before an individual could be reached. Time differences were another factor, and also many agencies were so small that the contact person was not always found at the listed phone number for long periods of time. Other concerns were, the number of incorrect telephone numbers, and the turnover among providers of health care for the homeless. After several weeks, the researchers re-assessed this approach, and decided to focus their efforts on homeless projects that were funded by the Stewart B. McKinney Act, the Robert Wood Johnson Foundation and the Pew Charitable Trust. It was felt that such agencies would be required to give feedback to their funding source and, therefore, would be able to provide the information requested in the proposed survey. Many of the smaller agencies contacted, provided services with few staff, and stated they had minimal record-keeping and evaluation procedures. Also, once the list of projects funded by these

TABLE 21.2
Development of Provider List

Primary Contacts
   Known homeless providers
   May 3–4, 1990, conference participants
   Other professional colleagues
   Division of Nursing grantees
Secondary Sources
   Referrals from primary contacts
   Mailing lists
   Nursing journals
   Other conferences
   State nurses associations
Funding Sources
   Stewart B. McKinney Homeless Assistance Act
Robert Wood Johnson Foundation/Pew Charitable Trust

two agencies was obtained, it became very apparent that this method not only would be cost-efficient but would also help to narrow the universe of providers.

Sample Selection

One hundred nine projects were funded by the Stewart B. McKinney Homeless Assistance Act, and these projects were evenly distributed nationwide within ten regions. Seventeen projects previously funded by the Robert Wood Johnson Foundation and the Pew Charitable Trust. There were eight identified university-supported programs.

A total of 287 agencies was identified which provided primary health care to the homeless. This number was derived from the Stewart B. McKinney Homeless Assistance Act programs, the Robert Wood Johnson/Pew Charitable Trust funded programs, the university and other programs. Of this 287, 87 or 30% were originally randomly selected to participate in the telephone survey.

Table 21.3 demonstrates the subgroups which comprised the initial sample.

It should be noted that, because several agencies received funding from several sources, these numbers were not mutually exclusive. It was decided that it would be interesting and helpful to subdivide the sample into four groups; Stewart B. McKinney Homeless Assistance Act funded, Robert Wood Johnson/Pew Charitable Trust funded, university sponsored, and other. This division was to allow comparisons among groups and possibly yield more comprehensive information. For example, all data collected by university groups might be similar, yet different from the larger and possibly more interdisciplinary agencies. The sample was further divided and two categories formed: those who would be requested to com-

TABLE 21.3
Identified Homeless Providers Sample Sub-group (N = 287)

Original 30% subgroup	87
Stewart B. McKinney Homeless Assistance Act	109
Original Robert Wood Johnson Foundation/Pew Charitable Trust Group	18
University Group	10
Other Funding Sources	63

* Numbers are not mutually exclusive due to overlap.

TABLE 21.4
Final Sample Selection (N = 252)

	N	Percent (%)
Total Agencies Selected for Mail Survey	156	62
Total Agencies Selected for Telephone Survey*	96	38

*Included Robert Wood Johnson/Pew Charitable Trust projects ($N = 17$), university programs ($N = 8$), and 30% randomly selected McKinney Funded Projects ($N = 71$).

plete a mail survey and those who would be requested to participate in a telephone survey (See Table 21.4).

Questionnaire Development

The questionnaire for use in the survey was developed using a structure-process-outcome framework. Structure items included information on size, staffing, available facilities, budget, location, etc. Process items focus on provider services for health care, that is, physical assessments, screening procedures, psychological assessments, dental assessments, services provided, patient/family education, medications, dressing changes, referrals to other agencies, and consultations. The outcome category included client-oriented aspects of care such as compliance, morbidity, return for follow-up, decreased signs and symptoms, health knowledge and attitude change, cost, and patient satisfaction. Participants at the May 3–4, 1990 conference served as experts and pilot tested the questionnaire.

The 87 selected agencies were to receive a questionnaire and a follow-up phone call to collect the data. Those telephone calls were to be scheduled in advance according to Don Dillman's recommended procedures. The other 173 agencies were to receive a questionnaire by mail and were to be asked to complete it and return it by mail. The full study was conducted during the summer of 1990. A total purposive sample of $N = 252$ was identified for the survey. Responses were received from 163 health-care providers, a 78.4% response rate. The data were analyzed, and the results have been published (Hunter et al. 1991).

Several recurring themes were documented from the initial phone calls and were discussed at the conference. These included: feelings of isolation and frustration, turnover of staff, funding concerns (i.e., "grant junkies"), paperwork required by funding sources, and the conflict between meeting requirements of funding agencies and providing service.

It should be noted that the need for support and networking varied with the location of the agency and its funding source. For example, the National Association of Community Health Centers publishes a regular newsletter STREETREACH and holds a national conference every year for the McKinney grantees. Other agencies were privately funded, and those providers indicated they had no linkage with other providers or agencies of like kind.

The response to the initial phone calls and the preliminary data suggesting that there was a great need for some health-care providers to have the opportunity to network with each other was substantiated by the conference participants. The data also supported Dillman's premise that if intangible rewards of positive regard, personalized contacts, and appreciation were communicated to the respondent, positive results would ensue.

The feedback also suggested that providers of health care for the homeless were seeking a means to develop a personal networking system with others to prevent burnout. The Nursing Center for the Homeless at the State University of New York at Buffalo assumed the responsibility for facilitating that process. Conference participants were provided the opportunity to speak with each other and to focus on specific issues and their specific concerns.

After the conference, the Nursing Center compiled a list of those persons who submitted their names, addresses, research interests, and areas of practice to the Center, and during the following months that list grew to approximately 130 health-care professionals. It was determined at the time of the conference that a newsletter should be started to provide the vehicle for networking, sharing information, and linking individuals with similar research interests. The first edition of the *Homeless Newsletter* was printed and distributed in March 1991.

The results of these research efforts have documented that evaluation of health care programs for homeless clients is recommended. Key outcome indicators of effectiveness need to be considered for evaluation of health care programs for homeless persons.

References

Cantor, J., Morisky, D., Green, L., Levine, D., and D. Salkenek, (1985). "Cost Effectiveness of Educational Interventions to Improve Patient Outcomes in Blood Pressure Control" *Preventive Medicine*, 14, 782–800.

Carrin, G. (1984). "Economic Evaluation of Health Care Interventions: A Review of Alternative Methods." *Social Science Medicine* 19(10), 1015–1030.

Dillman, D. (1978). *Mail and Telephone Surveys: The Total Design Method*. New York; John Wiley and Sons.

Hunter, J. K., Crosby, F. E., Ventura, M. R., and Warkentin, L. (December 1991). "National Survey to Identify Evaluation Criteria for Programs of Health Care for Homeless." *Nursing and Health Care* 12.10: 536–42.

A Nursing Center for Homeless Persons in Buffalo, New York. Final Report. Division of Nursing, HHS, USPHS, 5D10NU60003-03.

Smith, S. and Veglia, J. (1987). "Hospice Utilization of Hospital Services: A Cost Analysis." *VA Practitioner*, 72, 65–67; 82–86.

Warner, K., and Luce, B. (1987). *Cost Benefit and Cost-effective Analysis in Health Care: Principles, Practice and Potential*. Ann Arbor, Mich.: Health Administration Press.

Weinstein, M., and Stason, W. (March 31, 1977). "Foundations of Cost-effective Analysis for Health and Medical Practice." *New England Journal of Medicine* 296 (13): 716–21.

CHAPTER 22

The Role of Nurses and Nursing Schools in Health Services for the Homeless

Susan L. Kitchen

Abstract

*The financial and social burdens of providing health care to the homeless are de-
manding that more effective and innovative services be established to help serve the
needs of this growing population. Nurse practitioners at the Hampton University
Nursing Center, a nurse practitioner–managed primary-care facility, began providing health care to the homeless in targeted areas of Hampton and Newport News,
Virginia, in 1987. Health-care services initially were provided only to residents of
shelters for the homeless.*

*Collaboration among community agencies resulted in funding through the
Stewart B. McKinney Homeless Assistance Act of 1987. This grant helped to establish a local health care to the homeless project within which the Hampton University Nursing Center was contracted to provide health-care services. In 1988 these
services were expanded with the addition of a thirty-four-foot mobile home which
was renovated for the provision of health-care services. The Health Mobile provides health care on a daily basis at sites throughout the target areas.*

The financial and social burdens of providing health care to the homeless population in this country increase daily. The nursing profession is responding by offering
sensitive, humanitarian, and cost-effective care.

Hamptom University is taking steps to prepare nurses to care for this group and is
providing care at the local level. Founded in 1868, Hampton is a coeducational, non-
sectarian, historically black institution of higher learning located in Hampton, Virginia. The philosophy of the university is to provide its students with an "education
for life." The School of Nursing, led by Dr. Elnora Daniel, is the oldest continuous

baccalaureate nursing program in the Commonwealth of Virginia and has the first master of science in nursing program located in a historically black institution.

The Hampton University Nursing Center and Health Mobile are sponsored by the Hampton University School of Nursing with support from the Special Project Grants Program in the Nursing Education Practice Resources Branch, Division of Nursing, U.S. Department of Health and Human Services, Public Health Service, Health Resources and Services Administration, Bureau of Health Professions Administration. The Nursing Center was established in 1986 through funding by the W. K. Kellogg Foundation and offers affordable primary health-care services including health education, health screening, health counseling, and referral for medically unserved and underserved residents of the surrounding communities.

The Nursing Center also provides a non-traditional site for School of Nursing faculty practice and consultation and for undergraduate and graduate nursing students' clinical learning experiences. Students from other disciplines within the university, such as sociology and marketing, also utilize the Nursing Center for learning experiences.

The Health Mobile is a thirty-four-foot mobile home that was modified to contain one examination room, a multipurpose work station, a waiting area, a preliminary screening area, and bathroom and shower facilities. The Health Mobile is designed to facilitate multiphasic screening, group counseling, and health education services by increasing the accessibility of the population to the services of the Nursing Center. Extensive collaboration with and cooperation from community and civic organizations facilitates planning for the service delivery sites and the client services that are provided through the Health Mobile.

The Nursing Center became involved in providing health-care services to the homeless population of Hampton and Newport News, Virginia, in March 1987. A request for assistance from the director of the Salvation Army Family Shelter resulted in the formation of the Peninsula Homeless Coalition, a group composed of shelter managers and two Nursing Center nurse practitioners.

The initial needs assessment survey revealed seven major areas of concern that shelter personnel needed to address: 1) health screening, 2) illness treatment, 3) transportation to health-care sites, 4) health education and counseling, 5) referral resources, 6) staff training, and 7) school and camp physical examinations. Priority was given to the establishment of health screening, treatment, and referral services, with additional services to be added as expanded resources became available. Initially, one family nurse practitioner visited each of the five shelters for the homeless and the Battered Women's shelter once a week to provide services. Client education and health promotion, as well as education for shelter staff, were given on a one-to-one basis. The nurse practitioner assessed each resident for potential and actual health problems and developed a plan of treatment with the client and with input from shelter staff. Referral resources were those of the Nursing Center referral network, a group of physicians and health-care agencies who had agreed to accept clients from the Nursing Center who needed services beyond the scope of the nurse practitioners' practice or who needed specialty services not offered by the Nursing Center staff. Because of the limited on-site availability of a nurse practitioner, telephone consultation with the staff of the Nursing Center was available to shelter personnel at all other times.

The needs of the population and their response to services were even greater than anticipated and well beyond the scope of the original plans and personnel. Upon passage of the Stewart B. McKinney Homeless Assistance Act of 1987 by the U.S. Congress, the Peninsula Institute for Community Health, a federally funded community health center in Newport News, Virginia, applied for and was granted funds for the establishment of the local Health Care for the Homeless project.

The Health Care for the Homeless project serves homeless individuals in the cities of Hampton and Newport News, Virginia. The organization consists of a project coordinator, four case managers, and a secretary. Health-care management is provided through contract with the Hampton University Nursing Center. A nurse practitioner is assigned to the project daily. The project operates under a case management/outreach model. The case managers, all of whom have a background in social work, work with the shelter managers, soup kitchens, hotels, boarding homes, and other organizations working with the homeless to identify problems and offer services to homeless individuals and families. To establish a trusting relationship with the homeless clients, the case managers offer more than just access to medical care. The case managers provide food, clothing, transportation, or a listening ear to clients and give support to clients during episodes of crisis. The case managers assist clients through the social services system to insure that they receive the necessary services and do not get lost in the bureaucracy.

In March 1988 the Health Mobile began operation and was utilized to expand the services provided to the shelters and to reach the portion of the homeless population that was not housed in shelters. Health-care services are provided daily at rotating sites within the two cities. Sites are chosen on the basis of accessibility to the homeless population and the existence of other services for the homeless, such as a soup kitchen.

The Health Mobile is staffed by a family nurse practitioner, a driver, and a Health Care for the Homeless case manager each day. The physician consultant is there for one hour per day to evaluate clients referred by the nurse practitioner, review all client assessments, and prescribe needed medications. The nurse practitioner is responsible for client assessment and management, review of health records, referrals to specialists, and compilation of statistical data. Additionally, several family practice resident physicians donate time, on a rotating basis, one evening each week at the Salvation Army Family Shelter.

The Nursing Center's outreach program for health care for the homeless is an integral part of the curriculum for undergraduate nursing students in medical-surgical and community health nursing. Students are given the opportunity to assist in providing direct services and to learn about various aspects of the homeless experience through interviewing the clients, assisting the nurse practitioner with assessment and management, and visiting various shelters and soup kitchens serving the homeless population. Graduate nursing students in the areas of community health and mental health nursing also utilize the homeless outreach program for clinical experience. The complexity and multiplicity of the problems faced by the homeless client or family provides the graduate student with an opportunity to apply the advanced nursing principles contained in the curriculum to a nontraditional clinical experience.

The Hampton University Nursing Center and Health Mobile are an integral part of the successful implementation of this health-care project. Through the efforts of the Hampton University School of Nursing and local health-care agencies, the homeless population of the area is provided with accessible, high-quality health-care services and case management.

CHAPTER 23

Summary

Juanita K. Hunter

Homelessness is a complex societal problem that undoubtedly will continue to be a pressing concern into the next decade. The contemporary homeless have been described as a group different from those traditionally known to live on the fringe of society. The current situation has been described as the direct result of policy changes affecting housing, employment, public assistance, and health care. The increasing numbers of homeless people, particularly women, children, and families, poses many challenges for those individuals and those who provide care to them.

At the same time, health-care professionals have expressed concern about the multiple health and related needs of the homeless, and have involved themselves in gathering a data base about those needs, designing health programs, providing learning experiences for students, and implementing research efforts. Health care of the homeless has become a special concern for many nurses. The Special Project Grants Program in the Nursing Education Practice Resources Branch, Division of Nursing, U.S. Department of Health and Human Services, Public Health Service, Health Resources and Services Administration, Bureau of Health Professions Administration, has funded schools of nursing to demonstrate models that increase access to nursing services for disadvantaged populations, including the homeless. The Nursing Center for the Homeless, funded by the Division of Nursing, and sponsored by the School of Nursing at the State University of New York at Buffalo, in conjunction with four other funded projects, sponsored a national conference, "Homelessness: An Issue for the Nineties," on May 3–4, 1990. This book has provided the reader with the papers presented at that conference.

The papers included demographic data about specific groups of the homeless, and demonstrated a consistency with other published national data. The papers on issues related to homeless children identified that nursing roles of community public health nurse, nurse practitioner, and clinical nurse specialist are uniquely suited to meeting the needs of this special group. The innovative and creative learning experiences for students that were described also emphasized the benefits of exposing and sensitizing students to a population group most in need of health services, and without adequate health insurance. Further, the research papers highlighted the numerous unanswered questions, about quality of care, effectiveness of care, outcome criteria and data.

This book provides a source of information for examining the issues of homelessness, which go beyond just looking at the individual as cause and effect. Increased homelessness is associated with national policies, and it has been stated that coalitions must be forged in order to change the current lack of sufficient programs, to address the health care needs and other problems, of the homeless. Nursing has the expertise and the social responsibility to take the lead in designing, implementing, and evaluating health services for the homeless. This book demonstrates that nurses are in a unique position to assume leadership in designing the health-care system of the future, which will include care for all citizens.

Contributors

Beatrice V. Adderley-Kelly, Ph.D., R.N., Associate Professor and Chairman, Lower Division and Junior Studies, Howard University, College of Nursing, 501 Bryant Street, Washington, D.C.

Judith Anderson, M.S.N., Assistant Professor of Nursing, Psychiatric Clinical Nurse Specialists, Medical College of Ohio, School of Nursing, Toledo, OH

Andrea S. Berne, M.P.H., C.P.N.P., Senior Analyst, City of New York Department of Health, 125 Worth St., New York, New York.

Mary-Lynn Brecht, Ph.D., Principal Statistician, School of Nursing, University of California, Los Angeles, California.

Mary Ann Christ, Ed.D., R.N., Dean and Professor, University of Mississippi Medical Center, School of Nursing, Jackson, Mississippi.

Barbara Cross, A.D.N., R.N., formerly Homeless Specialist, Mental Health Case Manager, Western Psychiatric Institute and Clinic, Pittsburgh, Pennsylvania.

Candy Dato, R.N., C.S., M.S., Administrative Coordinator, St. Luke's Hospital Center, New York, New York.

Marilyn A. Davies, Ph.D., R.N., Assistant Professor of Psychiatry, Case Western Reserve University, University Hospitals of Cleveland, Cleveland, Ohio.

Strachan Donnelley, Ph.D., Ethicist/Director of Education, The Hastings Center, Manor, New York.

Marilyn R. Englert, R.N., M.S., C.R.C., Co-coordinator, Homeless Chronic Mentally Ill Veterans Program, Veterans Administration Medical Center, Buffalo, New York.

Kim Evans, R.N., M.S.N., C.P.N.P., Pediatric Nurse Practitioner, University of Texas Nursing Services – Houston, Houston, Texas.

Cathleen Getty, R.N., M.S., Associate Professor, Area Director, Graduate Psychiatric Mental Health Nursing, School of Nursing, State University of New York at Buffalo, New York.

Mary Margaret Gottesman, Ph.D., R.N., Assistant Professor and Project Director, School of Nursing, University of California, Psychiatric Mental Health Administration, Los Angeles, California.

Paige Gradick, R.N.-C., M.S.N., F.N.P., Charleston Medical Clinic, Charleston, South Carolina.

Joseph L. Halbach, M.D., A.B.F.P., F.A.A.F.P., Director, Department of Family Medicine, St. Joseph's Medical Center and Family Health Center, Yonkers, New York.

Catherine L. Hopkins, R.N.-C., M.S., F.N.P., Director, Outreach Health Care Unit at Homeless Services Network, Inc., Lienhard School of Nursing, Pace University, Pleasantville, New York.

Juanita K. Hunter, R.N., Ed.D., F.A.A.N., Project Director and Clinical Assistant Professor, School of Nursing, State University of New York at Buffalo, Buffalo, New York.

Bruce Jennings, M.A., Executive Director, The Hastings Center, Briarcliff Manor, New York.

Martha J. Kemsley, Ph.D., R.N.-C., M.S., Clinical Assistant Professor, School of Nursing, State University of New York at Buffalo, Buffalo, New York.

Mary A. Kiplinger, R.N., M.S.N., Clinical Nurse Specialist, Medical College of Ohio, School of Nursing, Toledo, Ohio.

Susan L. Kitchen, R.N., B.S.N., F.N.P., Family Nurse Practitioner, Hampton University Nursing Center, Hampton, Virginia.

Bernadine M. Lacey, R.N., Ed.D., F.A.A.N., Instructor and Projector, Howard University, College of Nursing, Washington, D.C.

Mary Ann Lewis, R.N., Ph.D. F.A.A.N., Professor and Chair of Psychiatric Mental Health Administration, University of California at Los Angeles, School of Nursing, Los Angeles, California.

Ada M. Lindsey, R.N., Ph.D., F.A.A.N., Dean, School of Nursing, University of California at Los Angeles, Los Angeles, California.

Diana J. Mason, Ph.D., R.N.-C., F.A.A.N., Director of Nursing Education and Research, Beth Israel Medical Center, New York, New York.

Martha J. Pituch, R.N., Ph.D., Associate Professor of Nursing, Medical College of Ohio, School of Nursing, Toledo, Ohio.

Tim Porter-O'Grady, R.N., Ed.D., C.S., C.N.A.A., President and Senior Partner, Affiliated Dynamics, Inc., Atlanta, Georgia.

Bob Prentice, Ph.D., Director of Homeless Programs, Department of Public Health, San Francisco, California.

Margaret Rafferty, R.N., M.A., M.P.H., Assistant Professor, Long Island College Hospital, School of Nursing, Brooklyn, New York.

Anne H. Skelly, R.N., M.S., ANP-C, Assistant Professor, School of Nursing, State University of New York at Buffalo, Buffalo, New York.

Jeanne Shipman, R.N., Ed.D., Director, Health and Safety, Shipman Printing Industries, Lewiston, New York.

Lillie M. Shortridge, R.N.-C., Ed.D., F.N.P., F.A.A.N., Professor and Associate Dean, Center for Nursing Research/Clinical Practice, Lienhard School of Nursing, Pace University, Pleasantville, New York.

Nancy L. Stokley, R.N., B.S.N., Child-Care Nurse Consultant, Seattle King County Public Health Departments, Seattle, Washington.

Jane C. Swart, Ph.D., R.N., Dean and Professor, Wright State University-Miami, School of Nursing, Dayton, Ohio.

Virginia E. Taylor, R.N., M.S.N., C.A.N.P., Erie County Health Department, Buffalo, New York.

Index

Abdellah, G., 47
Abuse
  child, 37, 86
  emotional, 3, 74, 110 *tab*
  physical, 3, 74, 108, 110 *tab*, 128
  psychological, 128
  sexual, 3, 86, 108, 110 *tab*
Abuse, alcohol. *See also* Alcoholism
  frequency by age, 41 *tab*
  as reported by homeless, 58, 59 *tab*
  treatment programs, 46
Abuse, substance, 3, 21, 35, 58 *tab*
  effect on children, 111
  frequency by age, 41 *tab*
  parental, 87, 111
  prior treatment for, 58, 59 *tab*
  as reported by homeless, 58, 59 *tab*
  treatment, 37, 46, 75
  underreporting of, 75
Acker, P., 85, 102
Activities of Daily Living, 40, 40 *tab*
  ability to meet basic needs in, 42
Adaptational Model of Poverty, 81–92
Adderley-Kelly, Beatrice, 201–205
Adler, P., 101, 102
Adolescents, services for, 35
AFDC. *See* Aid to Families with Dependent Children
Age, 34, 35, 38, 39 *tab*
  of children, 38, 39 *tab*
  and chronic illness, 57
Aggression, in children, 85, 111, 118
AIDS, 41 *tab*
  in children, 85
  counseling, 46
  homelessness resulting from, 21
  increasing prevalence in homeless, 86

Aid to Families with Dependent Children, 20, 45, 74
Alcoholism, 3, 21, 35, 52
  treatment, 37
Alienation, 128
Alperstein, G., 102, 118
American Nurses Association, 91, 119
American Public Health Association, 183
Amvets, 167
Anderson, Judith, 173–178
Anemia, 75, 129
  in children, 84
Anxiety disorder, 58 *tab*
  in adults, 41 *tab*
  Appleby, L., 152
Arce, A., 152
Arnstein, E., 118
Assessment
  health, 53, 118, 121
  models for children, 117–121
  needs, 53, 182
  psychosocial, 37
  of veterans, 161–162
Asthma, 41 *tab*, 75
  in children, 84
Atlanta Community Health Program for the Homeless (Atlanta), 11

Bachrach, L., 151
Bahr, H., 54
Bass, J., 72
Bassuk, E., 46, 52, 85, 86, 87, 117, 118, 152, 159
Bassuk, I., 72
Baxter, E., 60, 152
Bean, C., 153
Belcher, J., 152

225